An Aristocracy of Color

Race and Culture in the American West
Quintard Taylor, Series Editor

An Aristocracy of Color

*Race and Reconstruction
in California and the West,
1850–1890*

D. MICHAEL BOTTOMS

UNIVERSITY OF OKLAHOMA PRESS : NORMAN

Publication of this book is made possible through the generosity of
Edith Kinney Gaylord.

Library of Congress Cataloging-in-Publication Data

Bottoms, D. Michael, 1966–
An aristocracy of color : race and reconstruction in California and the West,
1850–1890 / D. Michael Bottoms.
p. cm. — (Race and culture in the American West ; v. 5)
Includes bibliographical references and index.
ISBN 978-0-8061-4335-4 (hardcover : alk. paper) 1. West (U.S.)—Race
relations—History—19th century. 2. Minorities—West (U.S.)—History—19th
century. 3. African Americans—West (U.S.)—History—19th century. 4. Chinese
Americans—West (U.S.)—History—19th century. 5. Mexican Americans—West
(U.S.)—History—19th century. 6. California—Race relations—History—
19th century. 7. Minorities—California—History—19th century. 8. African
Americans—California—History—19th century. 9. Chinese Americans—
California—History—19th century. 10. Mexican Americans—California—
History—19th century. I. Title.
F596.2.B68 2013
305.800978—dc23
2012023756

*An Aristocracy of Color: Race and Reconstruction in California and the West,
1850–1890* is Volume 5 in the Race and Culture in the American West series.

The paper in this book meets the guidelines for permanence and durability of
the Committee on Production Guidelines for Book Longevity of the Council on
Library Resources, Inc. ∞

1 2 3 4 5 6 7 8 9 10

For Anastasia

Contents

Illustrations

Acknowledgments

THERE ARE MANY THINGS I love about being a historian, but what I love most is the way that my job connects me with so many wonderful people. In the years—and *years*—it has taken me to complete this project, friends and family, scholars, teachers, and even complete strangers have kept me company and supported me in my work. I owe a great deal to a great many.

My greatest debt is, of course, to my advisor and mentor, Professor Stephen Aron. Steve's patience is magnificent. As I struggled through this project's first phase as a doctoral dissertation, Steve struck just the right balance between independence and firm guidance, allowing me to develop my ideas, test them, and rework them without demanding that my intellectual labors follow any strict timetable. As I struggled to transform the dissertation into a book manuscript, Steve regularly reminded me that, above all else, my primary goal was to "finish the damn book." He read endless drafts, some good, most awful, and never once let me get away with lazy thinking or sloppy writing. Through several incarnations of WHEAT (Western Historians Eating and Talking), Steve built a community of scholars of western American history that continues to sustain me even at a distance. At key moments too, Steve moved mountains to make sure that I had funding when I needed it. All of these overt contributions to my intellectual development, however, hid a deeper and more lasting influence. It is only now, after years of full-time teaching, that I have begun to realize that even as he helped shape my scholarship, Steve was teaching me how to teach. I find myself almost daily passing on to my own students lessons in research, writing, and critical thinking that I learned from Steve, and for that I am truly grateful.

A number of other scholars at UCLA played important roles in making this into a successful project. Ellen Carol Dubois and Clyde Spillenger read numerous drafts and continually reminded me that my work was worthwhile. Thanks, too, to Joyce Appleby, Daniel Walker Howe, Eric Monkonnen, Kevin Terracianno, Jessica Wang, and Mary Yeager. Also at UCLA, members of WHEAT—John Bowes, Anastasia Christman, Cindy Culver, Lawrence Culver, Chris Gantner, Samantha Holtkamp, Daniel Hurewitz, Jen Koslow, Shauna Mulvihill, Arthur Rolston, Rachel St. John, and Lissa Wadewitz—all provided me with a level of support, criticism, and friendship I can never repay.

The research and writing of this book was made possible through the generous financial assistance provided by George Mason University, the Fulton Junior Faculty Fellowship, the Bancroft Library at the University of California, Berkeley, the Huntington Library, the John Randolph Haynes and Dora Haynes Foundation, the Autry Museum of Western Heritage, and the Department of History and Graduate Division at UCLA.

Colleagues at George Mason University and Whitman College also deserve my undying gratitude. First and foremost is Paula Petrik, without whom I might never have reached the end of this process. Paula's generosity and enthusiasm are irresistible. I would also like to extend heartfelt thanks to Mason colleagues Sheila Brennan, Joan Bristol, Benedict Carton, Michael Chang, Rob DeCaroli, Christopher Hamner, Matt Karush, Meredith Lair, Alison Landsberg, Sharon Leon, Mike O'Malley, Zach Schrag, and Randolph Scully. At Whitman, Elyse Semerdjian, David Schmitz, and Lynn Sharp helped guide me through my first year of teaching and provided intellectual sustenance along the way.

I owe a special debt to my editor at the University of Oklahoma Press, Jay Dew, for gently guiding me through the publication process, and to Emily Jerman, Norma McLemore, and Anna María Rodríguez for their help in whipping the manuscript into shape. Matthew Whitaker, Al Hurtado, and anonymous outside readers offered constructive criticism and helpful suggestions that greatly improved the manuscript.

Family and friends sustained me throughout this process. In the San Francisco Bay Area, Tim O'Brien and Michele Ramirez opened their home and their refrigerator more times than I care to count. My mother, Janet Kempf, and stepfather, Ray Kempf, contributed meals and entertainment, laundry facilities, and occasional financial assistance when my car broke down. My mother deserves special thanks for gathering signatures and filing my dissertation for me, saving me the expense of a thousand-mile trip. My grandfather, Poppo, died before I could finish this book, but he never once doubted that I could do it, and I cannot begin to express my gratitude for all that he gave me. In Washington State, my father, Don Bottoms, read early drafts of every chapter and showed an enthusiasm for my work that to this day continues to amaze. My brothers, Brian, Dion, Brendan, and Rob, took my mind off of my work and enabled me to see more in life than the past. Ed Sheridan always, and with good humor, reminded me where I came from and why I'm no better than anyone else.

One friend in particular deserves special mention. Trey Proctor offered more help and encouragement through this ordeal than I had any right to expect. He read and diligently commented on early drafts, listened to me talk about my work with endless patience, and wrote letters of recommendation that were almost certainly instrumental in winning me the best job in the world. When I needed it, Trey distracted me with food, drink, and a cookie, and more than once that bottle of Maker's Mark in his desk preserved my sanity. Trey has been a better friend than I deserved, and if I spend the rest of my life repaying him, it still won't be enough.

Every page of this book carries within it the strength, wisdom, and love of Anastasia Christman. We met as this project began, married in its midst, and make a home together to this day. She endured far too many lonely weekends and summers while I worked on this book, and she wore her fingers to the bone typing every word of the manuscript. Without her my labors would never have borne fruit, and with her my life is fuller than I could ever have imagined. Because of her I am a better scholar, a better teacher, and a better man, and so it is to her that this work is dedicated.

An Aristocracy of Color

Introduction

IN 1867, CHARLES LORING BRACE, philanthropist and man of letters, found himself captivated by California. Brace, who had recently earned a reputation as an amateur ethnologist, had traveled to the Golden State in search of health and renewed vigor following a nearly fatal case of typhoid fever. Expecting to be confronted by a rude frontier setting, given the state's relatively recent admission to the Union, he was pleasantly surprised to find instead a bustling, sophisticated, and thoroughly American society perched on the western edge of the continent. San Francisco, he declared, had "the most exhilarating atmosphere in the world. In it, a man can do more work than anywhere else, and under it he feels a constant pressure of excitement." By any measure, California appeared to compare favorably with the more settled regions of the country, and as he traveled about the state, Brace began to suspect that in many ways California was superior to anything he had seen in the East. In San Francisco, the public buildings were "better than our new buildings in New York," and from those buildings the city was "governed much better than any of our eastern cities." San Francisco's more refined citizens had, with remarkable speed, and despite their seeming isolation from established cultural centers like New York and Boston, surrounded themselves with the trappings of "high civilization." Brace was pleased to discover well-attended churches, libraries, and social clubs, and well-appointed homes. The city's charms, moreover, were in no way limited to the upper classes. "Probably, in no city of the world," he claimed, "are the laboring classes in such prosperity. . . . As you go about the people, you hear of this lady's cook having a thousand dollars in bank, or this one's chambermaid owning a city lot, or another's hired man already possessing a farm worth a thousand or two." Nearly everywhere he looked, it seemed, Brace saw a promising future for the nation's new West.[1]

A visit to Yosemite during the summer of 1867 only confirmed his suspicion that California represented something new and special. The very land itself seemed suffused with vitality and power. Brace had already traveled extensively throughout Europe several times, but nothing in his earlier travels had prepared him for what he found when standing at Yosemite's Inspiration Point. "No aspect of nature I have ever looked upon," he later wrote, "was so full of the inspiration of awe as this first opening view of the Yosemite Cañon." He was stunned by the size of California's ancient sequoia trees, by the richness of the state's farmlands, and the quality of the state's wine. Even California's horses seemed an improvement on more familiar types. "No horses I have ever seen can compare, in ease of gait, with these California mustangs. . . . They feed on oat-straw, or mountain pasture, and bear the hardest usage with little damage." California's natural setting seemed to Brace to enhance everything it touched.[2]

As he continued his travels, Brace became convinced that there was a direct connection between California's environment and the apparent superiority of its social and political life. Nineteenth-century natural science suggested that such a connection existed, and Brace himself was deeply engaged in the effort to find proof. As a close friend of nineteenth-century scientific luminaries Asa Gray and Charles Lyell, he was intimately familiar with the latest thinking on such matters. Brace had been an early promoter of Charles Darwin's theory of evolution, and under its influence had recently published a lengthy study of human development titled *The Races of the Old World*, in which he explicitly linked "institutions [and] forms of government" to the "qualities of certain races." Applying these ideas to California, he came to the conclusion that what he was witnessing went beyond a simple narrative of social progress. The combination of Anglo-Saxon people and a new and vigorous climate would, he believed, "inevitably, in the long course of ages, form a fresh Race in the human family on the western shores of this continent." Something similar was already happening in the eastern states, where, he claimed, no one could "doubt that the physical beauty of the English-speaking race in America is improving." According to an optimistic Brace, "The same result, from more manifest causes, is taking place in California." On the West Coast, men would be stronger, women more fecund, and children healthier. By the end of his trip, Brace was certain he had glimpsed the nation's future glory. "Verily," he reported, "California is in the van of civilization."[3]

And yet, even as he extolled California's virtues, Brace also sounded a note of apprehension. The opportunity for racial progress might, he worried, be undermined by the diversity of races he found in the state. Under the influence of this apprehension, the superlatives that had defined Brace's optimism suddenly disappeared and were replaced by a wholly negative assessment of California's nonwhite residents. California Indians were, according to Brace, the "lowest tribe of the human race." Those he met on his excursion to Yosemite were "all disgustingly dirty" and possessed of a "long inherited listlessness, want of inventiveness, ignorance, [and] weak physique." The fact that they had enjoyed California's energizing climate for thousands of years without apparent improvement was, for Brace, proof of their racial inferiority. He dismissed the state's more recent rulers, the Californios, as drunken, inveterate gamblers whose poor farming skills justified the appropriation of their land. He praised the Chinese immigrants he met in San Francisco for their capacity to work long hours, and then condemned them as "meek, quiet, dreamy pagan[s]" who frittered away their hard-earned wages on opium, liquor, and prostitutes in the "fever nests" of the city's Chinatown. How, he wondered, could California's promise be rightfully fulfilled if such people, by their very presence, were allowed to interfere?[4]

In 1867, most white Californians would have agreed both with Brace's claims about their state's racial potential and with his identification of their state's central problem. For nearly two decades state and local politics had been shaped by debates over how to manage a depth and breadth of racial diversity few white Americans had ever contemplated, let alone experienced, prior to their arrival on the West Coast. The discovery of gold at Sutter's Mill in 1848 had triggered a massive international migration that drew people from all over the world to California and instantly transformed what had been a regional backwater into one of the most cosmopolitan and chaotic regions in the world. As a result, California quickly became the most racially diverse region in the United States, home not just to white Americans, but to blacks, Chinese, Mexicans, Hawaiians, California Indians, Irishmen, Frenchmen, and more. White Americans came to this scene from a society that had carefully nurtured the illusion of white racial supremacy by reducing race relations to a series of simple binary oppositions between white and black, a process made easier by Indian removal and African enslavement. In multiracial California, however, race relations moved in bewildering directions along several different axes at once and so defied the binary oppositions—black versus white, free versus slave, civilization versus savagery—that informed racial thinking in the eastern United States. Maintaining white supremacy in this new context was widely viewed among whites as essential to the success of their state.

Initially, white Californians dealt with their state's racial diversity by creating a legal regime that carefully reserved power and privilege for whites. Beginning with the first state Constitution in 1849, white Californians fashioned a familiar, if crude, binary racial hierarchy that divided the state's population into two broad racial categories: white and nonwhite. The state legislature and the state courts strengthened and extended that simple division over the next several years through laws and court decisions designed to banish all of the state's racial minorities to the political, legal, and social margins of California society. This legal regime was supported by a racial logic that defined each of California's racial minorities in terms of the weaknesses associated with the others. Black Californians, for instance, were tied to Indians through a rhetoric that defined both peoples as savages whose supposed childlike inability to acquire the trappings of civilization rendered them unfit. Chinese immigrants were linked to Indians through a rhetoric that defined both as pagans, and thus through a transitive racial property they were also linked to black Californians. All, under this conception, were deemed equally incapable of shouldering the responsibilities of civic and political liberty in a democracy.

Between this combination of law and ideology, California's regime of white supremacy achieved a remarkable degree of stability that lasted for more than a decade. Beginning in the 1860s, however, events outside California challenged whites' capacity to maintain that stability, particularly when it came to the law. When the Civil War broke out, California quickly declared for the Union and remained staunchly loyal throughout the war. But the issues that had led to war, and the issues that drove its prosecution, highlighted uncomfortable similarities between California's regime of racial discrimination and that of the slave South. Under the influence of wartime passions, some white Californians began to soften their stance toward the state's racial minorities, and calls for the repeal of some of the state's harsher laws slowly gained a wider audience. After the war and the abolition of slavery, the federal government's efforts to protect the rights of freed slaves in the South raised even more pointed questions about racial discrimination in California, and hints that federal initiatives might undermine the state's careful division between white and nonwhite began to provoke opposition. By 1867, the very moment of Charles Loring Brace's visit, many white Californians feared that the actions of the federal government in the South might imperil their own racial hierarchy.

Brace's arrival, in fact, coincided with a titanic political struggle over the place nonwhite racial groups would hold in California society. The central issue in the state elections of 1867 was whether California would support the ongoing federal program of southern Reconstruction by ratifying the Fifteenth Amendment to the Constitution, which would abolish racial barriers to voting. In so doing, it would extend the right to shape California's future to the state's black residents. To this extent, California's political controversy mirrored debates over the Fifteenth Amendment throughout the nation. But the presence of thousands of California Indians and tens of thousands of Chinese immigrants in the state provoked a level of racial hysteria unmatched anywhere else. Suddenly California's racial promise was in real jeopardy, and politicians in pursuit of power whipped up fears over the dilution of white privilege until the election became not merely a referendum on the Fifteenth Amendment but a referendum on the entire program of Southern Reconstruction. To Brace's surprise, the issues surrounding Reconstruction seemed as vital in California as they were in the South, and it appeared to him that "the old battle of humanity fought on our coast, of justice to the negro, is going on here in different form—of justice to the pagan."[5]

Historians have traditionally treated Reconstruction as an exclusively Southern phenomenon. On one level, this makes perfect sense. It was in the South that slavery took root and reached its fullest expression. It was in the South that a distinctive regional culture, rooted in the institution of slavery, diverged sharply from the rest of the nation over the first half of the nineteenth century. It was the South that had seceded from the Union, and it was there that the fighting during the Civil War had taken its greatest toll. But Reconstruction was ultimately a *federal* initiative pursued at the highest level of American government. While aimed at the transformation of Southern culture and society, its key provisions—the Thirteenth, Fourteenth, and Fifteenth Amendments, and the Civil Rights Acts that animated them—were *national* in scope and so had the potential to reshape race relations throughout the country.[6]

Nineteenth-century Californians were fully aware of Reconstruction's western reach and its potential to reshape their lives. While Reconstruction may have been a national initiative aimed at a distant region, from its very beginning Californians, white and nonwhite alike, experienced it as a fundamentally local phenomenon. White Californians saw in Reconstruction legislation a threat to the simple racial hierarchy they had so carefully built up during the 1850s. As those federal efforts progressed and radicals in Congress grew more powerful, white Californians turned against Reconstruction and began to actively oppose it both at home and, through their elected representatives, in Washington, D.C.

Nonwhites in California, on the other hand, quickly recognized in Reconstruction an unprecedented opportunity to reshape the state's race relations. The Reconstruction Amendments, and the Civil Rights Acts of 1866, 1871, and 1875 that gave them life, offered a formidable arsenal with which California's racial minorities might resist their state's regime of white supremacy. Black Californians and Chinese immigrants, in particular, eagerly seized upon federal Reconstruction legislation designed to protect the rights of freed slaves in the South, and drew it west into California. Armed with these new laws, California's racial minorities launched assaults on their state's edifice of white privilege and supremacy on a wide number of fronts, effectively turning the state's racial diversity to their advantage. As a result, they precipitated a monumental battle over the racial ideas that justified California's regime of racial subordination and began a process that ultimately complicated and reshaped the state's racial hierarchy.

The following pages trace the effects of federal Reconstruction legislation on race relations in California, and by extension throughout the American West. While California's large and diverse population and its dominant economic position on the West Coast offer the clearest illustration of the issues surrounding western Reconstruction, it is important to note that California's experience was in no way exceptional; the events in multiracial California were mirrored throughout the West. Conflicts over legal discrimination that gripped California between the end of the Civil War and the end of the nineteenth century were matched by parallel controversies in Nevada, Colorado, Oregon, and Kansas, and in the territories of Washington, Montana, Oklahoma, and Wyoming. While western struggles over the meaning and reach of federal Reconstruction were rooted in specifically western contexts, western judicial interpretations of federal laws reverberated throughout the nation and profoundly influenced the course of Reconstruction even in the South. In this sense, the western experience with Reconstruction stands as much more than a simple supplement to the "real" Southern story. Rather, viewing Reconstruction from the West suggests a radically different narrative, one that carries significant implications for understanding race relations in twentieth-century America.

Western Reconstruction moved in directions radically different from those in the American South. Under the influence of federal Reconstruction, the West's multiracial context enabled a wide range of vigorous civil rights activities designed to expand the rights of racial minorities. As these efforts unfolded, however, that same multiracial context also discouraged any cooperative effort among the West's marginalized groups. In California, where whites pursued a strategy that defined each minority group in terms of the weaknesses of others, the very nature of whites' objections to minority participation in California society tended to force each of the state's racial minorities to sever their efforts from those of the others. In effect, California's own racial diversity ultimately encouraged not cooperation, but a kind of destructive competition in which each group embraced the principles of racial difference and sought to elevate its own status at the expense of the others. Throughout the era of Reconstruction, minority efforts to reshape California's western hierarchy pursued two parallel paths. Each group engaged in a sustained act of racial self-definition by recasting themselves as worthy participants in the affairs of a democratic republic. At the same time, each group attempted to distance itself from the others by portraying them as hopelessly alien and permanently unworthy. As they did so, California's racial minorities articulated a new racial rhetoric that distinguished between minority groups, and their use of federal legislation in California courts helped drive that rhetoric from the margins to the very center of California's racial ideology. Ironically, Reconstruction legislation in this context became a crucial tool not for eliminating racial discrimination, but for strengthening positions within the racial hierarchy, effectively preserving it and supporting white supremacy.

Viewing Reconstruction through a western lens thus adds an important new dimension to our understanding of the construction and maintenance of regimes of white supremacy. Such regimes are traditionally viewed as systems of oppression imposed upon defenseless and marginalized groups from above by powerful elites, but the California experience reveals a more muscular dynamic. Given the new tools offered by federal Reconstruction, California's racial minorities were hardly powerless, and their efforts to resist white racial oppression placed real limits on white dominance. Far from being passive victims, California's racial minorities were instead active participants in the elaboration of the state's new racial hierarchy. Moreover, when white Californians pushed back against these early civil rights efforts, they often did so by adopting the very rhetoric that racial minorities had used against each other. This new rhetoric and the ideas it embodied were thus folded into both the fight against racial oppression and the ongoing defense of white supremacy. In this sense, minorities' constant negotiation for position had the perverse effect of reproducing California's racial regime through time. Thus a racial hierarchy rooted in and structured by white supremacy came to be built and sustained by all Californians, white and nonwhite.[7]

Historians have long known that Reconstruction's influence extended beyond the South. Over the decade following the Civil War, industrial energies unleashed by the conflict profoundly transformed American economy and society. Federal Reconstruction measures intended to secure black freedom in the South were bent to new and unintended purposes by capitalists determined to expand their power and control over labor and the processes of production. Recognizing this, many scholars have expanded their vision of Reconstruction to include the North. Historians of the era have explored the ways in which Reconstruction legislation reshaped the national economy and effected the parallel transformation of the American state. They have also demonstrated the ways in which Reconstruction outside the South opened opportunities for women and reoriented American ideas about gender. Even as these studies have dramatically expanded our understanding of Reconstruction's economic and social influence, however, they have had the concomitant effect of diminishing the role played by race. A smaller number of historians have ranged farther west in search of the wider effects of Reconstruction, and in the process they have begun restore race as a key component of the era's national discourse. Beginning with Eugene Berwanger's seminal work on the controversies over black suffrage in the West, scholars have widened their vision to address the role of Reconstruction in such areas as federal Indian relations in the western territories, the rise of Sinophobia on the West Coast, and the role of western identities in reshaping national character.[8]

This book builds on earlier scholarship by focusing on the tension between local desires and national initiatives that lay at the heart of Reconstruction. Californians, both white and nonwhite, essentially elaborated their new and more complicated racial hierarchy within the reciprocal dynamic between local setting and national context. Again and again, events on the national stage forced a reordering of California's racial hierarchy and a corresponding reformulation of the racial ideas that supported it. Each new reformulation blurred the boundaries of white supremacy and inspired nonwhites to look beyond California's borders for strength and salvation. In the process, California was drawn ever more completely into the ambit of Southern Reconstruction, and the destinies of state and nation were bound more tightly together.

The racial dimension of the western Reconstruction experience in turn relies on a large body of scholarship exploring the history of race relations in nineteenth-century California. These various histories have been mined mostly by social historians whose work has carefully detailed the daily struggles of California's racial minorities in an atmosphere of fierce white supremacy. While the vast majority of these works have emphasized relations between a single minority and the white majority, their depth and breadth offer the potential for exploring new directions in the history of California race relations. Taken together, these works provide a solid foundation from which to study the interactions between nonwhite minorities beyond their association with whites. Taking Michael Omi and Howard Winant's description of race as a socially constructed identity as a given, this book uses the competition between nonwhite minorities for position within California's developing hierarchy to explore the ways in which racial categories were constructed among nonwhites.[9]

To do this, *An Aristocracy of Color* traces the formation of racial ideas through the law, and as such is deeply informed by the work of scholars in the fields of critical legal studies and its corollary, critical race theory. In doing so, this book supports the position of critical legal theorists who argue for a more dynamic vision of the role played by law in American life. Here, the law is more than a ratification of already developed social ideas and practices. The racial legal structure that grew up around struggles over Reconstruction in California was both an expression of widely held racial ideas and a shaper of those ideas in its own right. As laws governing racial inclusion and exclusion operated in California, they defined relationships that, over the closing decades of the nineteenth century, achieved normative status. In the process, these legally defined relationships spawned new racial ideas of their own that strengthened and extended California's racial project. By detailing the legal restrictions, obstacles, and opportunities experienced by ordinary Californians, this social history of law grounds abstract racial ideology in concrete daily existence.[10]

In case after case, the political and legislative process served as the primary mechanism through which white Californians sought to coax order out of their state's racial chaos. And it was through their control and manipulation of the political system that white Californians achieved the most concrete and lasting expression of the racial ideas they developed amid California's racial diversity. The racial ideas developed in nineteenth-century California, in virtually every aspect of social and economic life, were distilled into laws, rules, and regulations via legislative and judicial processes. The rules that governed racial exclusion in nineteenth-century California were not unspoken rules everyone simply understood; they were, instead, inscribed in law to ensure that the hierarchy whites constructed was backed by the machinery of the state.

Chapter 1 describes the earliest iterations of that machinery in the 1850s by analyzing white Californians' initial efforts to create a binary racial regime and minority groups' resistance against that effort. The discussion centers on an examination of laws prohibiting nonwhite testimony in court cases involving whites. Because these laws could leave minorities' property, livelihoods, and even lives beyond the protection of the courts, they were easily the most dangerous of all the legal disabilities imposed by the state. For this reason, these laws were also their first target of resistance. In the 1860s, debates over these laws in the context of the Civil War and Reconstruction began the long process of redefining racial relationships in California.

The second chapter traces the early steps of that process by examining white Californians' growing alarm over the implications, national and local, of Reconstruction. As congressional intentions concerning black citizenship and suffrage became clear, white Californians felt betrayed by a federal government that appeared to reward their loyalty with laws designed to dilute white privilege. In the state elections of 1867, white voters repudiated Reconstruction by handing control over the state government to Democrats who promised to block its effects. Once in office, they moved to blunt Reconstruction's reach by rejecting both the Fourteenth and Fifteenth Amendments to the U.S. Constitution. The debates over these amendments exposed the ways in which black citizenship limited white legislators' attempts to defend white privilege.

Chapter 3 details black and Chinese Californians' use of the equal protection clause of the Fourteenth Amendment to try to force open their state's segregated public schools. In 1872, black Californians brought a test case before the California Supreme Court that ended up establishing the "separate but equal" principle in California twenty-two years before *Plessy v. Ferguson*. Chinese Californians followed suit with a test case of their own in 1885 that secured public funding for the education of Chinese children, but that ultimately failed to desegregate California's public schools. In the process, both groups advanced arguments that helped to reshape popular conceptions of citizenship in the American West.

Chapters 4 and 5 turn to the civil rights activities of Chinese immigrants. Chapter 4 recounts the transformation in racial thinking that led to the Chinese Exclusion Act of 1882 through a detailed examination of controversies surrounding the spread of Chinese laundries into white middle-class neighborhoods in San Francisco. In the 1870s and 1880s, a series of municipal regulations intended to harass Chinese laundrymen out of business prompted a flurry of lawsuits in defense of Chinese livelihoods. As white Californians increasingly described Chinese immigrants as a disease infecting the body politic, Chinese court challenges forced the U.S. Supreme Court to reinterpret municipal police powers in light of the Fourteenth Amendment and as a result played an important role in shaping national Reconstruction. Finally, chapter 5 describes the widespread disappointment among white Californians over the perceived failure of the Chinese Exclusion Act to rid their state of Chinese immigrants. Frustrated by this apparent failure, mobs of white Californians drove Chinese laborers and their families from dozens of towns in 1885 and 1886. The Chinese fought back in the courts, again invoking federal legislation directly related to Reconstruction. The ultimate failure of Chinese litigation in this case revealed the limits of Reconstruction in the American West and marked the establishment of a new pattern of racial interaction that would guide white Californians' response to successive waves of immigration from Asia in the ensuing decades.

All of these chapters rely heavily on court testimony, judicial decisions, and legislative debates transcribed in newspapers, pamphlets, ephemera, and personal letters. Unless otherwise noted, all direct quotations herein are printed exactly as they were found, including italics and idiosyncrasies of spelling and grammar. Out of respect for the people whose lives and struggles are described here, this work will avoid the use of the patronizing "[*sic*]" to mark those moments when too little education or too much enthusiasm may have led grammar astray.

In the second half of the nineteenth century, immigration from all over the world made the United States a remarkably diverse nation, but California was unique in its racial diversity. Nowhere else did so many free people of so many different backgrounds live and work together in such close proximity. Nowhere else in the United States did Americans, white or nonwhite, make the kinds of intellectual, economic, and social adjustments that Californians were forced to make, and nowhere else was American racial ideology more complicated. In this sense, California's experience with Reconstruction was also unique. The ways in which Reconstruction reordered racial relationships in California simply could not have occurred anywhere else, and it is perhaps for this reason that Reconstruction in California has been mostly overlooked, even by California historians. But in the years since Reconstruction, the United States has grown into a multiracial nation. In the process, many of the controversies and racial struggles that Californians experienced more than one hundred years ago have been repeated again and again across the nation. Seen in this light, California's experience with Reconstruction was a rehearsal for the nation's future. Now, as then, the ideas and relationships that define race in America are the products of the labor of all Americans, regardless of race, and to trace the roots of multiracial conflict and coexistence in America we must look to the beginning, to California.

Chapter 1
"Every Colored Man Is the Victim"
Race and the Right to Be Heard in
California's Courts, 1851–1872

ROBBING CHINESE MINERS DURING the California Gold Rush was never a safe proposition, but in the summer of 1853, a petty thief named George Hall made it a lot easier. In early August of that year, Hall, Samuel Wiseman, and another man who may have been George's brother, John Hall, attacked a group of Chinese miners in Nevada County, in California's northern gold fields. The three men fell upon the camp intending only to rob the Chinese of their gold, but when the miners resisted and took flight, George fired his shotgun, hitting a miner named Ling Sing in the back. Ling Sing died soon after the robbery, and when the Nevada County sheriff caught up with the outlaws, he charged all three with murder.[1]

The three men were tried separately, and of the three, George Hall appears to have fared the worst. The evidence against Hall, based on the eyewitness accounts of several Chinese miners, was overwhelming. Hall's attorney, J. R. McConnell, decided to rest his defense on a desperate gamble: he demanded that the testimony of the Chinese miners be excluded on the ground that the state law barred Chinese from testifying against whites. In fact, the law did no such thing. Section 14 of the Criminal Practice Act of 1850 did exclude the testimony of blacks, mulattoes, and Indians of full and mixed blood in cases involving whites, but it made no mention of the Chinese. Accordingly, the judge overruled McConnell's objections and allowed the Chinese testimony. The jury promptly convicted Hall, and the judge sentenced him to hang.[2]

A casual observer might be forgiven for assuming that the verdict and sentence signaled the presence of a stable and smoothly functioning justice system. In reality, the swift justice meted out in Hall's case

14

offered only the illusion of order. The California State Legislature had established a court system just two years earlier, and, while on paper it reigned supreme, in practice California's courts struggled for legitimacy throughout the 1850s. Inside the courtroom, the newly transplanted American legal system competed with, and was occasionally driven to accommodate, Spanish and Mexican legal traditions that had shaped the rules governing landholding, citizenship, marriage and inheritance, and crime and punishment in California for nearly eighty years. The Gold Rush, moreover, exposed a curious blind spot in American law. Before the discovery at Sutter's Mill, the United States had no mining tradition and so no established body of law that might impose order on the frenzied scramble for instant wealth in California's gold fields. In the absence of uniform standards, each mining camp developed its own mining code, effectively establishing a patchwork alternative to the disciplined harmony sought by the courts. Navigating these alternatives to established authority consumed much of the courts' energies in the first decade of American control and hampered their efforts to coax order out of frontier California's boisterous chaos.[3]

Outside the courtroom, faith in the courts' ability to secure public safety often collapsed in the face of a widespread perception that crime was out of control. California's mining camps and boom towns were filled with single men on the make who were eager to blow off steam after a hard day's work, and virtually every contemporary observer noted the miners' seemingly inexhaustible gifts for drinking, gambling, and fighting. In the early days of the Gold Rush, such behavior was widely tolerated so long as it didn't spill over into outright theft or murder. But as thousands of gold seekers became tens of thousands and opportunities for easy riches narrowed, some decided that lifting gold from the pockets of law-abiding miners was easier than the painstaking labor of drawing it from creek beds in the Sierra foothills. As the state's criminal element grew bolder and more aggressive, the courts often appeared overwhelmed. In such circumstances, ordinary citizens showed little hesitation in turning to more "democratic" remedies. On at least forty occasions, most famously in San Francisco in 1851 and 1856, Californians brushed aside established authority and formed vigilance committees to deal with rising crime. In each case, the courts reassumed their rightful place as defenders of public virtue once the danger had passed, but the ease with which they could be deposed did little to inspire confidence.[4]

Even when they were in session, the courts were administered by men who were often notably lacking in self-control. At a time when dueling was a wholly illegal and yet popular pastime, California's judges could be counted upon to participate in duels as often as they condemned them. United States Supreme Court Justice Stephen J. Field's experiences in California offer a particularly illustrative example. While practicing law as a young man in Marysville in 1850, Field ran afoul of the local district judge, William R. Turner, a Texan whom one observer described as possessed of "a narrow mind and bitter prejudices," with the "bowie-knife manners of that border state." In one case Turner fined Field $500 and sentenced him to two days in jail for being disrespectful. Field appealed to another local court for release, won it, and then apparently encouraged a drunken mob to burn Turner in effigy later that evening. When an enraged Turner threatened his life, Field took to carrying two pistols with him at all times for self-defense. Field would later sit on the California State Supreme Court with David S. Terry, who stabbed a member of San Francisco's Vigilance Committee in 1856, killed a sitting U.S. senator in a duel in 1859, and was slain in a California train station in 1889 by Field's bodyguard during an apparent attempt to assassinate the justice. Simply put, "order" was not a word generally associated with California's courts during the Gold Rush.[5]

In the face of such uncertainty and volatility, George Hall would have been foolish indeed to simply accept the jury's guilty verdict and the judge's sentence of death by hanging. Luckily for him, he had a tenacious lawyer, and McConnell refused to let the case end there. He quickly filed an appeal to the California Supreme Court, claiming that his client had been cheated out of a fair trial by the inclusion of damaging Chinese testimony. Before the court, McConnell argued that the intent of the legislature in enacting the testimony law had been to exclude not solely the testimony of blacks and Indians, but the testimony of all nonwhites. Its failure to mention the Chinese in the statute was merely an oversight, a consequence of the scarcity of Chinese in

California when the law was enacted. McConnell asked the court to honor the legislature's intention and to grant George Hall a new trial without Chinese witnesses.[6]

In a decision issued more than a year later, in October 1854, the court agreed with McConnell, asserting that the legislature's "evident intention . . . was to throw around the citizen a protection . . . which could only be secured by removing him above the corrupting influences of degraded castes." In sum, the court declared that section 14 of the Criminal Practice Act of 1850 should be extended to include the Chinese. To do so, Chief Justice Hugh C. Murray simply defined the Chinese as Indians and barred their testimony from all California courts. Justice Murray's decision placed the Chinese, along with blacks and Indians, firmly beyond the guardianship of California's legal system, reserving its protective embrace solely for whites. Hall's conviction was overturned, and he was eventually acquitted.[7]

Clearly, the *Hall* decision was tied to the maintenance of white privilege and control in California. Yet at the same time, Murray's reasoning in *People v. Hall*, by linking Africans, Chinese, and Indians together, and particularly by defining the Chinese as Indians, amounted to an act of racial classification, and, more important, inscribed that classification in law. In doing so, Murray touched on a larger intellectual movement that sought to explain racial differences using the vocabulary employed in the rapidly developing physical sciences. New principles and discoveries in physiology, archaeology, and medicine, as well as in less rigorous "sciences" such as phrenology, were broadly disseminated throughout American popular culture, and by the mid-1850s had won widespread acceptance. Murray's incorporation of these ideas into the law was, in some respects, the next logical step.

Nineteenth-century California was the most racially diverse region in the United States, and, for that reason, from the perspective of white American immigrants, it was also the most alien. White Californians dealt with that diversity by drawing a color line through their laws that divided the world into two simple categories: white and non-white. While white Californians were fully aware that developments in racial science in the eastern United States and Europe painted a much more complicated picture of the world, they consciously maintained a disjunction between theory and practice. In this, white Californians hewed to an American intellectual tradition that assumed a binary division between whites and all others, or between those who were considered capable of shouldering the responsibilities of civic and political liberty in a democracy and those who were not. Justice Murray's decision, by drawing Africans, Chinese, and particularly Indians in all their kaleidoscopic diversity into a single group, ratified that binary racial divide and confirmed its legal potency. Over the next two decades, however, as members of these excluded groups challenged that binary framework, it became clear that protecting white supremacy required a more nuanced system. Racial science demanded a much more complicated parsing of racial differences, and whites soon found themselves not only justifying the maintenance of white privilege, but also sketching out the details of an elaborate racial hierarchy that drew distinctions between peoples of color even as it set whites apart from, and above, other races.

Meanwhile, events outside California radically altered the legal and racial landscape at the national level and exerted enormous pressure on California's regime of white racial supremacy. The Civil War swelled the ranks of the state's small but active Republican Party and prompted many white Californians to question a racial regime that bore an obvious and uncomfortable similarity to that of the Confederacy. After the war, federal Reconstruction legislation originally intended to protect the rights of freed slaves in the South found its way to the West, and in the hands of California's nonwhites, particularly the Chinese, became a valuable tool in the fight for access to California's courts.

Nonwhites, particularly black Californians and the Chinese, responded to whites' racial classification project with a robust and often angry defense of their rights and dignity as full-fledged members of the human race. Yet at every step, their responses were conditioned by whites' increasing reliance on the theories of racial science. From the earliest appearance of the language of racial science in Justice Murray's 1854 decision to the final repeal of the testimony restrictions in 1873, California's nonwhite minorities struck back using the same language, all the while reshaping its vocabulary to suit their own purposes.

Their use of this language channeled their resistance down two paths that deeply influenced the shape of California's racial hierarchy. First, nonwhites resisted the project of racial classification by engaging in their own act of racial definition, explicitly challenging whites' description of them as degraded races. Black Californians emphasized their potential as productive and virtuous citizens, resting their arguments on the common moral and civic world they had long shared with whites, and on aspirations to middle-class status. The Chinese, on the other hand, demanded respect as representatives of an ancient and venerable civilization whose accomplishments compared favorably with those of the United States. Second, the very nature of whites' objections to nonwhite testimony and their justifications for the continued application of the law tended to force each of California's racial minorities to sever their efforts from those of the others. The logic of the developing hierarchy, by setting peoples of color apart from one another, encouraged each of the racial groups to compete against the others for position on the scale. The result was a racial hierarchy more complicated than any known in the eastern United States, and one not imposed from above by whites but created instead through the efforts of all Californians.

Life under People v. Hall

The first steps in the elaboration of California's racial hierarchy were taken by a chief magistrate whose sympathies clearly lay with white America. Depending on one's point of view, Hugh C. Murray either lacked entirely the sort of gravity and august authority needed to shape California's social order, or he was perfectly suited to elaborate the boundaries of legal apartheid. Appointed to the court in 1851 at age twenty-six, Murray was California's youngest chief justice. Murray's close connections with the Democratic Party and later with the nativist Know-Nothings lent his politics a strong racial dimension that would profoundly shape California's racial landscape. Widely known as a drunk, Murray fit comfortably into the rambunctious world of California's courts. Soon after his appointment to the state supreme court, Murray grabbed State Assemblyman John Conness by the throat and threw him against a crowded hotel bar after Conness, a future U.S.

senator, made some disparaging remarks about him. On another occasion, and again while sitting as a justice on the state's supreme court, Murray attacked a man on the street and beat him with his cane because the man had publicly described him as "the meanest man that ever sat on a supreme bench." As a young and evidently untutored lawyer, Murray owed his appointment to political patronage and commanded little respect as a jurist. His decisions tended to be brief and simplistic, often turning, as in the *Hall* case, on a single question of law. As one contemporary critic put it, Murray's decisions mixed "about equal portions of stupidity, dishonesty, malignity, and brandy."[8]

Murray opened his argument in *People v. Hall* with a rather baffling appeal to history. He decided that the central issue in the case was whether, in excluding black and Indian testimony, the legislature had used the terms "black" and "Indian" in a generic sense, or whether they had intended that the terms should refer to "specific types of human species." In addressing the question, Murray performed a remarkable series of semantic contortions to establish the legal principle he needed to protect white privilege. He reasoned that upon reaching the New World, Columbus, apparently under the impression he had reached Asia, had referred to the people he found there as "Indians" and that that moment should stand as the guiding precedent. "From that time down to a very recent period," wrote Murray, "the American Indians, and the Mongolian, or Asiatic, were regarded as the same type of human species." In other words, with Christopher Columbus as his guide, Murray determined that the term "Indian" was generic, not specific, and that the Chinese ought legally to be defined as Indians.[9]

The manner in which Justice Murray framed the legal issue signaled his direction and intent. By referring to various "types of human species," he assumed the role of scientist, and explicitly elevated humanity's taxonomic status from species to genus. Murray then went on to canvass the elements of scientific racial thought popular at the time in both the United States and Europe.[10]

Murray began by referring to older ideas that divided the human race into the traditional three groups—black, white, and red—and cited the well-known work of French naturalist and racial theorist Baron Georges Cuvier as an authority for continued acceptance of such a division. Cuvier, wrote Murray, broke those groups into numerous varieties and "tribes," and in this legal decision, Murray himself pushed the discussion by rooting the distinctions and similarities between these tribes in geography, physiology, and environment. The mountain ranges of both "Kamtschatka" and Alaska, he wrote, were "inhabited by a race who resemble, in a remarkable degree, in language and appearance, the Esquimaux, who again, in turn, resemble other tribes of American Indians." Spatial proximity signaled a much more important and much deeper connection between the peoples of Asia and North America. "The similarity of the skull and pelvis, and the general configuration of the two races; the remarkable resemblance in eyes, beard, hair, and other peculiarities . . . necessarily arise from the circumstances of climate, pursuits, and other physical causes." The difference between Asian peoples and Native Americans, Murray concluded, "was no greater than that existing between the Arab and the European, both of whom were supposed to belong to the Caucasian race."[11]

The *Hall* decision explicitly categorized the Chinese and Africans in terms of those whom whites considered the lowest common denominator, the California Indian. Whites' perceptions of their new, Native neighbors were conditioned by more than two centuries of accumulated experience with American Indians in the eastern United States and on the Great Plains. By the 1850s those experiences, alternately violent, commercial, and intimate, were for most white Americans filtered through a hazy film of romantic literature, lurid press reports of Native savagery, and an ideology of white supremacy rapidly hardening under the influence of racial science. Much of that science was devoted to classification schemes comparing the virtues of various peoples, and in California romantic, literary visions of the "Noble Savage" were quickly replaced by new visions that depicted California Indians as hopelessly primitive.[12]

Invidious comparisons were inevitable, and in press dispatches sent from the Pacific coast white commentators routinely grouped local native populations at the lower end of the developmental scale. "The Indians of California," claimed one writer, "may, without injustice, be classed lower in the scale of mankind even than the Esqimaux.

Equally inanimate and filthy in habit, they do not possess that inge-
nuity and perseverance which their northern neighbors can boast."
"The only thing that can be called human in the appearance of the
digger Indians of the Sierra Nevada," wrote another, "is their resemblance to the sons of Adam." The Gold Rush years saw every aspect
of Native custom and culture subjected to withering scrutiny, from
physical appearance and dress, diet and work habits, to family life and
spirituality. They were dismissed as "the most repulsive of all Indians,"
and as "small in stature; thin, squalid, dirty, and degraded in appearance." They were universally derided as "diggers," an artless term derived from the pervasive conviction that their diet consisted entirely
of "roots and reptiles, insects and vermin." Most tellingly in the context of the Gold Rush, California Indians were alternately described
as passively indolent and savagely violent. "Sullen and lazy," went one
common refrain, "they only rouse themselves when pressed by want;
and in the settlements of the missionaries, called Missions, where the
cravings of hunger and thirst are satisfied, coercion alone goads them
to labor." On the other hand, claimed a writer in San Francisco's *Daily
Alta California*, "Indolent and listless as they usually are, they are dangerous when aroused." Throughout the 1850s, panicked calls for military protection from Indian "hostilities" rang from every corner of the
state, initiating more than a decade of genocidal warfare that seemed
to confirm the Indians' irredeemable viciousness. While these images
might at first appear contradictory, they were in reality two sides of
the same coin: both images—passive indolence and bloodthirsty savagery—cast California Indians as obstacles to white American progress. Views such as these were unlikely to leave any place for Indian
peoples in the new American state.[13]

Whites' racial attitudes toward California Indians tracked neatly
with a longstanding national policy that sought to clear space for American civilization by removing Indian "obstacles" standing in the way of
American greatness to regions beyond the boundaries of white settlement. By the time U.S. forces occupied California in 1846, removal
policies had largely transformed whites' desire for racial segregation
into reality, at least east of the Mississippi River. But while the desire
for racial separation persisted during and after the Mexican War, the

seizure of California fatally undermined the policy of removal. Simply put, there was no place farther west that Indian peoples could be moved. The logic of this new reality exposed a basic truth: because continental expansion had always been a national goal, Indian removal had always been something of a fantasy, akin to the contemporaneous movement promoting African colonization. And yet, when confronted by this realization, white Americans in California chose to preserve the fantasy of separation by laying the groundwork for a new reservation system that would later become the model for a new national Indian policy. As has happened so often in the American past, the yearning for racial purity trumped physical reality.[14]

Beneath these desires for racial separation, however, lay a deeper and more terrible truth that drastically complicated white racial judgments of California Indians. Much as they might have wished for a racially segregated society, new arrivals in California quickly confronted the reality that Indian labor formed the backbone of California's economy. California Indians were unique among North American Indian peoples in that almost from the moment of European contact, they were critical participants in local labor markets. In the Spanish and Mexican eras, Indian laborers played a central role in the development of California's ranching and farming economies. As a result, locals muddled their racial judgments by regularly distinguishing between "wild" and "useful" Indians, according to the nature of their relationship to production. When gold was discovered in 1848, Indian laborers were among the first employed in the diggings, and as gold fever drained the state's labor pool, Indians became even more important to the state's agricultural producers. As a result, white Californians' desire for racial separation warred with the desperate need for Indian labor. One measure of that desperation can be seen in a law passed by the first California State Legislature titled *An Act for the Government and Protection of Indians*. Under this law, whose title should be judged a cruel joke, any Indian not obviously engaged in labor could be arrested and compelled to work for a term of up to four months; traditional Indian hunting and gathering practices were redefined as crimes carrying stiff fines that could be paid off only through labor; and Indian children could be bound out to white "masters" until they reached the age of fifteen for girls and eighteen for boys. Rather than protecting Indians, the law created a system of slavery in all but name that, as we shall see, contributed mightily to the rapid decline of California's Indian population. And, in contributing to that decline, the law ensured that California Indians would continue to be viewed as a servile, stunted, and childlike race—qualities that would soon be applied, as in the *Hall* case, to the Chinese.[15]

Simply tying these same qualities to the Chinese, however, was not enough for Justice Murray. Even as he pressed his argument behind the cold edge of science, Murray betrayed a visceral hatred of the Chinese in a tone that vacillated between panic and disgust. Sound public policy, he insisted, demanded that Chinese be excluded from the courts. "The same rule which would admit them to testify, would admit them to all the equal rights of citizenship, and we might soon see them at the polls, in the jury box, upon the bench, and in our legislative halls." Murray never explained just how removing a gag in court might lead to full inclusion, but he anticipated that inevitability with trepidation and placed himself firmly in its path. The depth of his trepidation, stated for the public record and established as a legal guide for California's courts, is worth quoting at length:

> The anomalous spectacle of a distinct people, living in our community, recognizing no laws of this State, except through necessity, bringing with them their prejudices and national feuds, in which they indulge in open violation of the law; whose mendacity is proverbial; a race of people who nature has marked as inferior, and who are incapable of progress or intellectual development beyond a certain point, as their history has shown; differing in language, opinions, color, and physical conformation; between whom and ourselves nature has placed an impassable difference, is now presented, and for them is claimed, not only the right to swear away the life of a citizen, but the further privilege of participating with us in administering the affairs of our Government.[16]

Clearly, Murray's racial fears were not reserved alone for the fates of criminals convicted on nonwhite testimony. In his mind, and in the minds of many whites in California, the issue of nonwhite testimony reached well beyond the witness box. Extending testimony privileges to the Chinese, for instance, also meant endowing the Chinese with the power to command white action. Testimony privileges would allow a Chinese immigrant to compel local sheriffs to arrest white suspects. A Chinese immigrant would have the power to compel a white judge to convene court proceedings, the power to subpoena white witnesses, and the power to compel twelve white men to expend time and energy as jurors. Testimony privileges meant, in effect, giving nonwhites an opportunity, however limited, to seize control of the levers of government. As Murray's decision shows, the prospect could push whites to near hysteria.

To this point, Murray had established a clear legal principle and accomplished his goal, but his special hatred for the Chinese prompted him to open a door to racial equality even as he closed another. Justice Murray's reference to "pursuits" as a causal factor in racial differentiation allowed him to define even finer distinctions between races. Many theorists of the day, following the evolutionary theories developed by French naturalist Jean-Baptiste Lamarck and championed in the United States by renowned Harvard paleontologist Louis Agassiz, argued that different cultural and political practices led to the development of racial characteristics. According to this theory, American civil institutions, for example, imbued Americans with a love of liberty and an egalitarian sense of fair play. Once acquired, such characteristics could be physically passed on to successive generations. For this reason, Justice Murray wrote, there were clear differences between "domestic negroes and Indians, who not infrequently have correct notions of their obligations to society," and "the more degraded tribes of the same species, who have nothing in common with us, in language, country or laws." Those nonwhites who had been raised in the United States and were familiar with republican institutions might in some limited sense be able to participate in American society. And although he would most certainly have denied it, his argument implied that perhaps even the Chinese, in time, might improve. Murray's admission breached the wall protecting white privilege, and over the next several years, nonwhites forced their way into the breach and widened it.[17]

That battle, however, was waged almost entirely by black Californians and the Chinese. Because the California Constitution of 1849 defined California's Mexican and Californio population as white, these laws did not, strictly speaking, affect them. Even so, legal status was no guarantee of equivalent social status, and in the years following American occupation, California's former rulers faced a steady erosion of their standing in the new American state. Gold seekers from the eastern United States brought with them a virulent vision of white supremacy, and under its influence they readily defined the Mexicans they met in the diggings as inferior. And yet, in the confusing mix of races occasioned by the Gold Rush, class affiliation could often mitigate racial judgments. Californio elites, particularly those in the southern part of the state, possessed a great deal of wealth in land and cattle, and as a result their racial status was as much a function of economic standing as it was of skin color. Wealthy Californios shrewdly translated their wealth into political influence and seats in the new State Legislature, where they sought to stave off their decline by joining their new American neighbors in defending white privilege. In fact, Californio members of the legislature repeatedly voted to support exclusionary testimony laws throughout much of the 1850s. It was only when, as we shall see, a member of the Californio elite was denied the right to testify in court for racial reasons that these legislators added their voices to the chorus of protest.[18]

California Indians, on the other hand, had worries much more important and immediate than their right to testify in court. The Gold Rush drew tens of thousands of people to regions of California that had largely avoided white encroachment in the Spanish and Mexican eras, with dire consequences for the local environment and the people who depended on it. Hordes of miners scared off game, filled salmon runs with silt, and cut down the oak trees whose acorns formed the core of the Indian diet. Ranchers and farmers claimed grasslands for themselves, and their new regime of private property immediately transformed Indian hunting and foraging practices into theft. Driven to near starvation, California Indians turned to raiding for survival, initiating a deadly cycle of retaliatory massacres. Frightened settlers demanded protection, and the state government obliged by funding militia expeditions that can be described only as pogroms. Worse still, state and local authorities began offering bounties for Indian scalps, encouraging even more indiscriminate slaughter. In this, white Californians' treatment of the state's native inhabitants ratified their judgments of them as something less than human. What followed was what nineteenth-century historian Hubert Howe Bancroft described as "one of the last human hunts in history, and the basest and most brutal of them all." Between wars of extermination and the labor regime established by the state's *Act for the Government and Protection of Indians,* California's Indian population virtually collapsed during the 1850s and 1860s. At the beginning of American occupation in 1846, the California Indian population stood at about 150,000. By 1870 their numbers had fallen to 30,000, and by 1890, forty-two years after the end of the Mexican War, the Indian population in California stood at just 16,000. Exclusion from the courts ranked a distant second to the struggle to survive, and in the end California Indians would serve more as rhetorical foils than as active participants in the elaboration of the state's racial hierarchy.[19]

While California's free blacks were not the victims of wars of extermination, their exclusion from California's courts could still make their daily lives precarious. Black Californians suffered from all manner of official discrimination, from limits on residence and hotel accommodations to restrictions in public transportation and public education. Until 1875, state law barred black Californians from practicing law, and on several occasions the state legislature debated and nearly passed laws barring African Americans entirely from the state. Each of these instances of discrimination drew the condemnation of black Californians and spawned civil rights activism, but none generated the same level of light and heat as the testimony laws. Simply put, this was because the prohibition on black testimony was by far the most dangerous of the legal restrictions visited upon California's black community. The 1851 law barring black testimony in civil cases left black Californians' property barely protected from fraud and theft. Land ownership, the primary symbol of masculine independence and, in Gold Rush California's speculative economy, a quick route to wealth, was especially untenable in the absence of real legal protection. A

white squatter could, with relative ease, push African American farmers and miners off of land they had worked for years. The courts could
intervene only if the victim's white neighbors demanded action and
were willing to testify publicly against another white.[20]

Simple fraud and theft, however, were far more common than
outright eviction. In December 1850, for instance, nineteen-year-old
Sarah J. Carroll stormed into the court of Sacramento Justice of the
Peace Charles C. Sackett and angrily demanded the arrest of her erst-
while friend, William Potter. Potter, she claimed, had stolen $700 in
gold and jewelry from her home and was at that moment aboard a
ferry planning to flee the city. The census of 1860 marks Ms. Carroll as a mulatta and one of eleven black prostitutes in Sacramento.
Ms. Carroll explained that Potter hadn't exactly broken into her home.
In fact, the two lived together and had done so "for some time past."
The judge accepted her story and swore out a warrant for the "arrest of
Wm. H. Potter f.m.c.," or "free man of color," assuming that their living arrangements meant that Potter, too, was black. Sackett's curt note
dismissing the case plainly reveals that he was mistaken. "Defendant
discharged, he proving himself a white man & none but Colored testimony against him." Potter was immediately back on the street and,
presumably, back on the ferry with Sarah Carroll's $700. Free blacks
in San Francisco and Sacramento were also routinely sued for fictional
unpaid debts by unscrupulous whites looking for easy cash, and confidence men throughout the state were careful to conduct business only
in the presence of nonwhites, safe in the knowledge that the law could
not reach them.[21]

The danger represented by the testimony exclusions was more
than financial; California's free blacks also ran a great risk of physical
harm, as in the case of Peter Lester, co-owner of San Francisco's Pioneer Boot and Shoe Emporium. In 1851, Lester was attacked in his
store and viciously caned by an unhappy white customer. Because of
the testimony laws, Lester "was compelled tamely to submit, for had
he raised his hand he would have been shot, and no redress." Newspapers of the period clearly show that black Californians were routinely assaulted or even killed, often in the presence of numerous
witnesses, yet convictions for such outrages were rare.[22]

Under California's exclusionary testimony laws, mining camps like the one depicted in this artist's rendering presented a tempting target for thieves. *Chinese Camp in the Mines*, lithograph by J. D. Borthwick, from *Three Years in California* (1857). (Courtesy, California Historical Society, CHS2010.431.tif.)

The Chinese, too, were no strangers to discrimination in California. Foreign miners' taxes and immigration restrictions, along with mob violence and criminal assaults of the sort practiced by George Hall, had for some time dominated the lives of Chinese sojourners on Golden Mountain. The exclusion of their testimony was a relatively new legal disability, but it was easily the most dangerous. Justice Murray's reasoning in the *Hall* decision effectively stripped the Chinese of all meaningful protection and appeared to imply that murder was an acceptable response to the presence of Chinese in California.

Through parallel civil rights movements, both groups vigorously opposed the world created by *People v. Hall*, but even as they challenged the testimony exclusions, California's racial minorities did not mount a direct challenge to the intellectual foundations of white supremacy; in fact, nonwhites often voiced their opposition in language that appeared to accept some basic assumptions of white supremacy. Even as they resented the line established by Justice Murray separating whites from nonwhites, they embraced the proposition that invidious distinctions should be made between the various races. At first, this acceptance was muted as both black Californians and Chinese each argued for inclusion by asserting their similarity with whites and their dignity as human beings. Yet as time passed, both groups showed an increasing willingness to attack each other and Indians in their efforts to gain respect among whites.

From 1851 to 1855, black communities throughout the state held small meetings in an attempt to organize resistance to the laws. Finally, in the fall of 1855, several prominent members of San Francisco's black community published a call for the first of what would be a series of statewide conventions of black Californians to organize and coordinate their efforts. When the convention met in Sacramento's Colored Methodist Church in November 1855, forty-nine delegates from ten counties quickly settled on a strategy that held for the rest of the decade. Taking a page from abolitionists in the eastern United States, the convention delegates decided to flood the legislature with petitions from all over the state calling for repeal of the testimony laws.[23]

Their chosen path is, in some ways, not surprising. Black Californians' exclusion from American political life did not isolate them entirely from American political culture. Even as American political practice reduced them to inferior status, American political ideals held out the potential for a better future. A lifetime on the margins of American politics had taught them the forms of American political culture, and they had watched other marginalized groups, particularly the Irish, avail themselves of those forms to move from the margins to the center of American political life. Practicing those forms independently was the surest way to prove their worthiness for inclusion. At the same time, many of the same leaders who called for a statewide convention had past experience in eastern abolition circles, and that experience had shown them that some whites were receptive to black aspirations. In California, then, blacks proceeded with a tempered optimism.

In each of the conventions, delegates argued over the tone of their petitions, and their arguments reveal how popular conceptions of racial science shaped the self-image of nonwhites as well as whites. Angry voices were raised in opposition to what one conventioneer called "the oft repeated taunt that we are but the connecting link between the monkey and the man," and delegates repeatedly reminded each other that "every colored man is the victim of bitter prejudice and unjust laws." But these voices were in the minority. The language used by most delegates implied that while black leaders refused to accept unequal treatment before the law, many were willing to defer to the authority of science, even to the point of conceding ideas of black inferiority espoused by racial science.[24]

The president of the first convention, William H. Yates, a former slave who had purchased his family's freedom while working as a porter for the U.S. Supreme Court, spoke for many when he appeared to accept the notions of black inferiority that supported whites' exclusion of black testimony. "While I acknowledge," he said, "that in form, appearance and education the African cannot compete with the Caucasian race, yet his sympathies are as warm, and his feelings as human. He can be grateful for kindness shown, and is ready to forgive the injuries done him—he loves his country as dearly as they." William Newby of San Francisco took Yates at his word and publicly forgave whites for having passed the testimony laws, saying that the legislature's handiwork derived from "an honest principle" and what "they believed to be a sense of duty." Even as the delegates decried the legal disabilities visited upon them by white Californians, many expressed a kind of gratitude bordering on filial piety for the gifts of white civilization. In the process, they revealed how powerfully the intellectual underpinnings of white racial superiority had influenced the thinking of all Californians. In another speech, Yates himself summed these feelings up, arguing that "if there are feelings of liberty within the breasts of those present, who but the Caucasian taught them to us?" In the end, each of the conventions adopted a conciliatory—one delegate called it "crouching"—tone for their petitions, positioning themselves more as supplicants than as equals.[25]

However "crouching" their tone, black Californians began staking out what would become a bold rhetorical position. Gaining access to the courts required that black Californians cast themselves as more intimately connected with white Anglo America than most white Californians were willing to allow. To forge that link, they fastened onto two subtle strategies. First, and most simply, black Californians took the initial steps in distinguishing themselves from other nonwhites by limiting their requests for a change in the law to themselves. The state convention's Executive Committee distributed preprinted petitions around the state which prayed for a repeal solely in relation to "those provisions of the law which disqualifies negroes and mulattoes from being competent witnesses in Courts of justice." This strategy reflected the feeling voiced by many leading black Californians that their lifelong association with the white polity entitled them to more consideration than other nonwhites.[26]

Second, black Californians extended this idea in the pages of the state's first black newspaper, the *Mirror of the Times*, which had been established at the behest of the delegates at the second state convention in 1856. As petitions from around the state poured into Sacramento, the editors at the *Mirror* attacked the logic of the testimony laws not by denigrating other nonwhites but by challenging the fitness of white immigrants. "We are men, and Americans," they wrote. "Free men; born on the soil, and claim all rights and immunities that any other class of men enjoy, not by adoption, but by right of birth." Their target was clearly the Irish immigrant, and their assessment of the Irish was harsh. "We want no laws in this State that decide the character of a man by the color of his skin," they wrote, "and we want no man who is unable to read and write his own name to dictate in the Councils of State what position we shall occupy on the soil of our nativity." "We are entirely unwilling," they concluded, "to be excluded from any participation in the Government which we contribute to support, while it elevates the ignorant foreigner, with the brogue on his tongue, for base party purposes." Black Californians were effectively attempting to cross Justice Murray's color line by muddling its precise position. Pointing to the Irish had the effect of breaking apart the notion of whites as a monolithic group at the same time that it reduced the distance between black and white. It also, by drawing invidious distinctions with the Irish, reversed a strategy pursued by the Irish themselves against African Americans in the East.[27]

Mifflin W. Gibbs (1823–1915). As co-owner of San
Francisco's Pioneer Boot and Shoe Emporium, Gibbs
was one of the city's most prosperous black residents.
In 1855, he was the editor of California's first black
newspaper, the *Mirror of the Times*. (Courtesy of the
New York Public Library, image 1169802.)

Such demands for equal treatment were not unique to California;
in fact, in the years to come, a similar pattern of black activism would
be repeated throughout the West. Drawing both on activist methods
developed in eastern abolitionist circles and on the experiences of
black Californians, black westerners formed committees, held conventions, and signed petitions, all aimed at ending discrimination.
In 1865, for example, the Nevada Executive Committee, made up of
black residents of Virginia City, Gold Hill, and Silver City, sent petitions to the state legislature calling for an end to discrimination and
"equal rights before the Law to all the Colored Citizens of the State

of Nevada." The following year, black Kansans held a convention in Lawrence at which participants questioned the racial logic that denied them access to the ballot box and pledged to be "a constant trouble in the state" until they had achieved equality. In Colorado, black men worked to block whites' movement toward statehood until the franchise was broadened to include them. Far from playing the role of passive victims, African Americans in the American West pushed back against discriminatory laws wherever they found them.[28]

Although the world created by *People v. Hall* left black Californians with little more than rhetoric as a defense, the Chinese occupied a somewhat different position. The Chinese arrived in California under the protection of treaty agreements that challenged white Californians' carefully constructed racial divide. However feeble and fractious it might have been, the Chinese Empire, by its very existence and age, offered some legal standing and a powerful rhetorical position for its subjects in California. The Chinese were foreign nationals. By the mid-nineteenth century, trade with China had become a significant contributor to the U.S. economy, and as a result the wishes of the Chinese government carried weight with American government officials. So while the law unambiguously subordinated black and Indian Californians, Chinese immigrants, as both a racial group and as foreign nationals, occupied a more nebulous legal space that whites eagerly labored to define more clearly.

Almost from the moment of their arrival, whites had sought to reduce the Chinese to the status legally established for blacks and Indians by linking them with California's other denigrated racial minorities. In a June 1853 editorial, for instance, editors at the *Daily Alta California* questioned the wisdom of unlimited Chinese immigration in terms that left no doubt about their views. The Chinese, opined the *Alta*, boasted "most of the vices and few of the virtues of the negro." They were "more clannish therefore more dangerous than the negro, more cunning and deceitful, *and less fitted to become menials or servants*." Worse still, the Chinese were "*not so provident as negroes*," were more offensive in their habits, and were "*mentally inferior to whites*." While the editors at the *Alta* firmly ranked the Chinese below blacks, others were less certain. An Englishman visiting San Francisco in the early 1850s wrote that "the Chinaman is looked upon by some as only a little superior to the negro, and by others as somewhat inferior." California Assemblyman J. E. Clayton deemed the Chinese "worse than worthless" and claimed that this distaste for the Chinese extended beyond whites. "The lowest digger Indian looks upon them with utter scorn," he cried, "and looks forward to the time [when] he can . . . exterminate these far away Indians, that they so much despise." Clayton's comments reflected the racial ideas embedded in the *Hall* decision, and his speech reinforced the diminished status decreed by Justice Murray. While such rhetoric justified distinguishing Chinese from whites more than it suggested real distinctions among nonwhite groups, the comparisons stung and provoked a strong protest.[29]

In the protest, a group of Chinese merchants, speaking for the Chinese community as a whole, combined an indignant defense of their status as a civilized people with a description of California Indians that showed they understood Murray's intentions perfectly. The merchants began by pointing out that they had come to America with high hopes and that initially they had been treated well. "But of late days," they wrote, "your honorable people have established a new practice. They have come to the conclusion that we Chinese are the same as Indians and Negroes, and your courts will not allow us to bear witness." The Chinese were clearly insulted at being classified with both Africans and Indians, but for the moment, they chose to focus their anger on being classed with only one of the other racial groups. "And yet these Indians know nothing about the relations of society; they know no mutual respect; they wear neither clothes nor shoes; they live in wild places and in caves." The Chinese argued they were neither slave nor savage; their race was instead suited perfectly for civilization, and China, as the oldest surviving civilization in the known world, was hardly to be classed with such peoples as these. "Can it be possible," they wondered, "that we are classed as equals with this uncivilized race of man?"[30]

The Chinese spoke through Reverend William Speer, a tireless champion of Chinese rights in California from the earliest days of the Gold Rush to the end of the century. Speer spent most of his adult life among the Chinese. In 1846, at the age of twenty-four, he was sent by the Presbyterian Board of Foreign Missionaries to Canton to minister to the Chinese in the midst of the Opium Wars. In 1852, Speer, by then fluent in both written and spoken Chinese, was reassigned to California and directed to minister to them in their own language. He spent the next thirty years defending the Chinese against discrimination and self-consciously wielded the power and authority of the clergy to accomplish his goals. In 1853, Reverend Speer was in Nevada County acting as interpreter for the Chinese witnesses in *People v. Hall*, and in 1855, Speer translated the first public protest transmitted to the State Legislature from California's Chinese immigrants.[31]

Over the next several years, as the legislature passed discriminatory legislation and toyed with innovative ways to halt Chinese immigration, Reverend Speer penned a series of learned and earnest appeals for a change in the testimony laws that built upon the arguments contained in the first. Embedded within these appeals were expositions on Chinese culture and civilization which, he hoped, would ease the ignorance of legislators and encourage more enlightened treatment of the Chinese.

In his appeals, Speer attacked the conclusions drawn from racial science by Justice Murray and others in anthropological and theological terms. He began by attacking the link between all three excluded groups established in *People v. Hall*. "I insist," he wrote, "that it is a violation of all right to include Asiatics in the category of either Indians or negroes." The Chinese, he felt, should be placed much higher in the scale of mankind being shaped in California. "They are as far removed ethnologically from either variety of the human race as we are." Speer's intention was not to break down the line forged by Murray, but to move it by establishing a closer affinity between the Chinese and whites. "If the Chinese are Indians, then *we* are Indians; if the Chinese are negroes, then *we* are negroes." For believing Christians, one conclusion to be drawn from Justice Murray's arguments was that God had created an "inferior species of mankind." Speer argued that this belief was unworthy of enlightened nineteenth-century men and cautioned against blasphemy, warning legislators against "heathenish ignorance." Holding such beliefs and incorporating them into law, he

Reverend William Speer's 1857 pamphlet, *An Earnest Appeal*, sought to persuade the California legislature to relax the state's exclusionary testimony laws by presenting Chinese immigrants as representatives of an ancient and advanced civilization. (Courtesy of the Bancroft Library, University of California, Berkeley, xF870.C5.C51 v.1:5.)

insisted, risked an end to God's grace in California and the very souls of the state's leaders.[32]

The all-white legislature's response to these arguments, black and Chinese, was hardly enthusiastic. In spite of the fact that both black Californians and Chinese immigrants had white allies and defenders, the majority of whites jealously guarded their state's color line, and their politics reflected that jealousy. Throughout the 1850s, the state government was dominated by the Democratic Party, whose legendary skill at manipulating racial anxiety for political ends at both the state and national levels is well documented. Lawmakers simply tabled Chinese petitions without comment, while suggestions that petitions from black Californians be thrown "out of the window" or "burnt" and never considered again were common. Sometimes white Democratic politicians went further, taking actions that sent a clear message to nonwhites that they risked more than rejection when they challenged white legal authority. In 1858, petition drives provoked the introduction of a bill designed to restrict further "negro immigration" into California, and even to deport those who refused to leave. This bill, along with a series of so-called "Coolie" bills encompassing the same object for the Chinese, stirred vigorous and vituperative debate, whereas the petitions had met with comparative silence.[33]

The message was clear, and, after 1858, nonwhite communications on the subject of the testimony laws all but ceased. Many black Californians, frustrated by the failure of their petitions and further demoralized by the Dred Scott decision in March 1857, declared the United States irredeemable and quit the state in a mass exodus for more hospitable society along British Columbia's Fraser River. The Chinese, equally frustrated with the world established by *People v. Hall*, concentrated on mining. California passed into the 1860s with its binary racial regime intact, but events outside the state soon offered new challenges and new opportunities.[34]

The Civil War

Between 1858 and 1861, on the surface at least, the matter of the testimony laws appeared settled. California's Democrat-controlled legislature had effectively threatened nonwhites into silence. Yet, despite legislators' efforts, faint rumblings of change could be heard beyond the legislative halls, as growing numbers of whites began speaking out against the laws. The rather sudden change in sentiment reveals the malleability of race thinking and underscores the ways in which the political, social, and economic considerations so often colored by racial thought might themselves shape that thought.

As national tensions over slavery worsened and the country moved toward civil war, many white Californians gravitated toward the Republican Party and grew increasingly uncomfortable with a racial order that appeared in many ways to match that of the slave South. Editorials appeared in Republican newspapers throughout the state demanding a repeal of the testimony laws. In 1857, the forces of racial inclusion acquired a staunch ally when Thomas S. King assumed leadership of San Francisco's *Daily Evening Bulletin*. King's brother, James King of William, had been murdered the previous year by a Democratic Party official named James P. Casey, precipitating the resurrection of San Francisco's Vigilance Committee and the destruction of the City's Democratic political machine. Over the next several years Thomas S. King shaped his newspaper into a powerful enemy of Democratic sentiment. King spoke out regularly and forcefully against the testimony exclusions. Calling the laws "contemptible, ignorant and narrow," King mercilessly ridiculed what he considered the blinkered prejudice of Democratic politicians, helping to shift public opinion all the while.[35]

Evidence that the efforts of King and others were having an effect can be found sprinkled throughout contemporary newspapers. Often, the change in whites' attitudes was a matter of self-preservation. In 1857, whites in the town of Bangor, tired of the murderers and thieves who hung about preying on local Chinese miners, lynched three "desperadoes" and promised more hangings if the testimony law was not changed. The nearby town of Long Bar forwarded a series of resolutions approving the action at Bangor to the legislature, claiming that "in the absence of all law to punish white men on Chinese testimony, it behooves each mining community to protect the Chinese" through vigilante justice.[36]

Also in 1857, Californios added their voices to the chorus demanding change. For most of the decade, the men who had once ruled

California stood with white Americans in excluding black, Indian, and Chinese testimony. The California Constitution of 1849 had ranked them with whites, and they zealously defended that status when the opportunity arose. But a controversial court case in 1857 changed the minds of many. The testimony of Manuel Dominguez, a signer of the state Constitution and a Los Angeles County supervisor, was excluded for his Indian heritage, prompting outrage in the Californio community. Pablo de la Guerra, who as a powerful Democratic state senator had quietly acquiesced in the existence of the testimony laws, now spoke out angrily against them.[37]

As long as the Democratic Party controlled the state government, there was little chance of change, but the party's days of glory were numbered. With the outbreak of the Civil War, the Democratic Party in California fell into disfavor, and its policies, particularly with regard to race, fell out of vogue. The secession crisis only mildly disturbed Californians, but the Union Army's loss at the first battle of Bull Run galvanized support for the Union, and in the elections of 1861 the Republican Party managed to gain an overwhelming majority in the Assembly, and a one-vote majority in the Senate. For the first time, there was a real chance that an assault on the testimony laws might be successful.[38]

For two months in the spring of 1862, California's legislative calendar was consumed by debate over two bills offered by Caleb Fay of San Francisco that intended to repeal the civil and criminal laws prohibiting black and mulatto testimony. The two bills both acknowledged the influence of national events on California politics, and in their limited scope reflected the strength of anti-Chinese sentiment.[39]

The urgency of the debates was heightened by the spectacle of the trial of Robert Schell, who was charged with murder in the death of a black barber in San Francisco. On October 29, 1861, Schell shot and killed George Gordon, who had been a delegate to the 1856 state colored convention. San Francisco's black community was incensed that the killing had taken place in Gordon's own barbershop, and their anger increased when the testimony of the only witness to the killing was dismissed.

At the trial, racial science was again injected into the justice system when Schell's attorneys challenged the legitimacy of the only witness, James C. Cowes. The judge was apparently unable to determine Cowes's race and so resorted to a novel solution. Cowes was forced to submit to an examination by two doctors who claimed to be able to determine his race through a close study of his hair. The press universally condemned the solution and ridiculed the two doctors of "hairology." Cowes did not help matters by showing up to court on the day of his examination wearing a wig. Despite the opinion voiced by several observers that Cowes was white, and by one in particular who claimed Cowes was a Jew, the two doctors determined that he was one-sixteenth African, and the judge excluded his testimony. The entire spectacle embarrassed the legal profession, and it made a mockery of the courts. Many whites who might otherwise have remained neutral on the subject of the testimony laws now agitated for change. Not long after the trial, state Senator George Perkins presented a letter to the Senate signed by every San Francisco judge but one and some 250 lawyers demanding repeal of the laws.[40]

Several state politicians read the change in public sentiment, particularly with regard to the secession crisis, and rushed to adopt positions in favor of a change in the laws. Assemblyman S. C. Bigelow, for instance, reflected popular sentiment when he took to the Assembly floor to state that he "was in favor of the bill because it would remove the last mark and badge, and burning brand of shame fixed upon this State by that class of men whose sympathies were with the men now in arms against the Government of the United States." Indeed, opening the witness box to black Californians seemed an easy way to relieve the state of the taint of secessionist leanings, and the debates surrounding Assembly bills 144 and 145 reveal a widespread willingness to accept black testimony for that reason.[41]

Fay's two bills promised to introduce flexibility into what had been a rigid binary system. The Civil War seemed to offer ample justification for the change, but a clever move by Assemblyman S. P. Wright of Del Norte County to include Chinese testimony suddenly made a far more elaborate justification necessary. From the moment Wright offered his amendment, debate shifted away from Civil War issues and instead focused on criteria for racial classification. Statements extolling the fitness of blacks to testify in court were coupled with statements denying the fitness and value of Chinese testimony. Opponents of the bills, horrified by the specter of black equality they represented, demonized the Chinese and constantly linked them and their supposed immoral behavior to black Californians, effectively using the Chinese as a foil to undermine popular support for black inclusion. Supporters of the bills scrambled to defend black Californians against these attacks, and in the process more sharply defined a set of distinctions between nonwhite races. The debates helped crystallize the arguments made on all sides regarding what each group felt should be the proper shape of California's racial hierarchy.[42]

The most common tactic employed by supporters of black testimony was identical to that which black Californians had been using for some years. In fact, whites adopted much of the rhetoric black Californians had developed during the 1850s. White Republican politicians urged their colleagues to recognize an affinity between black and white Americans that at once justified the inclusion of black testimony and the continued exclusion of Chinese testimony. Assemblyman William H. Sears was typical in this respect. According to a press report, in a brief address he carefully stated that "he had no objection to negroes or Indians, but he did object to the Chinese. There is no credibility in them." For Sears, the crucial distinction could be found in the common religion shared by blacks and whites. "The negro," he insisted, is "of the same religion as ourselves . . . the Chinaman believe[s] in a bamboo god." Similar sentiments were taken up and repeated throughout the debates over Fay's bills and mark an important change in attitude among many white Californians. In the 1850s, black Californians had been ranked with Indians and the Chinese. Now they were not only completely different from other minority groups, they were in many ways similar to whites.[43]

Black Californians advanced similar arguments, particularly emphasizing the common culture and religion of black and white Americans. The editors of San Francisco's African American newspaper, the *Pacific Appeal*, wrote, "We are Americans by birth, habits, custom, education and religion; we are part and parcel of the country, homogenous with the American people; 'natives here and to the manner born,' and we cannot be alienated nor driven away." Religious fraternity was especially important, and it was on these grounds that black Californians first directly attacked the Chinese. In a petition sent to the legislature in 1862, black Californians pointed to religion as the primary reason for continued exclusion of the Chinese. "We believe that the exclusion of a race of men, is never necessary unless of a race . . . having an idolatrous religion." Black Californians understood that if they were to win access to the courts, it would have to be at the expense of the Chinese, and they lost no time in joining the debate.[44]

California politicians combined their appeals to a common geography and environment with an elaborate scheme designed to justify racial discrimination. The scheme, which was drawn from the taxonomic work of natural scientists such as Carl Linnaeus and Georges-Louis Leclerc, Comte de Buffon, linked all of nature, from the simplest plants and animals to complex humanity, in a single "Great Chain of Being." The chain, while it confirmed the unity of the natural world, also through its very form implied a hierarchy that ranked nature from lower to higher orders of existence. Californians of all races used the scale developed by natural scientists to further explain racial differences and to defend their status in California society. In the hands of California politicians, the scale became infinitely elastic and could admit as few as three races and as many as thirty. To this scale, they added the increasingly influential theory of evolution, in their minds now synonymous with the American ideal of progress. The addition of evolution explained away awkward historical facts and allowed whites to claim top rank on the scale. For example, it was common knowledge in the nineteenth-century United States that while Europeans were still living in the forests and wearing animal skins for clothing, the Chinese were inventing gunpowder and paper. Coupling evolution with the Great Chain allowed Europeans to match and surpass the glories of Chinese civilization.[45]

Civilization, in fact, was the chief criterion by which white politicians judged other races in the testimony debates. All agreed that when it came to civilization, whites had a decided advantage over other races. But even within the race there were divisions, and the Anglo-Saxon was heralded as the greatest and most developed of all Caucasians. In wonderfully circular reasoning, their status in society stood as proof of the legitimacy of the racial scale, and their interpretation of the racial scale justified their position at the pinnacle of society. Whites rooted their success in Anglo-Saxon institutions, which, they claimed, were an inevitable product of Anglo-Saxon blood. The English and American Constitutions, their systems of law and economy, religion, and even architecture were evidence of a matchless level of civilized attainment. Politicians regularly congratulated each other on their descent from "the illustrious Barons of Runnymede and the sturdy men of Cromwell's days," and claimed that with the help of pure Anglo-Saxon blood this "nation would go on in the road of prosperity and happiness." It was against this ideal self-definition that whites ranked nonwhite Californians.[46]

Given the criteria whites used to define themselves, ranking California Indians was a simple task. By 1862, what remained of California Indian societies following the Spanish and Mexican periods had been almost completely erased. The labor system embedded in California laws governing Indians had so thoroughly demoralized them that by 1862, most whites' experience with Indians was limited to dime store novels and rumors of drunkenness and dissipation. Clearly, in the minds of California's whites, these were a people lacking entirely in any of the usual accoutrements of civilization. With no civic institutions, no legal system, not even a written language, and the crudest forms of agriculture and architecture, California Indians were relegated to the lowest rung on the racial ladder.[47]

The Chinese presented a thornier problem. California law had classed them with Indians, but clearly the Chinese possessed all of the same elements of civilization boasted by whites. White politicians dealt with this problem by claiming that moral turpitude had fatally undermined Chinese civil institutions. The Chinese, opined Assemblyman C. W. Kendall, were "a nation of bars. . . . They are educated to deception, gambling, drinking spirituous liquors with their food, and . . . there are few countries where prostitution is more widely practiced." All of these vices, Kendall implied, were the result of a decrepit legal system that not only allowed but encouraged such behavior. Worse still, the Chinese sent the worst of their population to California. Along with "the most vile and abandoned prostitutes,"

China sent "the gambler, the opium eater, the debauchee, who live with and upon these abandoned women and make the night hideous with the insane ravings of their intoxicated madness and the howlings of their strange excitement."[48]

Second, whites acknowledged the achievements of Chinese civilization, but, pointing to the age of the Chinese Empire, charged that China had slipped into stagnation. Here, the addition of evolution to the Great Chain of Being offered a powerful weapon. As all things in the natural world flourish and then decay and finally die, so too did races and civilizations. China, they argued, had long since grown moribund. "While the tribes, nations, and civilizations of the West have come and gone," wrote one observer some years later, "the Chinese have remained the same, generation after generation and century after century, content always to live and die in the conditions that Fate has imposed upon them in the Middle Kingdom." Such arguments helped white politicians anxious to pass Fay's bills establish distinctions between black Californians and Chinese, countering the links drawn between them by their opponents.[49]

Black Californians responded to the debates by reshaping whites' arguments in an effort to define themselves and assign themselves a rank that, if not equal to that of whites, was at least one higher than the Chinese had. The first step involved an acceptance of whites' assessment of Chinese civilization as a wedge separating the two excluded groups. "The Mongolian race," wrote the editors of the *Pacific Appeal*, "affords a striking example of inert civilization, if not of actual decay." "For hundreds of years," they continued, "their arts and sciences have stood where they are today. They have ceased to originate, and therefore to expand." This argument drew sharp and obvious distinctions between themselves and the Chinese, when stated in tandem with African American professions of patriotism, and undermined the logic of laws that defined both groups equally.[50]

The second step was much more complicated. Black Californians took whites' statements about their common religion and civic culture and placed them within whites' evolutionary scheme. They then used such statements as evidence of both their ability to improve and of their progress to date, thus driving a deeper wedge between themselves and the Chinese. "We are acquiring the energy, activity and enterprise of Americans, and the Colored American will, ere long, equal his white brother in all those attributes which tend to make the American character noticeable and enviable throughout the world." The editors of the *Pacific Appeal* even entertained the possibility that Africans might one day best the Anglo-Saxon race, turning whites' own rhetoric against them. "The Caucasian race . . . seems also to have approximated to the perfect ripeness that precedes loss of flavor and cessation of growth." "May there not come a time," they wondered, "when the Anglo-Saxon even—the present epitome of all that is strong, bright, good and impenetrable—shall have reached the end of its multifarious avenues of advancement?" All that was required for African Americans to rise, they argued, was an end to slavery. "Throw open to us the avenues of Wealth and Education, and in one generation we will compete with those who are now the favored classes. We, too, will have our bankers, our poets, and our artists."[51]

The mention of these three occupations signaled the middle-class aspirations of black Californians, and their claims to that status were embedded throughout such arguments. For some time, black leaders had been exhorting their communities to actively pursue the kinds of jobs and education that had so clearly led to white racial dominance. They counseled their communities to "abandon such positions as bootblacks, waiters, servants and carriers" in the belief that such positions led whites to look down upon them. "We should emulate, and if possible, excel white Americans in every sphere of life," they wrote. "We should apply ourselves to acquiring wealth, and obtaining education; we should learn all the arts, sciences, professions and trades which the progress of civilization had made necessary." In these statements, black Californians were informing white society that the distinctions whites wished to maintain between the races would not last.[52]

Their white supporters echoed these sentiments throughout the debates, pointing to the accomplishments of black Californians, their contributions to the state, and their successful adaptation. Politicians repeatedly pointed to the $2 million in property owned by blacks and the $300,000 paid annually in taxes by them. Black Californians had a higher literacy rate than did most white immigrant groups, and they promoted a vigorous press. Most telling, however, were their tastes and aspirations. As one white observer pointed out, "I have visited hundreds of colored families, and have found but one with good carpets and furniture. As a people they have a decided taste for the higher life, and a great desire to educate their children." Possession of the material elements necessary for American middle-class domesticity confirmed Californians, white and black, of the fitness of black Californians for the witness box. Middle-class aspirations and apparent success in achieving that status separated black Californians from Chinese and Indians, and these achievements made repeal of the testimony laws in their favor all but certain.[53]

Repeal, however, would have to wait another year. The bills passed the Assembly in 1862 but stalled in the Senate, where Republicans failed to muster enough of a majority to guarantee passage. Both bills were tabled indefinitely. But as the war with the Confederacy continued, the Republican Party in California, officially the Union Party as of 1862, gained in strength. The elections in the fall of 1862 marked an overwhelming victory for the Republicans, and they gained clear majorities in both houses of the legislature. With control assured, Senator George Perkins of San Francisco introduced Senate bills 2 and 3, which were nearly identical to Fay's bills of the previous session. With a minimum of debate, both acts passed, and the disability against black Californians was finally removed.[54]

The *Pacific Appeal* rejoiced in the passage of the bills, declaring, "We thank Almighty God that He has endowed our present rulers with a sense of justice that has prompted them to take upon themselves the responsibility of removing this foul stain from the statutebook." The editors professed the undying love of black Californians for the state and the Union, and called upon the black community to redouble their efforts in the nation's defense. Even so, the paper's editors remained mindful of black Californians' precarious position in California society. They recognized that the relaxation of the testimony laws in their favor meant more than access to the witness box and cautioned blacks against abusing their new privilege. "We should be more guarded than ever against committing any acts that might be construed, by the enemies of our advancement, as a consequence of the repeal of those unjust laws. . . . No suit should be entered merely because it can be entered." Repeal of the testimony laws had neither ended all prejudice nor erased discriminatory legislation, and the African Californian community needed to hold to the path of middle-class status if change was to continue.[55]

In passing Perkins's bills, the state legislature effectively dismantled the binary legal and racial regime created by Justice Murray's decision in *People v. Hall*. The issues surrounding the Civil War and the war itself strongly influenced events in California, not least by challenging white Americans to declare their loyalty to the Union and live up to the nation's founding principles. But while the war had provided the spark, it was the language of racial science that provided the engine for change. White Californians' embrace of that language offered not simply a rhetorical justification for the acceptance of black testimony but an intellectual one as well. More important, the language had provided the justification that white Californians needed to maintain the continued exclusion of Chinese and Indian testimony.

After 1863, California law recognized distinctions between nonwhite racial groups that elevated some at the expense of others. While these distinctions helped diminish the distance between black and white, the testimony debates exhausted white Californians' willingness to entertain any further movement toward racial equality. For the next two years, the war commanded Californians' attention, and questions about the shape of the state's racial regime faded into the background. Reconstruction, however, brought them back. Ratification of the Thirteenth and Fourteenth Amendments and passage of the Civil Rights Act of 1866 threatened to undo the barriers that white Californians had erected around the Chinese. After a brief period of quiet, California politics was suddenly again agitated by the subject of race. And once again, events outside California threatened to unbalance the state's carefully crafted racial order.

Reconstruction

Californians overwhelmingly rejected Congress's program of Reconstruction, despite support for the Union during the war and a willingness to relax the testimony laws in favor of black Californians. In the first statewide elections following the end of the war, the Democratic Party briefly reasserted its former dominance and attempted to roll back some of the advances registered under Republican control. The story behind California's rejection of Reconstruction will be detailed in chapter 2, but for now it is enough to say that as the intentions of the radicals in Congress became clear, white Californians recognized in them a threat to the racial hierarchy so painstakingly elaborated over the previous decade. More than that, they recognized in Radical Reconstruction a threat to their privileged position in California's racial regime.

Californians resented what they saw as an unwarranted federal intrusion into their affairs, and with the passage of each new Reconstruction measure, opponents of Radical Reconstruction searched for ways to blunt its effects in California. During the summer of 1867, newspapers around the state began reporting the efforts of supporters of racial exclusion to find a case to test the validity of the Civil Rights Act of 1866, and invariably the search centered on cases involving Chinese testimony. Judges around the state, particularly in San Francisco, began ruling "somewhat arbitrarily," admitting Chinese testimony to force a test. Finally, in November, a likely case was found and doggedly pursued. The case added a bizarre twist to earlier efforts to separate black Californians from Chinese immigrants and revealed the distance California had traveled from the world of *People v. Hall*.[56]

In October 1867, a black man named George Washington stole $25 in gold from a Chinese miner named Ah Wang in Nevada County. Washington was something of a hapless thief, however, and he was quickly surrounded by a group of Chinese miners who led him off to the sheriff. At trial, Washington's lawyers immediately moved for dismissal of the case on the grounds that the Civil Rights Act of 1866, which made citizens of blacks born in the United States, had effectively rendered their client legally white and thus rendered him immune from Chinese testimony. Judge A. C. Niles agreed with the argument and ordered the charges dismissed. The district attorney appealed to the California Supreme Court, and, once again, that court was asked to support the exclusionary testimony laws.[57]

In refusing Chinese testimony, Judge Niles had conceded the constitutionality of the Civil Rights Act of 1866. If the state supreme court accepted this argument and excluded Chinese testimony against black Californians, it would also be ratifying the right of Congress to pass legislation regulating state laws. For opponents of Radical Reconstruction, defendant Washington's fate was incidental to the danger such a position represented. As state Attorney General Jo Hamilton pointed out, either way, Washington was doomed. The Civil Rights Act, by establishing the inviolability of black civil rights at the federal level and enforcing those rights at the state level, effectively nullified all of California's racially discriminatory statutes. If the court found the Civil Rights Act constitutional, *all* testimony would be admissible, and Washington would be convicted. On the other hand, if the court rejected Congress's right to pass such legislation, then the barriers to racial minorities survived, and Washington was not equal to whites. Either way, his case fell.[58]

Hamilton found the prospect of abandoning California's carefully cultivated racial distinctions totally unacceptable, and he phrased his opposition in terms that echoed the testimony debates five years earlier. Californians may have reconciled themselves to black testimony, but this was a far cry from the sort of equality envisioned by Congress, and Hamilton would have none of it. The Civil Rights Act, he argued, compelled the state to accept "that each and every one of the human race having the attributes of *man*, whether he be negro, white, Chinaman or Digger, whether he be sane or insane, creditable or infamous, is entitled to be a witness in Courts of justice." Hamilton's inference that the Chinese merely possessed the "attributes" of man and that their testimony was as valueless as that of the insane or infamous simply rehearsed the same justifications employed by the state legislature in 1862 and 1863. But his argument went further and attempted to limit any further black advances by challenging Congress's right to make citizens of black Californians. In a comment that erased years of Civil War, Hamilton insisted that the *Dred Scott* decision remained the law of the land, in spite of at least two cases upholding the constitutionality of the Civil Rights Act of 1866. "The term 'citizen,'" he urged, "does not include 'negroes' or mulattoes." The court had little choice, according to Hamilton, but to stop the Civil Rights Act at the California border.[59]

The court's decision, written by Chief Justice Augustus L. Rhodes, neatly avoided these problems by tying the Civil Rights Act to the Thirteenth Amendment's guarantees of personal as opposed to political liberty and emphasizing the use of the word "citizen" in the Civil Rights Act. The act, which grew out of the Thirteenth Amendment, guaranteed equal treatment only to citizens of the United States, and since the vast majority of Chinese in California were immigrants without citizenship, they were not covered by the act. Moreover, the Civil Rights Act covered only civil rights as opposed to political rights. Nineteenth-century jurists made much of the distinction between the two, and often, as in this case, used that distinction to maintain the stability of racial categories. Civil rights were defined as "those which have no relation to the establishment, support or management of Government," or those liberties that protected a person in the enjoyment of life and property. Political rights were those that "consist in the power to participate directly or indirectly in the establishment or management of Government" and included the franchise and the right to hold office. Neither the act nor the Thirteenth Amendment conferred on anyone the right to vote, hold office, or even to attend the same schools. In other words, Washington was protected from Chinese testimony. In his *civil* rights he was equal with whites, but not in his political rights, and so black access to the levers of government might still be blocked. The Civil Rights Act of 1866 was constitutional, and California's racial barriers remained intact.[60]

At the time of Washington's arrest, the Civil Rights Act of 1866 was in effect, but the Fourteenth Amendment had not yet been ratified. By the time the trial reached the Supreme Court, the Fourteenth Amendment was the law of the land, but the court decided the case without reference to it because Washington's crime had been committed prior to its ratification. Justice Rhodes did, however, note that his decision really held only for this specific case. The Fourteenth Amendment, by adding the word "person" to that of "citizen," did demolish the barriers erected against nonwhites and "may supersede all that our Constitution contains on that subject."[61]

Following ratification of the Fourteenth Amendment, opponents of Radical Reconstruction again searched for a case that would shield

California's racial regime from congressional oversight, and again their efforts focused on the issue of Chinese testimony. In the first such case to reach the Supreme Court, lawyers for the Chinese victim of a white robber argued that the Fourteenth Amendment guaranteed equal protection to all persons in California and that the testimony laws deprived the Chinese of equal protection.[62]

The court, in a 4–1 decision, disagreed. Employing tortured logic, the justices claimed that the law did not discriminate against the Chinese and so did not run afoul of the Fourteenth Amendment. The law, they argued, "affords the Chinaman every means of bringing the facts to the knowledge of the Court . . . that is afforded to the white man." Chinese could not rely on Chinese testimony, and neither could whites. Both groups were treated equally. Advocates for the Chinese countered that a white man could testify in his own behalf, while a Chinese victim could not. The court confessed itself "unable to see the force of this position" and insisted that if no white witnesses were available, that was the fault of the victim for associating solely with his own kind, not the fault of the law. The legislature, the court argued, was empowered to ensure that testimony brought before bar was reliable. Children, the insane, and convicted criminals, along with the Chinese, had been deemed incompetent to testify, and the court argued that the Fourteenth Amendment had not been intended to interfere with the state's power to exclude them. That the Chinese were incompetent to provide reliable testimony was not the fault of the law.[63]

The court had placed itself firmly in the path of Radical Reconstruction and declared its undying opposition to congressional attempts to dismantle California's racial hierarchy. But the court was fighting a losing battle, and in the 1870s, the Republican Party regained control of state government. Attitudes among many whites softened with regard to the testimony laws, and public opinion diverged from the state court's. Editorials around the state appeared that chastised the supreme court for its embarrassing reasoning and demanding a more enlightened attitude toward the Chinese. Some of the agitation grew out of the anti-Chinese riots in Los Angeles in October 1871. Nineteen Chinese immigrants were lynched in a daylong orgy of violence that nearly destroyed the Chinese quarter of the town. Many Californians were outraged when the perpetrators of the riot, "ruffians who, under legal protection, were guilty of arson and murder by wholesale," were acquitted of any wrongdoing in the absence of admissible testimony. The *Daily Alta California* demanded "repeal of that disgraceful clause of our law which excludes" Chinese testimony. "If there is one law upon our statute books, which more than another should be repealed, it is that which forbids the introduction of Chinese testimony in courts of justice," wrote another editor. As in the late 1850s with African American testimony, judges who had grown uncomfortable with the law began ignoring the law, admitting Chinese testimony in spite of the state supreme court's decision in *People v. James Brady*.[64]

The change in public sentiment encouraged state politicians and when, in 1872, the state legislature overhauled and revised the state's laws, the law excluding Chinese and Indian testimony was quietly, and without debate, omitted. After years of struggle and angry polemic, California's prohibitory testimony laws quietly passed into oblivion without protest. By 1872, most white Californians had come to recognize if not the injustice of the laws then at least the danger such laws represented to their own interests. Moreover, in the years since the end of the war, racial politics had fastened onto other topics that now drew the attention of all Californians, white and nonwhite. Reconstruction threatened to break down barriers whites had erected around the ballot box, and in hotels, trains, streetcars, occupations, neighborhoods, and schools. In the face of such momentous changes, and especially given the presence of African American congressmen, defense of the testimony laws may well have seemed a waste of time and energy. The project of racial classification embedded in the debates over nonwhite testimony shifted in the early 1870s to match and mirror issues that consumed the nation at large.[65]

Conclusion

Throughout the 1850s and 1860s, California's nonwhites labored under a legal regime of racial exclusion and discrimination in which the testimony laws played an important but by no means exclusive role. The testimony laws were unique, however, in two ways. They differed, first, in the explicit link between all three excluded groups drawn by

Justice Murray's decision in *People v. Hall* and, second, in the vocal, public opposition that link generated. Nonwhites opposed all the various forms of oppression under which they suffered in California, but nowhere is that opposition more visible than in the disputes over the testimony laws. Both black Californians and Chinese immigrants took bold steps into the public arena that showed courage and a remarkable faith that American institutions would respond. By embracing the language of racial science, their assaults on California's binary racial regime, with the help of events outside the state, forced white Californians into an elaborate defense of white privilege that created an ever more complicated and variegated racial hierarchy unique in the American experience.

The distance Californians traveled between 1854 and 1872 is perhaps best captured by the case of George Washington in *People v. Washington*. The case starkly exposes the level to which black Californians had risen in status by the end of the Civil War, and the level to which the Chinese had sunk at the same time. Admitting African Californian testimony was more than a concession to Union sentiment. It amounted to acceptance of the notion that blacks were capable of at least some degree of participation in American civic life, and that admission opened a door that could never be closed. Moreover, the fact that Washington chose to use federal laws designed to combat racial oppression as a weapon against another minority signaled a conviction, apparently a well-founded one, that whites would view blacks in a better light than they would Chinese or Indians. The *Washington* decision showed very clearly that the line dividing those considered capable of shouldering the responsibilities of civic and political freedom from those considered incapable had blurred. Over the next two decades, Californians, both white and nonwhite, worked to clarify that line, and the struggles would always revolve around issues raised by federal Reconstruction.

Chapter 2
The Apostasy of Henry Huntley Haight
Race, Reconstruction, and the Return of the
Democracy in California, 1865–1870

ON A COLD, GRAY morning in December 1867, Henry Huntley Haight took to a Sacramento stage and delivered a furious denunciation of the Radical Reconstruction policies pursued by Congress. Haight's speech on this day echoed sentiments he had expressed publicly, and with increasing ferocity, over much of the preceding year, but now he spoke for the first time as governor of California. His inauguration staged the final act in a political revolution that swept the Republican Party from power and delivered the state into the hands of the Democrats, a party that only a year earlier had seemed so blackened by the stain of rebellion that few thought it would ever rise again. Just two years after the end of a bitter war, and with the Republican Party ascendant across the nation, white Californians overwhelmingly repudiated the party of Lincoln and embraced the party of slavery and treason. That repudiation was led, symbolically and literally, by Henry Haight, a man who, seven years earlier as state chairman of the Republican Party, had vigorously campaigned for Abraham Lincoln.[1]

Haight's victory as a Democrat shocked Republican stalwarts across the nation. Throughout the war, California had been a staunchly loyal state, whose politics under Republican leadership had embraced, along with a bloody war for the preservation of the Union, the full breadth of the Republican prescription for American progress. Under the guidance of Governors Leland Stanford and Frederick Low, California had poured its energies into the construction of the transcontinental railroad, its gold into the war effort, and its troops into battle. The state had also, with some difficulty, begun to accept the spirit of Republicanism by liberalizing its exclusionary testimony laws, at least with regard to black Californians. And yet, in the intervening years, something had changed. How had Californians become so dissatisfied with Republican leadership? And how, for that matter, had Henry Haight moved from Republican Party leadership in 1860 to open apostasy in so short a time?[2]

Haight's inaugural address offers some clues to his change of heart, and that of many Californians. Haight claimed that Congress, "under the leadership of extreme men," was brazenly subverting the purposes for which the war was fought, and the consequences of this subversion, he feared, would be disastrous. "The late war," he insisted, "was waged on our part to enforce the authority of the Federal Government in the Southern States and prevent the disruption of the Union." It was not waged, he contended, "to destroy the liberties of any portion of the people, or create a negro empire on our southern border." As the rest of his speech made clear, this last was the consequence he feared most. Nine months earlier, the Radical Congress had extended the franchise to blacks in the District of Columbia and the territories, and, six months earlier, it had enfranchised freedmen throughout the South. For Haight, of all the "usurpations" perpetrated by Congress, this was the worst. "This is briefly the nature of the reconstruction policy of Congress," he said. "It takes from the white people of ten States their constitutional rights, and leaves them subject to military rule; and disfranchises enough white men to give the political control to a mass of negroes just emancipated and almost as ignorant of political duties as the beasts of the field." Haight warmed to his subject as he continued, and his language purpled with outrage. Neatly turning Radical idiom back on itself, he told the crowd, "Thus, the reconstruction policy of Congress is the . . . abolition of those personal rights guaranteed by the Constitution and . . . the subjection of the white population of the Southern States, men, women, and children, to the domination of a mass of ignorant negroes."[3]

Here was the panic that had brought California's dissenters to the polls. The notion that black men might control the levers of power anywhere in the United States was appalling in itself. But Haight reminded his audience that the reality was in fact much worse: "The national legislature enacts . . . that the political power . . . shall be given

Henry Huntley Haight (1825–1878). As the tenth
governor of California, Haight led the fight against
Reconstruction and persuaded the State Legislature
to reject the Fifteenth Amendment. (Courtesy of the
Bancroft Library, University of California, Berkeley,
California Faces: Selections from the Bancroft Library
Portrait Collection.)

to the negroes, who can thereby control their domestic administration and send to Congress negro senators and representatives, to assist in making laws to govern the white people of the North." Black men now had the "power to participate in federal legislation," and Haight was incredulous. "That any white man could be found on this continent to sanction a policy so subversive of rational liberty, and in the end so fatal to the Union and the Government, is a subject of unceasing astonishment." "These measures," he said, "are a violation of the fundamental principles of the Constitution and of liberty; of every dictate of sound policy; of every sentiment of humanity and christianity; and are a disgrace to our country and to the age in which we live."[4]

At least one historian has argued that western engagement with Reconstruction was on the wane by the winter of 1867. He contends that once congressional control of Southern affairs was secured through passage of the Reconstruction acts and that eventual Southern reintegration with the Union was thus assured, westerners turned away from national events in favor of local concerns. Yet as the controversies over their state's exclusionary testimony laws demonstrate, Californians experienced Reconstruction not as an abstract national question but as a profoundly local one. To Californians, what happened in the South was by no means a matter of minor import, diminished by distance. Like Americans all over the West, Californians recognized from the beginning that congressional efforts to rebuild the South might reach into their lives as well. But how one felt about Reconstruction or whether one supported Congress, was, at bottom, not a question of loyalty to the president or of the limits of federal power versus states' rights or even of Southern sympathy. It was instead, as Governor Haight's inaugural address makes plain, a question of local racial attitudes. As Congress focused ever more closely on preserving and expanding the rights of freed slaves, white Californians recognized in the deliberations a threat to their dominance over the racial order they had so carefully constructed.[5]

In a small but significant way, pressures related to the Civil War and Reconstruction had already altered that order. Black Californians had won the right to testify in California's courts, and to that limited extent had been invited into what had been an exclusively white public realm. In the process, the simple binary racial hierarchy that had tied each of the state's nonwhite racial groups together was undone. In its place, a more complicated and more ambiguous hierarchy began to take shape. Californians of all races quickly grasped that their state's racial diversity lent an added dimension to the national influence of Reconstruction legislation. While in the South that legislation altered the relationship between white and black, in California racial change would take place along three, or even four, axes.

Their worry became more urgent as Congress began debating the possibility, and later, the necessity of black suffrage. Even as newspapers around the state followed arcane debates surrounding such issues as whether the rebel states were in or out of the Union, the central concern for white Californians was the dilution of white political power. Some local Republicans, soul mates to the Radicals in Congress, argued that simple justice demanded the extension of the franchise to black Americans. Even in their own party, however, their voices were a minority. Most white Californians simply refused to see justice in a policy that lent equal weight to the voice of what they held as an inferior and enervated race in determining American destiny. At the same time, the prospect of black suffrage struck directly at a key component of white American male racial identity. White men's exclusive exercise of the franchise had, since the spread of universal white male suffrage earlier in the century, stood as the clearest and most potent expression of white racial superiority. Admitting black men to the vote thus threatened to undermine the very foundation of that superiority. Within California's unique multiracial context, white Californians feared that black suffrage was only the first step in the inevitable elevation of all nonwhites. This underlying horror infected debate over every Reconstruction issue and gathered in its orbit everything from religion and sex to the Chinese and Charles Darwin. Most important, it led the California legislature to reject the Fourteenth and Fifteenth Amendments to the federal Constitution, drove the tenor and direction of California politics well into the next decade, and revived the Democratic Party throughout the state.

Wartime Politics and Reconstruction Fears

At the close of the Civil War, politics in California was, on the surface, a harmonious affair. With few exceptions, the State Legislature had approved Lincoln's conduct of the war, even to the point of publicly endorsing the Emancipation Proclamation. Throughout, Union victories had been occasions for exultant legislative celebration, while Union defeats drove the state's public servants to don sackcloth and ashes and lament the passing of the Republic. When the Thirteenth Amendment came up for vote in Congress, the State Legislature again approved and directed its representatives to support the amendment. Dissenters who clung to the old precepts of the Democratic Party and refused to accept a changed world were brushed aside as atavistic symbols of failed glory. Motivated by a strong desire to preserve the Union, California's political leaders, much like political leaders throughout the American West, managed to set aside their local differences and on national issues presented as united a front as could be expected.[6]

Even so, these outward acts of patriotism rested on an unstable political coalition that grew tenuous with the end of hostilities in the South and the opening of the Reconstruction Era. Since the beginning of the war, California's politics had been led by the Union Party, a restless and potentially volatile coalition of Republicans and loyal Democrats. While the war raged, the two constituencies worked together, but within weeks of Lee's surrender, buried tensions rent the party fabric. The Democrats, who had chafed under Republican domination in the Union Party, began to flex their muscles, bolting in minor municipal elections in an effort to gain control over local party machinery. In these early betrayals, the "bolters" cast their actions as purely matters of candidate preference rather than party antagonism. It was not long, though, before old party distinctions emerged, and when they did, race served as the entering wedge.[7]

The first sign of a Democratic revival occurred at the Yuba County Union Convention in July 1865. There, the "short hair" faction of the Union Party adopted a platform resolution clearly calculated to appeal to the county's low-lying Democrats by making an issue of Republican pronouncements regarding Reconstruction. Adopting a tone of affected and strained magnanimity, the "shorts" declared that "while we are willing to extend to the African or negro race upon the continent all their natural rights, and protect them in the enjoyment of the same, we still believe this to be a 'white man's government,' and that allowing or permitting the negro to vote would be the introduction of a system unnatural, impolitic, and degrading."[8]

Few were fooled by the feigned concern for the African's "natural rights," least of all the Union Party convention in neighboring Butte County, which adopted a series of retaliatory resolutions that at once exposed the short-hair strategy, and at the same time acknowledged the power of racial politics. They began by accusing the shorts of disloyalty. "Parties of men," they proclaimed, "who advocate the dissolution or disorganization of [the Union] party can be successful in their desires only by open affiliation with secessionists and copperheads." Such an accusation, however, was weak in the face of a history of wartime cooperation among the short-hair leaders, and subsequent resolutions by the Butte County convention shifted strategies by dismissing the local relevance of Reconstruction in an effort to hold the Union Party coalition together. "The question of 'negro suffrage,' upon which the so-called democratic party is endeavoring to force upon the union party of the union, and of this state," read one such resolution, "is one which belongs in the non-seceding states, exclusively to the states themselves, and as yet in this state is not an issue to be presented to the people for their action." The short hairs responded to such pleas by working even harder to undermine the Union coalition.[9]

Matters came to a head at the Sacramento County convention on July 25, 1865. When the long hairs, who held a majority, elected a convention secretary who was unpopular with the short-hair faction, the shorts reverted to their old habits and attacked. A five-minute brawl ensued in which each side reached for whatever weapon was handy—canes, chairs, ink stands, spittoons—and laid into each other with great enthusiasm. In the end, the long hairs were driven from the meeting hall, some through windows. The fracas, however, proved the undoing of the short-hair rebellion when public outcry prompted their political leaders to repudiate such violent tactics and to support the long-hair candidates.[10]

The Union Party maintained its hold over the state government in the 1865 elections, but the racialized rhetoric of the short hairs exposed the key weakness in the coalition, and on that front the party's ability to contain dissent was severely undermined. In five counties where bolters fused with what was left of the Democratic Party, Democrats managed to win seats in the Assembly. More important, a sizable portion of the San Francisco electorate, whose numbers guaranteed a disproportionate say in California government, had shown a willingness to vote Democratic. To this point, only a handful of Californians were yet ready to openly break with the policies of the Union Party or with their president on matters of war and Reconstruction, but race was potentially another matter. Across the state, the racial issues raised by the short hairs clearly touched a nerve and generated a strong response. The rhetorical and political efforts of the short hair faction of the Union Party laid the foundation for California's political response to the battle between Congress and President Andrew Johnson over Reconstruction, which began soon after the 1865 elections.[11]

Reconstruction Fears Realized

The platform fights at Yuba and Butte and the embarrassing brawl at Sacramento were especially galling to many if not most Californians, coming as they did so soon after President Abraham Lincoln's assassination. In the months and days before his death, Lincoln had spoken often and eloquently about his hopes for a "righteous and speedy peace" and the need for a national reconciliation. He had always held the opinion that if the nation was to be made safely whole again, the Union's Reconstruction policy had to be guided by principles of generosity and forgiveness. And in such matters, Californians appeared willing to follow their President's lead. When, in December 1863, Lincoln announced his plans for Reconstruction and amnesty, the State Legislature embraced the President's posture of conciliation even as they condemned the rebellion as "a war of the southern slave owning aristocracy against the democracy of the nation." But when word of President Lincoln's assassination reached San Francisco, the news hardened the hearts of loyal Californians. Aggrieved and angry mobs attacked the offices and destroyed the presses of five newspapers whose Democratic persuasion had offended public honor, and thus they described the limits of forgiveness and conciliation.[12]

While many Californians may have been willing to follow their president's lead before his death, many members of Congress were not. Lincoln died without having secured anything approaching consensus over the matter of Reconstruction even among members of his own party. His initial proposal, dubbed the "10 Percent Plan," was charitable indeed and was rooted in Lincoln's belief that power over Reconstruction policy rested in the executive office. Lincoln proposed to offer amnesty to all but the most prominent participants in the rebellion, provided they pledge loyalty to the Union and accept the abolition of slavery. Once 10 percent of a state's eligible voters had made this pledge, they might then form a new state government and rejoin the Union. Lincoln had tested his plan in Louisiana, where Union control had been reestablished in 1862. Republicans in Congress were dismayed by the results. Former slaveholders, among whom feelings of contrition were noticeably absent, attempted to reestablish slavery in all but name through violence and intimidation, while former slaves demanded more of their newfound freedom than even many white northerners were willing to accept. To many, the result was chaos, and even Lincoln conceded that events had hardly been encouraging.[13]

Some of the more radical members of the Republican Party's congressional delegation felt that the 10 Percent Plan was far too magnanimous and that a more exacting peace was required of the rebellious South. They argued further that the former Confederate states were now conquered territories, and so the task of Reconstruction more properly lay in the hands of Congress. Two, Senator Benjamin F. Wade and Representative Henry Winter Davis, proposed a more stringent set of requirements. Where Lincoln's plan required that only 10 percent of a state's eligible voters take an oath of allegiance, the Wade-Davis bill demanded that the oath be taken by a majority of the state's voters before restoration to the Union might be considered. Under the congressional plan, only those who had never actively fought against the Union could participate in the new state governments, and Confederate leaders were to be permanently disfranchised. Lincoln felt that this plan went too far, but at the same time he knew that he needed consensus within his party's ranks if Reconstruction was to be at all successful. And so, even as he quietly disposed of the Wade-Davis bill with a pocket veto, Lincoln sought out congressional leaders in an attempt to reach a compromise. An assassin's bullet, however, brought those efforts to an abrupt and brutal halt, leaving the nation both leaderless and without a coherent plan for Reconstruction. And there matters stood as a far lesser man, Vice President Andrew Johnson, stepped in to fill Lincoln's shoes and conclude his peace.

The Republican congressional delegation viewed Johnson's elevation to the presidency with cautious optimism. In the decades before the war, Johnson had built a successful political career in his home state of Tennessee and, later, in Washington, D.C., as a member of both the House of Representatives and the Senate. That career, however, had blossomed entirely in Democratic soil, and it was clear to all that Johnson's Jacksonian roots ran deep. Johnson, moreover, had once been a slaveholder and had defended slavery and the South throughout the crisis years of the 1850s, evidence that he did not entirely share Republican values. And yet, throughout his political career, Johnson had often displayed an independent streak that led him to oppose the political will of the Southern planter elite. When the South moved toward secession, Johnson was violently opposed to the dissolution of the Union, and while he failed to prevent his own state from seceding, Johnson himself was the only Southerner to remain in the U.S. Senate as the war began. As vice president, Johnson won over Radical Republicans by angrily denouncing Confederates as "infamous of character and diabolical of motive" and remarking that "treason must be made odious." Where Lincoln counseled forgiveness and reconciliation, Johnson told the Union faithful, "I would arrest them; I would try them; I would convict them, and I would hang them." Given such pronouncements, Radicals dared hope that Johnson would work with Congress to punish treason properly. Upon Johnson's inauguration, no less a Radical than Benjamin Wade congratulated the new president, exclaiming, "Mr. Johnson, I thank God that you are here. Lincoln had too much of the milk of human kindness to deal with these damned rebels. Now they will be dealt with according to their deserts."[14]

Johnson took office within a window of remarkable opportunity. The Radicals who were swept into office with Lincoln in the November elections of 1864 would not take their seats until December 1865. As a result, throughout the summer and fall of 1865 Johnson was free to pursue his own policy of Reconstruction without congressional interference. He began by extending amnesty to all who were willing to take an oath of allegiance to the Union, even those who had actively fought in the war. The only exceptions were those whom Johnson blamed for the conflict, Confederate leaders and the wealthiest planters. Under the new president's plan, these men might rejoin civil society only through personal appeal to Johnson himself. Johnson appointed provisional governors to oversee state affairs while each state's citizens formed new governments. Once each new state legislature had renounced secession, repudiated the Confederate debt, and ratified the Thirteenth Amendment, they would be restored to the Union. Each of the states quickly conformed to Johnson's demands, and before year's end the nation had been made whole again.

At first, Republicans in Congress were pleased with Johnson's progress. After so much bloodshed, reconciliation came remarkably smoothly as one state after another bowed to the president's demands and began the process of rebuilding. Even the Radicals in the party were cheered by Johnson's apparently hard-line approach to Confederate leaders. But dismay quickly replaced their optimism as a parade of Confederate leaders made their way to the White House, where they easily secured Johnson's pardon. Johnson's generosity convinced some in Congress that these pilgrimages were more about satisfying the president's vanity than about exacting punishment. Worse still, upon returning home, Southern voters promptly elevated the pardoned Confederate leaders to state and even federal offices. Once in office, the former rebels worked to reverse the changes in Southern life that had followed the Union victory. One after another, the newly reconstituted states passed "black codes" designed to severely circumscribe the rights of freed slaves and in effect return them to their former condition of servitude. These events mocked the Northern victory, spurning its sacrifice and eviscerating its meaning. Northern Republicans demanded that Johnson intervene, and his inaction convinced many that he could not be trusted with responsibility for Reconstruction.[15]

Johnson, for his part, saw little that could or should be done. In December 1865, as the 39th Congress convened, Johnson sought to defend his actions. In his annual message to Congress, the president lectured congressmen about the respective duties and responsibilities of the legislative and executive branches and about the proper relationship between the federal government and the states. Even as he affirmed the supremacy of the federal government, however, Johnson insisted that his powers to protect blacks were limited. The newly reconstituted state governments, he argued, were now responsible for prosecuting crimes within their borders and thus for protecting blacks' civil rights. Some had suggested that what blacks needed to secure their rights was access to the ballot box, but here again, Johnson declared his hands tied. The Constitution simply did not allow it. For him to have imposed black suffrage upon the states, he said, would have been "an assumption of power by the President which nothing in the Constitution or the laws of the United States would have warranted." As for suggestions that Congress might engage directly in the labor of Reconstruction, Johnson flatly declared the "work of restoration" all but complete. The only role Congress might legitimately perform was to seat the newly elected Southern delegates.[16]

Johnson's refusal to yield, along with the deteriorating situation in the South, provoked an inevitable confrontation with Congress. Republicans who had campaigned with Lincoln during the darkest days of the war found themselves asked to share power with many of the men who had precipitated the conflict. Determined to honor the sacrifice of so many, Northern Republicans refused to seat the Southern delegates and then moved to assert control over what they had concluded was a corrupted process. They began by passing a bill strengthening the Freedman's Bureau, established the previous spring to defend the civil rights of freed slaves, and by establishing a Joint Committee on Reconstruction to design a Reconstruction program that would more firmly impose the results of the war on a recalcitrant South. Further, Congress began work on a civil rights bill that would extend and guarantee to black Americans the same civil rights enjoyed by whites. Under the bill, anyone born in the United States, including former slaves, would automatically be a citizen, with the rights to be heard in court, to make contracts, and to be protected in both person and property. More significant, the bill revoked all state laws to the contrary and empowered the federal government to intervene in state affairs in defense of civil rights. Some Radicals even went so far as to propose amending the Constitution to extend suffrage to black Americans as a means of protecting blacks' civil rights and the Republican majority in Congress.

As tensions between Congress and the president rose, whites throughout the West grew increasingly uneasy over how Radical Reconstruction plans might alter their region's racial landscape, particularly with regard to suffrage. In Nevada, Republicans in the state legislature quietly approved of Johnson's vetoes out of a widespread apprehension that Radicals' plans might extend to the Chinese. In Kansas, and in the Montana, Colorado, and the Indian Territories, whites fearful of the prospect of black suffrage stepped up their efforts to maintain white privilege. In California, the depth of racial diversity threatened to dilute the white vote in ways distressingly similar to the prostrate South, and the prospect generated outrage. The end of slavery had meant the death of the federal Constitution's infamous three-fifths clause, and Congress had now to refashion the basis for congressional representation. If the newly freed slaves were fully counted, the Southern states would add a significant number of seats in the House of Representatives and potentially gain dominance over the federal government. This loyal Unionists could not abide. Instead, Radicals advocated basing apportionment on total population, with a proportional reduction in representation for those states choosing to deny the right to vote to nonwhite males over the age of twenty-one. For Southern states with large black populations, denying blacks the right to vote would then mean a diminution of Southern representation, while extending suffrage to blacks would virtually guarantee a strong Southern vote for the Republican Party. Either way, under the plan Republicans stood to maintain control of Congress.[17]

Most Northern states, with tiny black populations, could continue to deny blacks the right to vote and suffer not at all. But Californians, and westerners in general, quickly realized that their region's distinctive racial makeup placed them in a position more like that of the Southern states than those in the North. "There are in this state at least 60,000 persons of the inferior races," wrote the editors of San Francisco's *Daily Alta California*. Because together these sixty thousand people meant one more member of Congress for California, the Radicals' plan could prove awkward. "If they are to be deducted hereafter," the editors continued, "our political power in the councils of the Nation will be diminished accordingly; and we will have to suffer that diminution or engage in the hazardous experiment of putting ballots in the hands of persons who can have no just conception of their value, force or effect." The clear implication was that the Radicals' plan stood to undermine California's regime of white supremacy. The irony was not lost on white Californians. They had vigorously supported the Union throughout the war, yet they were now to suffer the same fate as states that had attempted to destroy that Union.[18]

Adoption of the congressional plan had potentially explosive consequences for the survival of the Union coalition in California, and so the editors of the *Daily Alta California*, among others, inclined toward the president's solution, which would base congressional representation on the number of qualified voters in each state. Adult white males were still by far the largest segment of California's population, and so under the president's plan the state stood to increase its seats in the House from three to five at the expense of more settled states with larger populations of women and children. At the same time, white privilege would be preserved. For this reason, most white Californians struck a tone of moderation and support for the president as the crisis brewed in the nation's capital. The *Daily Alta California* captured the public mood in an editorial published on February 13, 1866, in which editors cast the growing bitterness between Congress and the president as mere "disagreements." The editors sought to downplay the "disagreements" and hold the Union Party together by confidently assuring their readers that there was "really no difference in principle between the majority of the House and the President," and that fault for the discord lay with a minority of "ultra and uncompromising" legislators.[19]

That confidence was sorely tested in late February and again in late March when President Johnson moved to block congressional efforts to intervene in the process of Reconstruction by vetoing first the Freedman's Bureau bill and then the civil rights bill. In explaining his vetoes, Johnson spoke directly to the fears harbored by those white Californians who had begun to question Radical goals. Beyond the fact that he could identify "no immediate necessity" for the Freedman's Bureau bill, Johnson worried over the expansion of federal power that such a measure would effect. He made the same point more explicitly in his rejection of the civil rights bill, all the while stoking white racial anxieties. The provisions of that bill, he explained "interfere with the municipal legislation of the States . . . an absorption and assumption of power by the general government which, if acquiesced in, must sap and destroy our federative system of limited powers, and break down the barriers which preserve the rights of States." He was especially appalled at the way the bill barred states from "exercising any power of discrimination between the different races." Johnson worried that black Americans were not yet ready for all the responsibilities of freedom and implied that such discrimination might yet be necessary. They were, after all, only recently released from bondage. "Can it be reasonably supposed," he asked, "that they possess the requisite qualifications?" Johnson also strenuously objected to the prospect of extending citizenship to Chinese and Indians, and even went so far as to insist that "the distinction of race and color is, by the bill, made to operate in favor of the colored against the white race." In short, President Johnson cast the two bills in precisely the way white Californians were increasingly inclined to see them: as a massive assault on white privilege.[20]

The vetoes stunned many Republicans who had assumed that Johnson would be a "sincere friend of the negro," and they fractured California's Union Party. Around the state, confusion reigned as the party's opinion makers adopted conflicting positions. In San Francisco, the editors of the *Daily Alta California* remained supportive of the president but around the state, stalwart Republican papers turned on Johnson with a vengeance. The *Stockton Independent*, for instance, issued repeated calls for impeachment, while the *Sacramento Daily*

Union flung vitriolic condemnations at Johnson. The Union Party's state executive committee attempted to heal the growing rift by issuing a tepid set of resolutions that called for "patience, discretion, and deliberation." They decried any appearance of sympathy with the "copperhead sympathizers of San Francisco," and hoped "that President Johnson [would] remain true to the constitution and his pledges" to act in the best interests of his party.[21]

The Union Party's elected officials attempted to quell the confusion by staking out a clear position in the State Legislature. After weeks in which competing resolutions warred in both the Senate and the Assembly, the Union delegates finally closed ranks in an impressive display of party unity. Just three days before the legislative session ended, Union Party members passed a series of resolutions they hoped would rally the faithful, but that in the end had disastrous consequences for the party. Coming down firmly on the side of Radicals in Congress, the California State Legislature insisted that "all questions pertaining to the status of the late rebel states . . . belong to the legislative and not to the executive department of the federal government." The legislators signaled a clear break with Johnson when they stated, "that any attempt by the national executive to control the questions, would be an invasion of the rightful authority of the people, and dangerous to republican liberty." They also registered their hearty approval of a constitutional amendment, then making its way through Congress, that would enshrine the provisions of the recently vetoed civil rights bill in the nation's organic law. Having thus made their position clear, the legislators adjourned and returned to their home districts to face an angry public.[22]

Instead of drawing the Union Party faithful together, the resolutions only drove the party's competing factions farther apart. Whether the state's politicians had based their stand on the courage of their convictions or on a disastrous misreading of public opinion, their decision fatally wounded the Union Party and opened a golden opportunity for the Democrats. By endorsing what eventually became the Fourteenth Amendment, California's Union Party publicly embraced a national policy that would allow Radicals in the federal government to dictate racial policies in the states. White Californians had come to fear a federal assault on white privilege, and now they saw their own representatives joining in. In April 1866, the state's lawmakers left Sacramento and returned to home districts more fractured than ever. Over the next several months they watched in dismay as their coalition party broke into distinct Radical and Johnson factions, each holding its own convention and publishing its own resolution on Reconstruction.[23]

As Californians argued over Reconstruction, the Fourteenth Amendment gained two-thirds majorities in both the U.S. House and the Senate, and Congress reported the text to the states for ratification. The amendment arrived in California while the State Legislature was in recess. California had recently adopted a system of biennial sessions, and the legislature would not reconvene until December 1867. Governor Frederick F. Low had the option to call a special session to consider the amendment, but he declined to do so. Why he declined to call the special session remains unclear. Given the firestorm that followed the Union Party's endorsement of the Fourteenth Amendment, he may have feared that the state's legislators would be unwilling to go further and actually ratify it. Such a failure would be deeply embarrassing. At the same time, given the current uproar over Reconstruction, he may have felt that the people of California deserved the chance to speak on the matter first through the electoral process. Whatever the reason, Governor Low left the Fourteenth Amendment on his desk for, he hoped, the next Union Party governor. But in the long gap between California's biennial legislative sessions, the state's political landscape tilted drastically.[24]

The Election of 1867

The gubernatorial campaign of 1867 opened early in California. While the general election would not be held until the first week of September, political machinations at the ward level began in early spring in preparation for the primary elections that would send delegates to the state nominating conventions held in June. Control over local primary elections could make or break a candidate for statewide office, and these early contests of the political cycle were often bitter and even violent. Bad feelings generated in the rough and tumble of ward politics could poison formerly warm political relationships and undermine party unity in the general election. Ugly local battles occasionally doomed a party's effort even before candidates for state office were chosen. In 1867, just such bitterness led to a disaster for the Union Party. For the Democrats, early control coupled with a racialized agenda led to a smooth nomination and a successful campaign.[25]

The Democrats began by choosing at their state convention a platform with a content signaling that race and Reconstruction would occupy center stage as the primary issues of the campaign. Fully half of the resolutions adopted by the convention dealt with Reconstruction, and in each of those, state Democrats condemned the policies of the Radical Congress and denied the right of that body to legislate for the states or interfere with the president's prerogatives in binding the nation. The seventh resolution brought Reconstruction home to multiracial California in terms that echoed the president's objections to the civil rights bill. "We believe it impracticable to maintain republican institutions based upon the suffrages of negroes, Chinese, and Indians, and that the doctrines avowed by the Radical leaders of indiscriminate suffrage, regardless of race, color, or qualification, if carried into practice, would end in the degradation of the white race and the speedy destruction of government." Since by the time of the state Democratic Convention, which opened on June 19, 1867, Congress had extended the franchise to African Americans in the District of Columbia and throughout the South, the issue of black suffrage was fresh in the minds of most Californians. Inclusion of Chinese and Indians in the plank served to remind voters that what Congress did in other states, it might do in California.[26]

Even as the platform signaled the direction of party rhetoric, the Democrats' choice for gubernatorial candidate signaled an intent to steal votes from the Union Party using race as a wedge. To understand how that strategy was intended to work, one needs to understand the candidate. If nothing else, on the surface Henry Huntley Haight seemed an unlikely choice. Publicly, Haight claimed that he detested politics. As governor he would complain incessantly about having to work with the legislature, an activity he called "dabbl[ing] in the filthy pool." He felt that politics brought out the worst in human nature and despaired at the "profundity of rascality" he detected in California's legislative body. Before his run for governor, Haight had never held public office of any kind. And yet, despite his public protests, he had been deeply involved in politics for most of his life.[27]

Henry Haight was born in Rochester, N.Y., to parents of English descent, in 1825. As a young man he attended Yale, graduating in 1844. Soon after graduation, Haight moved to St. Louis, where he read law in his father's firm. While in St. Louis, Haight dabbled in politics for the first time, editing a Free Soil newspaper on the side. When gold was discovered in California, he pulled up stakes and headed west.[28]

Haight arrived in San Francisco in January 1850 and quickly determined to mine the miners rather than the mines. He set up what would become a successful San Francisco law practice with two men who would later serve as the first of many important political connections upon whom Haight would rely in his race for governor. The first was his father, who followed him from St. Louis in 1851. The elder Haight gave the firm local respectability and considerable influence when he was appointed to a post as federal district judge for the southern region of the state. The second was James A. McDougall, who had been attorney general of Illinois in the early 1840s and was elected to the same post in California in 1850. He went on to a term as U.S. congressman in 1853 and was one of California's U.S. senators when Haight ran for governor.[29]

In 1856, Haight supported the first Republican presidential candidate, John C. Fremont. It is likely that he was drawn to the Republican Party out of his earlier Free Soil sympathies rather than by the new party's antislavery stance. Haight's later race panic, evident throughout the 1867 campaign, fits neatly with the fear, prevalent among Free Soilers, of the connections drawn between labor and color in the argument over slavery. Following Fremont's defeat, Haight stuck with the Republican Party, rising to the post of state chairman of the party in 1860, and in that position he was responsible for organizing the effort to elect Abraham Lincoln. Haight, however, almost immediately regretted his support for Lincoln. Soon after Lincoln's inauguration, Haight wrote in a letter dated May 3, 1861, that he considered his vote a mistake.[30]

Although he never made his reasons clear, Haight's break with the Republican Party was complete. By 1863, he had embraced the

Democratic Party, in spite of its taint of treason, and briefly appeared
that year as a candidate for state supreme court justice. Haight politely
withdrew from the race before it ever started, but managed to poll a
thousand votes in spite of his withdrawal. The timing was no coinci-
dence. On New Year's Day, 1863, President Lincoln had made good
his promise to change the nature of the war by publishing the Emancipation Proclamation. In California, the announcement was greeted
by many with dismay, and soon after that Haight came out publicly as a
Democrat. In 1864, Haight campaigned vigorously for George B. Mc-
Clellan, the ineffective former Union general whose bitterness drove
him to an ill-fated attempt to unseat Lincoln. During the campaign,
Haight was reported to have been publicly unkind to Lincoln and his
cabinet, referring to the president as a "vulgar jester," and to Secretary
of War Edwin M. Stanton as a "liar and dirty dog."[31]

This was strong language for a man who by all accounts was
deeply sensitive. At 5 feet, 6 inches and 170 pounds, Haight was a
short, round man whose stiff, gray beard lent him a public aura of
gravity and dignified detachment that hid a more sensitive nature evident in his role as a devoted husband and father of two daughters. Like
many nineteenth-century men, including his nemesis Lincoln, Haight
could also be sentimental. According to a friend, he "disliked to hear
bloodcurdling tales. He seemed to have a very sensitive nature, more
like a woman in that respect." In 1867, Haight, in addition to being a
lawyer, was also a Presbyterian minister and a Mason. In spite of his
stated dislike for politics, he was so well connected in both major parties and in California society in general that he was in reality an ideal
candidate. And, as it turned out, Haight had a flair for oratory.[32]

Following the Democratic Convention, Haight held a series of
rallies in the northern part of the state, focusing on San Francisco and
Sacramento. In speech after speech, he expanded upon and refined
the meaning of the Democratic platform, whipping up Californians'
fears of racial amalgamation and degradation, and especially of black
domination, all the while linking both with the Republican program
for Reconstruction. As he did so, Haight reached deep into the rhetoric of California's recent racial past. He approached the racial issues of

the contest from two different directions. First, he sought to reverse some of the gains made by black Californians during the war years by challenging their status as more deserving of inclusion than the Chinese and Indians. Second, he sought to establish a clearer description of a white racial ideal that would forever limit, if not bar, nonwhite participation in public life. Democratic newspapers supported his efforts by printing editorials undermining the Union cause and insisting that "universal suffrage" was the only important issue of the campaign, and that a vote for the Union Party was a vote for black suffrage.[33]

Haight delivered what was probably his most important speech of the campaign at San Francisco's Union Hall on July 9, 1867. The centerpiece of the speech was Reconstruction. Haight began by hinting that Radicals in Congress were engaged in a conspiracy to elevate blacks at whites' expense, placing white Americans "under the heel of the negroes," and he challenged the loyalty of Radicals by loudly proclaiming such a policy "not American." That such a thing had happened in the South, all present in Union Hall knew. But those in the hall also knew that their state's racial diversity posed special problems, and Haight made sure to render his audience personally threatened by making a bogeyman of the Chinese and considering what would happen in California should Radical policy reach the Pacific. "Suppose," he asked, "you had in this State a Chinese population of 100,000 males over 21 years, and a white population of 120,000 males over 21—and suppose you had rebelled against the Government. . . . What would you think . . . if, to punish you it should disfranchise half your white population, and by military force give the Chinese population the right of suffrage?" Here, without ever mentioning black Californians, Haight neatly linked the two races together. In doing so, he began a process of collapsing the racial categories and distinctions that had been so carefully marked by the Republican-controlled legislature during the debates surrounding California's exclusionary testimony laws in 1863. Haight scoffed at the Radical Republicans' call for "manhood suffrage" and suggested that death would be better than such a dishonor. "Would you not rather have all property confiscated and every tenth man hung?" And here, in his dreadful rhetorical choice, Haight began to describe, in outline, a self-definition of the ideal white American man that would both gain strength and coherence over the next four years and also sustain the Democratic hold on power in the state.[34]

Haight articulated his ideal through a series of one-sided oppositions, describing nonwhites in negative terms and leaving to his audience the task of collectively drawing conclusions about what such terms said of themselves. "The Chinese," he exclaimed, "have no intelligent idea of Republican government." This was true, Haight believed, because God lay at the center of such governments. "Indeed, no race can permanently maintain free institutions which has no faith in God." The Chinese, it was well known, were "pagans," a fact repeated almost daily in California newspapers. The obvious implication was that a proper American was a Christian. This much had long been established in discussions concerning the immigration of Chinese and Chinese testimony in California's legislative halls over nearly two decades. It was an old criticism but an important one. Possession of Christian morals and knowledge of Christian strictures were essential to proper comportment in civilized society.

More important was the type of character required to build up such republican governments. "Our institutions are the result of centuries of struggle and sacrifice," claimed Haight. The "admirable framework of [American] government has resulted from the labor and study of some of the greatest and best men who have ever lived." Struggle and sacrifice, labor and study, all were virtues of personal character that, for Haight, added up to the key virtue of American government: "its harmonious adjustment of local reserved authority, with national control." In other words, its order. All individual citizens were properly a reflection of such good order. They would be men whose knowledge of right thinking and action were internalized to such an extent that exterior bonds of social control became unnecessary. The ideal embodied the capitalist demand for the self-denial of material gratification and the profoundly eighteenth-century republican virtue of self-sacrifice in search of the common good.[35]

Whether any white Californian could be said to meet such a standard was, for Haight, irrelevant. The more important point was that the Chinese, and by extension black Californians, could never attain such a standard. "Shall we entrust this fair fabric to the custody of a servile, effeminate and inferior race of Mongolians," he asked? Beyond their lack of Christian understanding, the Chinese, "whose want of truthfulness, of courage, of moral stamina, of every quality which fits a man to govern himself, is . . . a race whose men are inferior in every quality." Such men would stand neither the struggle nor sacrifice, and possessed neither the knowledge nor strength to even begin to develop the virtues necessary for "self-government," in both personal and civic senses. He closed by reiterating the links that defined California's nonwhite racial groups as equally unworthy of participation in the white polity. For Haight, and for his audience, it was "sufficient for the Chinese, Indians and negroes that they enjoy the protection of the laws, and they are guaranteed equal and just taxation with the whites." It would be a kind of velvet cruelty, suggested Haight, to offer them more. "It is for the good of the Mongolian and Indian and African that suffrage should be confined to the white race."[36]

The following day, at Platt's Hall in San Francisco, the Union Party candidate responded to Haight's speech. Against Haight, the Union Party, which by now was the Republican Party in all but name, had chosen George C. Gorham as its standard-bearer. Gorham proved to be a fiery speaker and an able politician, but his nomination process, unlike Haight's, had been wrenchingly painful.

Like Haight, George Gorham had never been elected to a statewide public office, but also like Haight, he had a strong political background and powerful connections. A decade earlier he had clerked for state Supreme Court Justice Stephen J. Field, whose patronage would prove vital throughout his political career. That position led to a clerkship at the U.S. Circuit Court in San Francisco and important connections with local politicians. Capitalizing on these connections, Gorham managed to secure a position in the administration of Governor Frederick F. Low in 1863. As personal secretary to the governor, Gorham built up a powerful position as a leader of the short-hair faction of the Union Party and was known as a skilled ward-level political operator. With the help of another political patron, Senator John Conness, and some unsavory politicking in San Francisco and Sacramento, Gorham managed to secure the nomination following a bitter four-way contest.

The backroom dealing that Gorham's victory required occasioned a great deal of controversy and alienated some of the more powerful long-hair leaders. In the end, the Union Party convention in Sacramento was tartly characterized by famed local poet and all-around social commentator Bret Harte as "a spectacle of corruption unexampled even in the palmiest days of New York municipal politics." These leaders were so angered over the manner in which Gorham's nomination had been secured that they bolted and ran a candidate of their own, thus officially and irrevocably splitting the Union Party. The split proved fatal to the party, as well as to Gorham's candidacy.[37]

Gorham's response to Haight the following night exposed the weakness of the Union Party position in California, and its failures would be mirrored in the meek Republican response to Haight's administration for the next several years. Gorham publicly accepted Haight's contention that Reconstruction was the central issue of the campaign, but in doing so, he also explicitly accepted the racialized framing constructed by Haight, thus ceding any control over the shape of the contest. In his speech, Gorham waved the bloody shirt, telling his audience that "it is plain to all but those who are determined not to see, that the accursed spirit of slavery is not conquered, that the 'snake is scotched—not killed.'" Gorham warned his listeners that should the Democrats gain control of even a few Northern states, they might regain control over the Senate and, worse, over presidential electors. For the Democratic Party in general, he reserved his strongest language. "I believe them to be of the brood of Satan," he said. "The Democratic Party, as it at present exists in this country, is . . . the highest expression of the will of the Prince of Darkness among men." In the end, Gorham offered little resistance to Haight's racial message, and he danced around the issue of black suffrage. "I know of no party or faction," he claimed, "which favors 'indiscriminate suffrage.' Let the elective franchise be restricted to native Americans, exclusive of Indian tribes, and to persons of foreign birth who can come up to the requirements of the naturalization laws, and the country will be safe." Safe, because as his listeners certainly understood, California's Indians had largely faded from view by 1867, and since only whites could be naturalized as citizens, naturalization would only increase the white vote. Having thus conceded the merit of Haight's racial complaint, Gorham was left with little more than a strategy devoted to impugning the character of the white men supporting Haight. It was a strategy almost calculated to fail.[38]

Democrats capitalized on Gorham's shrinking eloquence by articulating a racist ideology that bordered on zealotry. A few days following Gorham's speech, the San Francisco *Daily Morning Call* published a brief column by its editors titled "The Negro's Natural Place." Denying the equality of the African with the European, the editors appealed to their readers not to be deceived by black Americans' new status as free men. While the African was indeed free, they argued, he was only free to the extent that he might capably exercise that freedom, and his nature clearly militated against his full participation in the political or social realms. "There are different breeds of men, as there are different breeds of brutes. All, according to their capacities, are capable of improvement." Blacks, they said, were susceptible to slight improvement under Caucasian tutelage, but that improvement could never hold on its own. "Bolster him with Caucasian enlightenment, and his imitative faculty results in a sort of caricature of civilization. Remove it, and he sinks." Put simply, the black man, according to the *Call*, lacked any faculty that might prove conducive to improvement. The obvious implication was that efforts to force progress on Africans were unnatural and that the only responsible course was to limit black access to the public realm whenever possible. "And yet," they said, "a combined sentiment of fanaticism and morbid conscientiousness insists on advancing him to place and power."[39]

In this, the *Call* took up where Haight's speech of two weeks earlier left off. Haight, remember, had begun the implicit process of articulating a white ideal to complement the sort of unsavory negative black ideal advanced by Democrats like the editors of the *Call*. Concealed within their virulent attacks on American blacks was a sort of silent praise for the white American. Whereas for Haight, America's republican institutions were the culmination of years of struggle and learning, for the *Call* no span of time, and no amount of study would ever yield a similar achievement for blacks. "We cannot, of ourselves, elevate him; that must be his own work. Our race has shown him what

This 1867 political cartoon, which satirizes the gubernatorial campaign of George Gorham (depicted carrying California's minorities on his shoulders), captures both the complexities of California's racial diversity and white Californians' fears over the potential effects of Reconstruction. (Courtesy of the Bancroft Library, University of California, Berkeley, BANC PIC 1953.013—B.)

a people may do. The faculty of self-improvement and elevation is organic. It cannot be created or transferred. It seems wanting in the negro." The changes in blacks' legal status over the previous several years
prompted whites to harden their rhetoric and deny even the possibility of self-improvement. No example could be found, they argued, of
the African ever living up to the ideal set by the United States, in spite
of numerous attempts. Those attempts in fact constituted the "greatest proof of the inferiority of the negro." The black man's greatest fault
"is his instinctive clinging to, and imitation of, the Caucasian." "Were
he possessed of proper individuality he would scorn to endeavor to
associate on terms of social and political equality with a race by whom
he is instinctively avoided." The mere wish for equality was taken as
proof that African Americans did not deserve it. Their wish amounted
to little more than "striving against Nature."[40]

This form of opposition to black equality, which would become
even more important during the debates over the Fifteenth Amendment, drew heavily on well-known theories of evolution, recently lent
even greater weight by the work of Charles Darwin. Indeed, the editors' references to "Nature" and "progress" as the primary engines
and obstacles to human improvement represented a new departure
for California's racial hierarchy. As recently as 1863, much of the debate over racial difference had taken its foundational premises from
the Bible. Now, four years later, God was conspicuously absent from
the discussion.

Across the United States, scholars and scientists, and particularly the medical profession, relied more and more on a peculiarly
American interpretation of Darwin's theories to explain the problems
of population facing the country and, more important, to prescribe the
solutions. As Californians debated the merits of black suffrage, American scientists embraced Darwin's promise of limitless evolution for
whites, but drew nonwhites out of the picture, claiming that natural
selection no longer operated for them. If this were true, the question
of black suffrage would take on special urgency. Their interpretation
had potentially dangerous consequences for nonwhites in the United
States, and their arguments quickly seeped into public discourse when

it was discovered that they offered a convenient justification for whites' racial beliefs.[41]

As the gubernatorial campaign wore on, Henry Haight continued to stoke the fires of racial hatred. Throughout the summer, he confined his political peregrinations to the northern end of the state, but this in no way implied that he had written off the still largely Spanish-speaking "cow counties" of Southern California. Both Haight and southern California's Democratic candidate for Congress, Samuel B. Axtell, published speeches in Spanish for local consumption. Both men reiterated the racial elements of the Democratic Party platform and their firm belief in the rightness of that platform. "I positively oppose the creation of a community of equality between the Chinese, negro and Indian," wrote Axtell, before going on to decry Congress's Radical policies. Haight, for his part, claimed he would always oppose attempts "to force me into a state of political equality with negroes." Equally important, both men continued Haight's practice of collapsing nonwhites into a single racial category.[42]

The Spanish broadsides published by both Haight and Axtell reflected the ambiguous position that Californios occupied within the state's racial hierarchy. As numerous historians have shown, Californios and Mexican Californians had suffered discrimination and racial opprobrium from the moment white Americans arrived in California. Sonoran miners had been driven from the gold fields, and Californio landowners had been bankrupted and displaced when they were forced, in a hopelessly corrupt process, to defend their titles in American courts. By both social and legal convention, all Latinos, whether Californio, Mexican, or Chilean, had been defined as a criminal element within California society. And yet, across the state, and particularly in the southern counties, Californios retained a great deal of political and economic power. That power secured for Californios several seats in the State Legislature, the office of state treasurer, which was almost a sinecure for Californios, and the deference of politicians like Haight and Axtell. The speeches also implied a racial affinity between white Californians and Californios of a certain class that required a concerted defense against nonwhite encroachment. This awkward position, in which California's Spanish-speaking population could be both racial ally and racial enemy, persisted until well into the 1880s and faded only when Californio economic power diminished and sapped their political strength.[43]

Black Californians watched Haight's campaign with growing alarm. Black San Franciscans had been among the first to recognize the potential for national black suffrage in the Radicals' control of Congress. They were also among the first along the Pacific to recognize President Johnson's intransigence and to call for his impeachment. As early as March 1866, black Californians had begun calling for black suffrage in California, claiming that "there is such a strong desire in the minds of colored men to possess this right, so highly do they prize it, that they would undergo any privation to obtain it." Suffrage, they argued, would finally be "evidence of that American citizenship for which we have so long been yearning." Haight's increasing popularity, and the split in the Union Party caused by Gorham's backers, demoralized black Californian society. That demoralization, however, did not prevent them from challenging Henry Haight's attempts to define them out of the ideal republican polity.[44]

Black Californians first parried Haight's attacks by championing the hierarchy articulated during the testimony debates of 1863. In those debates, their Republican defenders had carefully established distinctions between the African and Asian races, and in relaxing the exclusionary laws with regard to black Californians had effectively written those distinctions into law. In part, that effort had been successful because of plausible assertions by both white Republicans and black Californians that the latter adhered to precisely the same Victorian, middle-class values as whites. Haight's definition of the ideal had implicitly challenged black Californians' efforts to attain middle-class respectability by classing them with the Chinese, and it was against this slur that they first directed their response.

The editors at the *Elevator* refused to accept any such link, particularly when it came to fitness for suffrage. Haight had, from the beginning, used the presence of Chinese in California as a weapon against black suffrage, arguing that "if we admit the negro to the vote we must grant the same privilege to the Chinese." "There is no analogy between the cases," they said. "The negro is a native American, loyal to the Government, and a lover of his country and her institutions—American in all his ideas." In essence, they rehearsed the same arguments they had advanced in delimiting themselves from the Chinese four years earlier, and establishing their middle-class American credentials. Blacks were born American and Christian, and so had a stake in the well-being of the nation. "In every war in which our Government has been engaged . . . the negro has borne a prominent part," and for that, they argued, they deserved a voice. The Chinese, as "sojourners," had no care for American progress; they only wanted to make money. They had "never raised a sword or fired a gun in defense of the country which gives them protection." Most important, the Chinese, they said, "are foreigners, unacquainted with our system of government, adhering to their own habits and customs, and of heathen or idolatrous faith."[45]

As they had during the testimony debates ten years earlier, black Californians complicated whites' color-bound racial categories by redefining Irish immigrants as less than worthy participants in the public realm. In accepting Haight's emphasis on self-control and republican knowledge as befitting a man for suffrage, black Californians sought to drive a wedge through the white population. The editors at the *Elevator* explicitly challenged the fitness of many of Haight's own supporters for the suffrage. "In reference to the ignorance of the negro, why, the most ignorant plantation slave knows more about the politics of the country and its institutions than one-half of the European immigrants on their first arrival to America." Given the fact that black Californians likely had a significantly higher literacy rate than did Irish immigrants, this was a particularly telling accusation.[46]

The reference to immigration was clearly a swipe at San Francisco's burgeoning Irish population, a group whose infamous antagonism toward African Americans was enthusiastically returned. In this, the editors at the *Elevator* were tapping into a deep reservoir of unease and resentment against the presence of a large and unpopular element of the white community. Looking back some twenty years later, Hubert Howe Bancroft remarked that his support for the Democratic Party's exclusion of black Californians from the franchise might have been more enthusiastic had it also included the "low Irish." At the time,

Bret Harte blamed the Irish for the political turmoil at the Union state convention and doubted their loyalty during the war. When the editors at the *Elevator* expressed invidious distinctions between themselves and the Irish, they emphasized loyalty to the nation as well as their own respectability.[47]

The role of the Irish in California's racial politics exposes the fluidity of racial definition in the state. In the East, the Irish went through a long, linear process of racial assimilation before finally achieving "white" status in American society. In California, the Irish appear initially to have been accepted as white during the Gold Rush years. Yet as California's frontier qualities softened and cities like San Francisco and Sacramento acquired cosmopolitan respectability, the Irish seem to have experienced a loss of status that rendered their connection to Anglo-Saxon society ambiguous.[48]

Social commentators often reflected the confusion over Irish status, and more often helped to exacerbate it. Referring to the "blind hatred and active malice of our Celtic citizens," Bret Harte repeatedly lampooned Irish pretensions, coupling ethnic prejudice and anti-Catholicism. "Convinced from the beginning of the superiority of freckles, red hair and brick-dusty epidermis . . . they at once put the Mongolians in the level of the African, and abused them on theological grounds. It was only when they attempted to settle the question of average brain capacity, by breaking the Chinese head to more conveniently examine its contents, that they were checked." Disgust with Irish social behavior often led critics to link the Irish with nonwhite groups in ways similar to those employed by Henry Haight and the Democratic Party. Bret Harte, for instance, claimed that the Chinese were a better class of immigrant. "As servants they are quick-witted, patient, obedient and faithful, and the old prerogatives of Bridget and Norah . . . are seriously threatened by the advent of these" more pliable immigrants.[49]

Clearly, black Californians recognized in the Irish an opportunity to both resist Haight's attacks and to rise in the esteem of California's better men at the same time. The strategy reversed that used by the Irish themselves against African Americans in the East and was similar to that deployed in the testimony fights. Black Californians embraced a piece of the opposition argument, in this case the element of Haight's ideas that emphasized moral character, and they challenged its racial element by invidious comparison with another racial group. Whereas four years earlier the racial group had been the Chinese, now black Californians added the Irish.

In the end, however, Henry Haight crushed George Gorham in the election. Haight won by more than nine thousand votes and carried with him the entire Democratic ticket, ending Union-Republican domination of the state for the rest of the nineteenth century. Republicans in California and around the country expressed shock and dismay, but none were as bitter as black San Franciscans. Both black Californian newspapers, the *Elevator* and the *Pacific Appeal*, condemned the Union Party bolters and the racists who had engineered Haight's victory. While the editors of the *Elevator* tried to remain optimistic about the future, those at the *Appeal* could muster nothing but vituperation, sackcloth, and ashes.[50]

Henry Haight settled, if a little uncomfortably, into office and created a strongly Jacksonian administration stressing a policy of limited government and liberal use of his veto power. Haight lost no opportunity to rail against Radical Reconstruction and voice his support for Andrew Johnson. Shortly after his inauguration, Haight wrote to President Johnson, praising his fight against the Radicals and begging him to stay the course. Haight did his part by leaving the text of the Fourteenth Amendment, forwarded to his predecessor by Congress more than a year earlier, on his desk where he found it. Haight never transmitted the amendment to the State Legislature, and in any event it was unlikely that the newly elected Democratic majority would ratify it. His overriding worry was, of course, black suffrage. "The northern people," he wrote, "will pronounce against the policy of negro and military rule by an overwhelming majority. . . . The elections last fall have given of this sufficient proof." For the next several years, Haight continued to fight and speak against what was to all intents an inevitability.[51]

The Democratic sweep in the elections of 1867 secured California against black suffrage for the moment. Haight's victory, though, offered a precarious sort of security for whites hoping to avoid the fate of the Reconstruction South. When Congress submitted the Fifteenth Amendment to the states in late 1869, Democratic race panic accelerated and generated several weeks of angry, anguished debate in January 1870. The crisis began with Haight's submission of the amendment to the legislature along with an intemperate message suggesting that the legislature reject it.

The Fifteenth Amendment Debates

Haight began his message by saying that race had nothing to do with the Fifteenth Amendment, an odd statement in itself, considering its purpose. He then offered a dry, workman-like canvass of legal and constitutional issues that read more like a legal brief than the fiery speeches that had won him his office. The question at hand was one of states' rights, he claimed, whether "Congress ought to restrict the people of the several States from exercising their own independent judgement on the subject" of suffrage. As dry as it was, Haight's message struck right at the heart of white self-conception. Should the legislators fail to understand or recognize the vital constitutional issues, they would also, then, fail the key test of republican manhood. "To say that the people of California should tie their hands upon this subject, is to charge upon them either incompetency to comprehend what is expedient and just to those within her jurisdiction, or unwillingness to be governed by justice and sound policy." With this statement, Haight managed to bring race into the question without actually mentioning it. If white Californians gave up the power over the vote, that would prove them unfit for self-government. The implication was obvious: giving up power over their own affairs was the same as becoming black.[52]

In the end, though, Haight could not help himself, he simply had to bring the race issue into the open, in spite of his initial assertion that it wasn't relevant. The old stump orator came out as Haight once again brought Reconstruction home to Californians. "If this amendment is adopted, the most degraded Digger Indian within our borders becomes at once an elector, and so far, a ruler. His vote would count for as much as that of the most intelligent white man in the State. In this event, also, by a slight amendment to the naturalization laws, the Chinese population could be made electors." Once again, Haight clearly linked Indians and the Chinese with African Americans. He did so, however, very quietly, managing to submit a thirteen-page message on the Fifteenth Amendment without ever mentioning the racial group it was specifically designed to help. And in case any of the legislators had missed his earlier point about the danger of race degradation the amendment represented, he closed his message with a slavery metaphor whose implication was abundantly clear. Beseeching his readers to stand firm even in the face of the inevitable, he wrote that even "if it were true that the . . . majority of the Northern States were so far misled by their political leaders as to look on with complacency while chains were being placed on their own necks and on those of their Southern brethren, we would still owe it to ourselves and to the cause of constitutional liberty throughout the world, to raise our voices in condemnation and warning."[53]

In the debates that followed Haight's message, Democratic legislators refined their self-definition and their definition of African Americans. The story of the Fifteenth Amendment in California is the story of Charles Darwin and the Democrats. The Democrats, who had never really accepted the racial hierarchy developing in California, now embraced it. Their arguments betrayed an oddly enthusiastic acceptance of Darwinian evolution, all the while carefully excluding nonwhites from the Darwinian promise. Their arguments followed three basic lines of defense, and many legislators wove all three together through weeks of speeches in both the Assembly and the Senate.[54]

The first line of argument was most ably presented by the first senator to speak on the amendment, William M. Gwin, Jr., on January 13, 1870. Gwin took up Haight's charge that to accept this new congressional usurpation was to engage in the degradation of whites. The amendment, he argued, would cause the government of California to "degenerate into a government of mixed races," reducing white to a level with black. When the Republican Party, which he sarcastically referred to as the "party of progress," accomplished its goals in the South, he claimed, it will "inaugurate its policy on this coast. The contest that has been carried on there will be transferred here—the only difference will be the substitution of the Chinaman for the negro."[55]

Gwin's inclusion of the Chinese in the equation is important for understanding how Democrats understood the problem. For one thing, it again rendered Reconstruction a local issue. It also, however, offered an important new claim about the relationship between black, white, and Asian. "The radical party is a revolutionary party. Its chief glory . . . will be the degradation of the white race to the political level of the negro; its next greatest achievement will be to assert the equality of the Mongolian." Implicit in this statement is an argument about African Americans. While contact between the races lowers whites and raises the Chinese, the black remains in place, frozen in evolutionary time by the limits of his biology. This theme of degradation and subordination was played out again and again in the debates, each time raising and lowering whites and Chinese, but leaving blacks stagnant.[56]

The second line of defense evident in the debates constituted the strongest denunciation of the presence of blacks in American political society and built upon Gwin's degradation argument. Appealing to the black's supposed incapacity for self-government, R. M. Martin of Siskiyou canvassed a number of regions where such an experiment had been tried. In all such places, he found that blacks "began to retrograde" once the bonds of slavery had been lifted. Freed of restraint, blacks ceased working and proceeded to "idle away their time, lying at all times of the day at their ease, or asleep, reeking in foul odors—depending entirely for subsistence upon the spontaneous products of the earth for a livelihood." The image that Senator Martin described depicted blacks as animal rather than human, as insensible rather than rational, and he was clearly playing off of antebellum portraits of African slaves and the definition of the ideal American developed during Haight's 1867 campaign.[57]

African licentiousness was not confined to idle play. It could also explode in violence—passions one way or another were not controlled by reason in the African. Senator Martin described black uprisings in the Caribbean in which women "were violated in order to sate their brutal passions," and "children's heads were cut off, stuck on poles and paraded through the streets." All of this was done while Africans "possessed all the political power necessary to carry on an Independent government." The implication was clear, and the danger immediate. Black Californians could be trusted only to destroy everything whites had built.[58]

William Gwin offered an important variation of the argument from idleness and brutality by linking black profligacy to private property. Should black Californians and the Chinese become voters, "they will destroy all equilibrium between the property taxpayer and the poll taxpayer." While he was careful to avoid arguing for property qualifications lest he alienate working-class voters, he argued essentially that propertyless race inferiors would vote for expensive improvements at others' expense, reducing the state to penury. The South offered a clear example. "The negroes," claimed Gwin, "too indolent and improvident, ever to become property holders, are ruining the South."[59]

Perhaps the most eloquent of the speakers during the debates, if "eloquence" can be used to describe such an aggressively hateful purpose, was Senator John S. Hager. Hager suggested that those who questioned a future in which black Californians vote need look no farther than Africa itself. "In his native Africa . . . he remains . . . unchanged and unimproved. Still devoted to fetish worship; still engaged in human sacrifices. . . . We have seen him on this continent at Hayti attempting to build a government upon the ruins of one of the white race; imitating all the tawdry tinsel of royalty . . . and yet we find there degeneracy and decay." The best that blacks might hope for, according to Hager, was mimicry and blood. The black's barbarism and licentiousness rendered him incapable of political participation of any kind.[60]

The final tack taken in the debates stirred fears of the disappearance of the white race entirely. No two races could coexist, they argued, under a republican government without dire consequences. "It is against human experience," said Senator Barclay Henley of Sonoma, "and our knowledge of man's nature, for any two races of people to live together harmoniously under a Republican form of Government in the equal enjoyment of political rights, unless they intermarry or amalgamate." This, of course, spelled race suicide. "I do not think the donkey is the equal of the thoroughbred," said Senator Hager, "nor do I think our radical Congress can legislate him into a horse, or into social equality with the horse. You may cross them, and you have a hy-brid—the mule—but you cannot propagate a race of mules. You may cross the white and the negro races, and have the mule, or the mulatto, which I believe is a synonymous word, but you cannot propagate a race of mulattoes. You must return to the original stock, on the one side or the other, or they become extinct." Hager went on to explain in detail how this had happened again and again in history, and he pointed to Mexico as evidence of the degeneracy of such a racial policy.[61]

Throughout all of these arguments, California's Democratic politicians appeared to finally embrace a hierarchy that drew distinctions among races. Indeed, many of the arguments they offered against the amendment required such distinctions if they were to make sense. Perhaps the best articulation of this came from Senator Hager in a speech that finally closed the debate. Hager's articulation also offered the most clearly Darwinian interpretation of California's population yet.

Hager began with the monkey. "As we walk along the streets we see the organ grinder with his monkey . . . and we are amused and surprised at his displays of watchfulness and intelligence. He looks and acts somewhat like the common brotherhood . . . but we do not recognize him as such." Hager traced what he conceived as, if not the human line of descent, at least the human taxonomic pedigree through chimpanzees and gorillas, noting at each level of the ladder the increasing biological similarity with *Homo sapiens*. From the gorilla, it was but a short jump to "the Australian savage . . . indulging in unintelligible gibberish, and fleeing from the face of the white man, like the beasts of the forest." Hager wondered whether at this point he had reached the line dividing man from beast, but then implied that he had not. He proceeded to list the "types of mankind," rising "through the Digger Indian and the Esquimaux, the lowest of the race on this continent; through the Kanaka, the Hottentot, the Arab, the Mongolian, etc.," until he finally arrived at the pinnacle, the white man. The hierarchy, derived from unassailable science, offered proof that the various racial groups could neither breed nor govern together. The lines separating each rendered them almost totally different species, and justified the permanent exclusion of those whose natural condition left them unfit for self-government. This was the verdict of progress, not prejudice.[62]

John S. Hager (1818–1890). As a state senator
in 1867, Hager fought against ratification of the
Fifteenth Amendment. In the 1880s, as collector
of customs for the Port of San Francisco,
Hager would suffer withering criticism for his
handling of Chinese immigrants. (Courtesy of
the Bancroft Library, University of California,
Berkeley, California Faces from the Bancroft
Library Portrait Collection.)

In the end, Hager was preaching to the converted. Few in the
California State Senate disagreed with his assessment of the relative
values of nonwhites, just as few of the men who had been swept into
office with Henry Huntley Haight had any intention of voting to diminish white privilege. On the same afternoon that Hager expressed

his views on race, the Senate voted overwhelmingly against black suffrage. The following day the California State Assembly concurred with the Senate, and California officially rejected the Fifteenth Amendment. The rejection of both the Fourteenth and Fifteenth Amendments placed California at odds with much of the rest of the nation. California's racial diversity had driven whites to align themselves, at least in terms of racial ideology, more closely with the South than with their former Union allies. And yet, even in the South the Fourteenth Amendment had been ratified by every state as a condition of readmittance to the Union, while ratification of the Fifteenth Amendment was required of the unreconstructed states of Georgia, Mississippi, Texas, and Virginia. In many ways, California stood as the most "unreconstructed" state, if only for a short while. The Democrats' victory for white supremacy was both hollow and brief. Within days of the vote in California, the Fifteenth Amendment achieved the necessary approval and became part of the nation's organic law.

Conclusion

Democrats' embrace of a more complicated racial hierarchy signaled an important shift in race-thinking in California in several important ways. The notion of a complex racial hierarchy had been championed by California's nonwhite minorities and their white, Republican allies since the mid-1850s, and so in simplest terms, acceptance of that notion by white Democrats represented the achievement of a kind of consensus regarding race. More substantively, through the nature of their opposition to the Fourteenth Amendment and particularly the Fifteenth Amendment, Democrats transformed the role played by hierarchy in California's race relations. Whereas supposedly common racial characteristics had once linked nonwhites in common degradation and thus justified racial exclusion, now hierarchies of difference served the same purpose. Whereas those hierarchies of difference had once been used by black Californians as the fulcrum by which they lifted themselves into white society, blacks now saw whites turn those differences against them. The more complicated hierarchy blacks had seized upon to raise themselves up was now a tool for their oppression. In this sense, California's experience with Reconstruction fundamentally altered the way Californians approached race, at least intellectually. California's experience with Reconstruction also transformed California state politics. Democrats had been out of favor in California since the beginning of the Civil War, and in San Francisco since the mid-1850s. Now, because of the actions of the federal government, with Republicans in power, California's Democratic Party was revived and would be a serious contender for power for the rest of the century.

Perhaps the most important transformation concerned the context within which racial conflict took place in California. Ratification of the Fifteenth Amendment meant the end of white men's unique status as political beings and masters of American destiny. Now, black Americans would have a hand in shaping the nation's future, and a key component of white privilege was undone. Over the next several years, white officials in some voting districts attempted to block black efforts to exercise their new political rights, but those efforts never came close to matching the mass disfranchisement of the Jim Crow South. Instead, the majority of white Californians appear to have quietly accepted blacks' new political status. Yet, even as whites accepted a new political landscape, they still felt a pressing need to maintain racial distance between themselves and California's nonwhites. When Reconstruction reconfigured the political sphere, social distance became more important than political distance, and the wider cultural and social ramifications of Reconstruction became arenas of racial tension. Access to schools, hotels, theaters, employment, and housing would soon become the sites of racial conflict. In the South, Reconstruction became Redemption and finally came to an end in 1877 when federal troops finally pulled out of the former Confederacy. But in California, Reconstruction continued to transform race relations throughout the 1870s and into the 1880s as blacks and Chinese sought to expand the freedoms and rights embodied in the Fourteenth and Fifteenth Amendments.

Chapter 3
"The Most Satanic Hate"
Racial Segregation and Reconstruction in California Schools

In children thus divided by law, the most Satanic Hate is likely to be engendered. This, no one who has studied human nature will deny. This hate "grows with the growth and strengthens with the strength." What children are in the school-room, they are when manhood has come over them, and what feeling the schoolroom fosters appears in after life in the shape of a monster called law.
—Proceedings of the State Convention of Ohio Negroes, 1849

IN JUNE 1872, MARY FRANCES WARD was eleven years old. Every morning, she walked from her home at 1006 Pacific Street to San Francisco's "Colored School," which the white men on the city's Board of Education had placed at the top of Russian Hill, at the corner of Taylor and Vallejo Streets. Today, Vallejo Street, west of Mason, climbs sharply for one short block, then disappears into a steep rock wall lined on one side by an equally steep concrete stairway. In 1872, Mary Frances, without benefit of a stairway or sidewalks, would most likely have avoided Vallejo Street and chosen instead to trudge up the busy, rutted, and often treacherous thoroughfare known as Broadway. The worry this dangerous daily trek caused her parents, A. J. and Harriet Ward, was compounded by the humiliation of being forced to send their daughter to a racially segregated school. Worst of all, however, each day on her way to what they felt was an inferior education, Mary Frances walked past the spacious and well-appointed grammar school reserved for white children on Broadway.[1]

By the end of June, Harriet Ward had had enough. On July 1, 1872, she presented her daughter to Noah Flood, principal of the whites-only Broadway Grammar School, and requested that he find a space for Mary Frances in the sixth-grade class. Flood, court documents would later show, without pausing to ask after her abilities or residence, "at once politely but firmly and definitively declined . . . to admit" Mary Frances. His one and only reason for this, according to Harriet Ward, was that Mary Frances "was black and there was a special school for black children." Harriet and her husband found a lawyer and sued, claiming that the city and state laws that supported Noah Flood's decision violated both the letter and spirit of the Fourteenth Amendment's guarantees of equality before the law.[2]

In the surviving court documents, Harriet Ward's is the only testimony offered in defense of her daughter's education. Her husband and the black community whose lot the case stood to improve are conspicuously absent. On the surface, at least, Harriet Ward appears as a lonely crusader, courageously stepping beyond the limits of her station to win a brighter future for her daughter. In reality, Mrs. Ward's suit grew out of a long struggle over black access to the Broadway school and was part of a carefully orchestrated assault on the racial barriers white Californians had raised around their public schools. *Ward v. Flood* was, in fact, a test case, deliberately designed to capitalize on the earlier successes of the civil rights struggles of the 1860s and on the changes wrought in American law by the passage of federal civil rights legislation during the early years of Reconstruction.

In the simplest practical terms, the suit proposed to end segregated schooling in California and win access to better schools, better opportunities, and better lives for California's black children. Full access to the fruits of education had been a goal for black Californians ever since the first statewide civil rights convention met in 1855, but that goal had been repeatedly set aside in the face of more urgent demands, such as the rights to testify in court and to vote. With those rights secured, black Californians felt free to pull Reconstruction more deeply into the West and make an issue of California's segregated schools. On a deeper level, the suit represented an attempt— through the state's system of public schools—to redefine the meaning and scope of Reconstruction and the terms of black citizenship. To do this, black Californians self-consciously manipulated and reshaped the racial ideas supporting their state's racial hierarchy in light of the legal transformations wrought by Reconstruction. As citizens of the Republic, black Californians now occupied a new legal and political space, and in the 1870s, they used the fight over school segregation to expand their achievements into the social realm.

For whites, the suit struck an equally deep chord. In spite of the difficulty that successive state superintendents of public instruction had in securing funding for the public schools, white Californians regularly acknowledged their importance. In an era still infused with a Jacksonian distrust of government, government-run public schools were almost universally promoted as an absolute civic necessity. Indeed, white Californians embraced a set of widespread beliefs about education and public schools that were central to the concept of American citizenship, a concept that Harriet Ward's suit threatened to dismantle. It was in the public schools that young citizens learned of the profound meaning embedded in the liberties guaranteed them by birthright. It was also in the public schools that young citizens were instructed in the web of civic and social obligations those rights implied. Schools, then, served a political purpose and produced loyal, disciplined, virtuous citizens.[3]

Such citizens embodied traits that, in the minds of many white Californians, blacks were constitutionally incapable of acquiring. Embracing such rigid racial distinctions allowed white Californians to continue denying their black neighbors full social and political inclusion, regardless of the Fifteenth Amendment. Whites interpreted black demands concerning schooling as a demand for a degree of civic inclusion far beyond that which whites understood was decreed by the three Reconstruction Amendments. Given the schools' political function, to admit black children into white schools was to train black children in the same civic lore as white children and so admit black citizens fully into the white republic. In the midst of the argument, many white Californians, especially white Democrats, claimed that blacks and their white, Republican allies were seeking something that, to their minds, constitutional amendments had no power to mandate: nothing less than full social equality.

Historians often dismiss the warning of impending social leveling as a racist rant, a cynical appeal to the baser instincts of that class of white Americans predisposed to vote in defense of racial superiority, or worse, as a hysterical call to arms in defense of the purity of white women. But however accurate and trenchant such historical judgments might be, judgment cannot replace an analysis of white racial anxieties. Moreover, such judgments tend to obscure California's distinctive multiracial context. Even though black Californians, as in previous years, limited their demands for racial inclusion to themselves, white Californians feared those demands would widen a tear in the wall surrounding white racial privilege and allow Chinese immigrants and California Indians to come rushing through. Because of these fears, white Californians took the matter of social leveling very seriously and devoted a great deal of energy to anguished public debate over the question.

Black Californians often vigorously denied the charge of social leveling, but, in fact, this was precisely what they were seeking. Unlike whites, they interpreted the end of slavery and the advent of Reconstruction as an end to the caste system that had left them to languish on the margins of American politics and society. In the years immediately following the Civil War, they were repeatedly frustrated by their continued exclusion from trolleys, omnibuses, theaters, hotels, and, most humiliating of all, public schools. By the 1870s, black Californians were no longer content to simply demand that white Americans live up to the ideals professed in the Declaration of Independence and the Constitution. Like black Americans across the nation, freedom and necessity transformed black Californians from deferential petitioners to legal innovators. In pursuit of social equality, a realm over which many argued the law held no sway, black Californians consciously sought to draw the law into the fray. They demanded more than equal treatment before the law—they demanded that the definition of legal protection be expanded into daily social life and that legal authority be employed to shape social attitudes. This demand formed the foundation of *Ward v. Flood* and similar cases, including California's contribution to the famous *Civil Rights Cases* ten years later, and it represented a fundamentally different conception of freedom than that held by white Californians in the aftermath of the Civil War.[4]

From Unfettered Citizens to Responsible Patriots

Californians had a highly developed sense of the purpose behind their public schools. While the traditional "3 R's" formed the core of the curriculum, Californians also expected their schools to produce good citizens. On a purely prosaic level, this meant that schools should promote an orderly society by placing children firmly on the path toward virtue rather than vice. To this end, a portion of every school day was devoted to moral instruction, and the practice aided in the development of a cottage industry devoted to the publication of textbooks providing lessons in "moral science." In his official report to the legislature in 1867, State Superintendent of Public Instruction John Swett recommended one such textbook, which was part of the state-mandated curriculum, and he discussed its value in terms that both expressed the desired outcome of such instruction and implied some of the deficiencies he saw in California classrooms. Marcellus F. Cowdery's *Elementary Moral Lessons*, he argued, would instill "habits of personal cleanliness, neatness in dress, order, obedience, and politeness." Its "simple stories" would "illustrate the virtues of honesty, truthfulness, and kindness to one another, and to animals." This last was a necessary addition, given the rude state of many California schools, in whose playgrounds, according to one observer, "cattle and hogs dispute with the children."[5]

The state's Californio children were deemed especially vulnerable to the temptations of savagery, and this judgment demonstrated once again the racially ambiguous position of the state's former rulers. D. S. Woodruff, superintendent of Contra Costa County Schools, warned his superiors that "there is not enough pains taken to entice the uneducated boys and young men of the native stock. . . . Many of them learn quickly when they attend school, but it requires a great effort to keep them there, and it seems to me that they are going to furnish little better than banditti as they reach maturity, unless they can be persuaded to attend School more regularly, thus filling the rich

John Swett (1830–1913). As state superintendent
of public instruction, Swett worked hard to open
California's public schools to racial minorities. His
efforts on behalf of public education in California
earned him fame as the "Horace Mann of the West."
(Courtesy of the Bancroft Library, University of
California, Berkeley, California Faces: Selections
from the Bancroft Library Portrait Collection.)

soil of their minds with good, instead of leaving it to grow to thorns
and brambles." Los Angeles County Superintendent John W. Shore
also employed a metaphor of cultivation as he described in detail the
criminal talents of Californio offspring. Even the parish priest in his
district, claimed Shore, "recently said that the materials were here for

the worst banditti in the world." In school, he insisted, Californio children often proved excellent students. "Out of school," however, "they learn . . . but in a very different way. Many of them can ride a horse to perfection; shoot a revolver from a horse's back as they run . . . or lasso a bear to admiration. They are, out of school—a rich soil left to thorns and thistles." As in Contra Costa though, all hope was not lost; the schools offered a defense against vice. "Readily enough, they learn the vices of Americans, and add them to the vices of their fathers; and they can be gathered and taught the virtues and knowledge of Americans too." Such vivid fears testified to a common perception that Californio children lacked the self-control thought of as natural to white children. And yet, the remedy suggested by California's educators also implies a widespread belief that Californio children would respond to training and a widespread willingness to conduct that training in publicly funded schools alongside Anglo children. In this, Californio children were afforded a racial capacity that white opinion denied black children.[6]

Californios were by no means considered the only children at risk, and parents, educators, and politicians around the state regularly suggested that compulsory education offered the key to an orderly society. The editors of the *Los Angeles Star* argued for just such a law in an editorial in which they decried the "large class of people who . . . being themselves ignorant, permit their children to grow up in ignorance, leading inevitably to vice." The city superintendent of San Francisco blamed miserly city officials and asked "if it is economy to allow hundreds of our children to ramble through our streets, to acquire vicious and idle habits?" Responsible citizens breathed a sigh of relief when compulsory education finally became law in 1874.[7]

On another level, Californians, like Americans elsewhere, expected their public schools to produce patriotic citizens properly fitted for republican self-government. Good citizens were expected to pay attention to civic events and to be vigilant observers of their leaders' political behavior. When called upon, they were expected to participate in civic life. The founders had envisioned a constant dialogue between the people and their elected leaders and worked to ensure that a mechanism for that dialogue would always exist. An essential but now often forgotten feature of the First Amendment is the right of petition, and in the nineteenth century, as one historian has pointed out, "the modest exercise of signing a petition was a chief way the public made known its sober will to its representatives." That will, it was to be hoped, was one tempered by education. Good citizens, in other words, needed to be instructed in order to properly instruct their government.[8]

At the founding of the Republic, and into the first half of the nineteenth century, the emphasis in that instruction was on helping citizens acquire the tools they needed to recognize potential demagogues and tyrants. Citizens were educated in their rights to know when to defend them and in their responsibilities to know how. Californians considered this an essential element of a child's education and wrote that belief into the state school law. The law made civic instruction part of a teacher's official duties, and explicitly linked that instruction with the moral education provided by the daily curriculum. "It shall be the duty of teachers," the State Legislature solemnly decreed, "to impress on the minds of their pupils the principles of morality, truth, justice, and patriotism; to teach them to avoid idleness, profanity, and falsehood; to instruct them in the principles of a free government, and to train them up to a true comprehension of the rights, duties, and dignities of American citizenship."[9]

In antebellum America, white male Americans were free to define the style and tenor of their political behavior. Antebellum politics was a tumultuous, chaotic, and often violent affair, and its practitioners considered heated partisanship an indispensable ingredient. Antebellum schools were expected to support political diversity by instructing children in their civic rights and duties without reference to partisanship; they were expected to rise above party squabbling and teach commonly held principles along with the rules of the game.[10]

With the onset of rebellion, the public school came to be seen as a tool to overcome politically dangerous ideas. Civic responsibilities became more important than the liberties American children had long been taught to vigilantly defend. "The events of the great rebellion," reported Superintendent Swett, "have shown conclusively the necessity of inculcating the lessons of patriotism by means of history.

The law ought to require . . . the study of . . . State and National Government, and the duties of citizens of the republic." The rebellion replaced a discourse of rights with a discourse of duties. Increasingly, duty to community replaced duty to individual freedom, and patriotism became synonymous with loyalty. After the war, Californians consciously reconstructed their schools, transforming the schools' mission to support political diversity into a mission to promote homogeneity. Only by taming the boisterousness and diversity of prewar politicking could another national tragedy be averted. Textbooks published after the war reflected this transformation in political thought and behavior. One author advertised his text as "the only work calculated to perpetuate the American Government by familiarizing the popular mind with its principles, and thus fortifying public opinion against the assaults of treason and corruption." This would be accomplished, he wrote, by "explaining and defining 'loyalty' in the United States, and the proper relation between patriotism and party."[11]

These changes in California's political and educational outlook mirrored changes in the rest of the United States. Across the country, politicians, commentators, and educators looked to the schools as a hedge against disorder. Many Americans felt that while the war was over, it would take little to plunge an exhausted and fractured nation back into chaos. Many also saw the national divide between North and South repeated in lesser, but no less vital, rifts between native-born and immigrant, Catholic and Protestant, Democrat and Republican. Binding the nation's wounds, some argued, would require a commitment to common principles and a dedication to social as well as national unity.[12]

In the early 1870s, a number of prominent Republicans began arguing for a federal role in education. One suggestion was the creation of a cabinet position and the elevation of famed educator William Russell to the post of secretary of education. Massachusetts representative George Frisbie Hoar introduced a bill in Congress designed to create a national system of education that symbolized the nationalizing influence of Reconstruction. Hoar's bill moved Henry Wilson, chairman of the Republican National Committee, to publish an article in the *Atlantic Monthly* calling for "the public school to become the centerpiece of a new Reconstruction of all of American society, North as well as South."[13]

In the South, religious aid societies were pursuing the same goal in their efforts to educate and elevate former slaves. Much of the curriculum there was designed to train black students to support established economic relationships and to provide Northern entrepreneurs with a stable workforce. Black Americans in the South also received training in their duties as proper citizens, an element of their education that took on a special urgency with the extension of the franchise to southern blacks in 1867. The restrictive message embedded in the philosophy of civic responsibility was explicit in Southern black schools, where, in the words of one historian, education was meant "to bind, not to liberate."[14]

Race in the System

In California, however, the creation of responsible patriots was widely seen as a project limited to white children. State politicians and educators had long believed that the principles of proper civic behavior were beyond African Americans. It was precisely those "rights, duties and dignities" so carefully imparted in the classroom that state legislators, while debating the ratification of the Fifteenth Amendment in early 1870, had argued black Californians could never comprehend. To reinforce those beliefs, race was woven into California's education system through the laws that governed it and the curriculum that fulfilled its mission.

The issue of race first appeared in the California school law of 1855. Prior to that, state funds were apportioned to local districts according to the number of school-age children in each district. In 1855, the legislature inserted the word "white" into the law, explicitly linking funding only to white children. Before the change, State Superintendent John G. Marvin had simply assumed that state-funded public schools would be segregated and left local districts to their own devices. With the change in the law, local districts were actively encouraged to exclude black children.[15]

Black children, however, were not the only children driven from the schools by the new law; the law also, by extension, excluded Chinese children. What little education of Chinese children existed in the early decades of statehood was provided by missionary schools in San Francisco, Sacramento, and Los Angeles. Contemporary commentators assumed that the Chinese were mainly interested in learning English and claimed that they left the schools once they had acquired basic skills. Contemporary reports further suggested that Chinese parents and students were put off by the paternalistic version of Christianity they found in the mission schools and that they rejected the prospect of attending schools with black children. In other words, it was widely assumed that Chinese immigrants had little interest in placing their children in public schools and as a result, during the first three decades of statehood, Chinese in California hardly figured in debates over schools except as foils in the arguments between black and white Californians. As we shall see, however, the Chinese did make an issue of segregated schools in the 1880s, long after the issue had been settled for black Californians.[16]

California Indians occupied a more complicated space. Most Indian children were either running for their lives or living on federally administered reservations, and so did not come under the purview of state schools. The school law did, however, admit Indian children living with white parents. The *Law for the Government and Protection of Indians,* passed in 1850, allowed whites to essentially kidnap Indian children and "employ" them as servants. It also expected whites to provide for their education and training for adult life, hence the provision in the law. It is unknown how often Indian children in such circumstances appeared in school, but it is doubtful that it was a common occurrence. Indians, then, also appeared in the discussion largely as foils for debate.[17]

Despite these restrictions, nonwhite children did occasionally attend school with white children, often through the generosity of liberal-minded local school officials. By the end of the 1850s, it was clear to the new state superintendent, Andrew Jackson Moulder, that such encouragement was not enough to prevent race mixing in his schools, and he asked the State Legislature for the authority to punish districts that violated the law. "I regret to announce," he began, "that the odious tastes of the Negrophilist school of mock philanthropists,

Andrew J. Moulder (1825–1895). During a long
career as a public educator, Moulder dedicated
himself to maintaining strict racial segregation
in California schools, and he ended his career
by denying Chinese children access to public
education.

have found their way . . . into California. In several of the Counties,
attempts have been made to introduce the children of Negroes into
our Public Schools on an equality with whites."[18]

Moulder was especially disturbed by a recent imbroglio in his own
hometown of San Francisco, in which a prominent black businessman
named Peter Lester had presented his daughter for admission to the
public high school. The request precipitated a crisis among the members of the city's school board and a flurry of editorials demanding the

protection of the purity of white children. Most editors agreed with the *San Francisco Daily Evening Bulletin*'s position. "We hold it to be wise and true policy to maintain the social distinctions between the white and inferior races in our State, in all their strength and integrity." Arguing that the success of Britain as a colonizing power was ascribable to its strict policy of racial separation and that the failures of France and Spain were due to the absence of such a policy, the editors called for the continued exclusion of black children from the schools. "We think," they wrote, "that history demonstrates the wisdom of keeping . . . all the natural prejudices against the amalgamation of the races. . . . Nothing could possibly have so powerful an effect in destroying these prejudices as educating the two races together."[19]

Moulder agreed with this assessment and claimed in his report to the legislature that "this attempt to force Africans, Chinese, and Diggers, into our white Schools . . . must result in the ruin of our Schools." By defining black, Chinese, and Indian together as equally ruinous of white education, Moulder reiterated the distinctly circular reasoning that had marginalized all nonwhites since the *People v. Hall* decision five years earlier. Black aspirations had been repeatedly thwarted by the claim that their racial affinity with Chinese and Indians rendered them unworthy of full inclusion in American society. Chinese immigrants and California Indians, by the same token, were unworthy of full participation because of their racial affinity with blacks. To allow black children into classrooms with white children was to undermine all racial restrictions. To do so, moreover, was really nothing more than cruelty to the black children. Mixed-race education would encourage a belief in equality and could "only bring mortification and chagrin . . . when time disabuses them of this idea." Moulder asked that his office be given the authority to withhold funds from districts that violated the law, but softened the blow by adding that local districts could, if they chose, open separate schools. This was suggested, wrote Moulder, not out of "any prejudice against a respectable negro—in his place; but that place, is not . . . an association on terms of equality, with the white race." Moulder, in other words, argued that the state should not attempt to challenge the "natural" order but should instead devote its energies to promoting it. The following year, the State Legislature granted Moulder's request and effectively pushed black Californian children from the public schools.[20]

The exclusion of black Californian children from the classroom could only have encouraged the belief among white children that black Americans were not suited for full participation in civic life. This belief was reinforced in daily lessons throughout the state, particularly through instruction in geography. In their geography lessons, California's schoolchildren learned about the world around them, from local landscapes and the important geographical features of their state and nation, to distant, exotic lands and continents. Each lesson followed a similar pattern: first topography and climate, then vegetation and animal life, and finally human inhabitants. It was here that many of California's white children had their first experience with other races, and what they learned colored their views on civil society for the rest of their lives. Nineteenth-century geography textbooks, in fact, probably contributed more to the propagation of racialist ideas in America than any other feature of American life following the death of slavery, making later racial regimes such as Jim Crow more palatable and even logical to white Americans.[21]

Typically, in such popular texts as *Cornell's Primary Geography*, Arnold Guyot's *The Earth and Its Inhabitants*, and Guyot's *Earth and Man*, the regions of the earth were ranked according to climate. According to nineteenth-century science, the type of climate determined the type of vegetation, which in turn determined the type of animal life. While each of the regions, or "zones," was inhabited by "mankind," and "all climes provided him materials for food, raiment, and shelter," some were clearly considered better than others. The most salubrious regions, according to universal acclamation, were the temperate zones. Those regions in the temperate zones most conducive to animal husbandry and wheat cultivation—meaning Europe and the United States—were deemed most likely to produce industry, economy, and morality.[22]

The temperate zones were taken as the ideal, by which all others were defined, and from which all others deviated. "In the temperate zone," for instance, were found "not only all those plants and animals most needful to civilized man, but also a great abundance of the most useful minerals." "The climate," moreover, was considered "such that man can easily perform the labor necessary to obtain and make use of" that abundance. For all other zones, the greater the distance from the ideal, the greater the savagery of the natives the children were taught to expect. "The most luxuriant vegetation is found in the moist portions of the torrid zone; that is, in South America and India," claimed Guyot. This was important because all agreed that the more exotic the vegetation, the less pliable the animal life. "The largest and fiercest animals, as the elephant, lion, tiger, are found in the dryest continent of the torrid zone; that is, in Africa." This Guyot contrasted with what he considered the ideal. "Nearly all those animals most useful to man in performing labor, or in furnishing him food and clothing, are natives of the temperate zone."[23]

This heavy dose of environmentalism also extended to the local human inhabitants, with those outside the ideal zones often reduced to little more than another form of animal life. It was in the temperate zone, that the "most highly civilized nations" were found. The tropics, on the other hand, were "unsuited" for civilization because "the climate is so warm as to make people weak and indolent." People who inhabited such regions were "almost constantly at war among themselves, and are generally very cruel to their enemies, but are often kind and faithful to their friends."[24]

More detailed distinctions between the peoples of the earth were normally collected in the final chapter under the title "Types of Mankind." Here the authors refined the crude distinctions rooted in climate into a complex and often bewildering arrangement in which human "types" gradually modified with distance from the ideal. At the primary level, geography textbooks rendered these deviations in simple, blunt terms. "The people of the United States," explained Guyot, "are generally well educated, and are remarkable for their industry, intelligence, and enterprise." To the rest of the world, Guyot was less kind. "The African and the Australian, or black races, the Malay and the American race, have very little civilization, and a large proportion of the people are entirely savage." Among the least of humanity were ranked the original inhabitants of California. "The 'Root Diggers' of California and Nevada," he wrote, "are very miserable and degraded creatures." Another author of a primary textbook reduced Arabs to "a wandering race of people," and described Abyssinians as "very rude and brutal in their manners and customs."[25]

Older children were treated to more complicated language and schemes that drew distinctions between peoples of similar regions. Guyot's *Intermediate Geography*, for instance, located the "cradle of the human race" in Persia and claimed that the first people were Caucasian and represented the ideal. "Europeans and their American descendants," Guyot's readers learned, "form part of the same great branch of the white race, have in general, less regularity of features and harmony of proportions than the Persians and Armenians; but the face has more animation, more life and expression; the beauty is less physical, more moral and intellectual." As students shifted their studies away from the "geographical centre of the races," they found that "the regularity of features diminishes, and the harmony of features disappears." The Arab's "head is less symmetrical, while his complexion varies with the climate to tawny and even to black." Gradually, humanity grew less white, and less beautiful, until the survey ended with a bump in Tasmania, where people were "among the ugliest of mankind, with gaunt body, meagre members, bending knees, hump back, and projecting jaws." Students could trace these changes by studying the detailed woodcut illustrations that accompanied the text, which faithfully depicted the decline from noble beauty to enervated degradation.[26]

In the same way that whiteness and beauty diminished with distance from the "centre," so too did mental and moral capacity as well as civilization and good government. California's schoolchildren learned all this and more in daily geography lessons administered by teachers schooled in the same lore. The most complicated of all the textbooks was Guyot's *Earth and Man*, which was part of the standard curriculum at the state normal school, where the state of California trained its teachers.[27]

Race could occasionally burst beyond the walls of the classroom and dominate political discussion. In 1862, the only statewide office up for election was superintendent of public instruction. The contest was widely seen as a referendum on California's loyalty to the Union, and a test of the still-young Republican Party's power in the state. The Republicans put up a popular young school principal named John Swett as their candidate and prepared a campaign that emphasized loyalty and hatred of treason. But they soon found themselves on the defensive when the Democrats began slinging accusations of race amalgamation.

It all began when a broadside, which was first posted throughout San Francisco and later distributed around the state, accused John Swett of violating the school law prohibiting interracial education. In the broadside, published by San Francisco City Superintendent of Schools Henry S. Janes, an ardent Democrat, Swett was accused of running a school in which *"negroes were taught and classed upon terms of equality"* with whites. For weeks, the public, in newspapers, speeches, and counter-broadsides, angrily argued over this "monstrous doctrine." Swett himself vigorously denied the charge in an open letter to the *Sacramento Daily Union*. Laying responsibility for the situation at the feet of the female principal of the primary school—Swett was principal of the attached grammar school—Swett admitted that "two very light mulatto girls" had attended the school unknown to him. When he found out, he wrote, "they remained against my protest." In the end, in spite of the Democrats' loud denunciations of "Mr. Swett's abolition and amalgamating proclivities," loyalty to Union won out, and Swett was elected.[28]

Swett's election was, as many historians—including Swett himself—have pointed out, the most important event in the history of California schools. Later known variously as "the Horace Mann of the West" and the father of California's public schools, Swett was a tireless educator who managed to secure permanent funding for the school system and to greatly expand and professionalize it. His election also presaged a Republican sweep in the next year's elections that would result in a relaxation of the state's exclusionary testimony laws for black Californians and, more important for this chapter, a change in the school law. In spite of his public distaste for interracial education, Swett firmly believed that nonwhites had a right to an education and, given their payment of taxes, a right to expect state-sponsored schools. He also believed that it was in the state's interest to educate potentially criminal elements. Throughout his tenure in office, Swett urged the State Legislature to provide for nonwhite education, and near the end of his term Swett got his wish. A provision was added to the law mandating the creation of a separate school should the parents of at least ten nonwhite children in a district wish it. The provision also stipulated that if there were fewer than ten nonwhite children in a district, they might be admitted to the white schools. It was a small step forward, but an essential one nonetheless. Where black Californian children had been all but excluded from the public schools, they were now guaranteed an education at state expense in their own schools. The liberal atmosphere of the war years in California soon came to a crashing halt, however, as the war ended and as Californians overwhelmingly rejected Congress's program of Reconstruction. In the first major statewide election held after the war, Californians ousted the Republican Party and established Democratic majorities around the state. Educational prospects for black Californians in particular suffered a blow as the election replaced John Swett with Democrat O. P. Fitzgerald as superintendent of public instruction.[29]

The Broadway School

Soon after winning control of the state government, local Democrats in San Francisco moved to limit the influence of federal Reconstruction by excluding black Californians from as many arenas of public life as possible, chief among them the schools. On July 2, 1868, the San Francisco Board of Education voted to close the Broadway school for "colored children," an act that led directly to Mary Frances Ward's arduous daily trek up Russian Hill and the Wards' suit four years later. The action was taken after little debate and with little fanfare. San Francisco's black community was absolutely flabbergasted. The school, which stood on Broadway, between Powell and Mason Streets, had been built at city expense in 1864 for $10,933, and had, on average, taught some one hundred black children each day. Now, suddenly, and for the first time in many years, San Francisco's black community was without a school at all.[30]

In spite of white Californians' ceaseless efforts to exclude them, black Californians had long numbered among the state's most dedicated educators. William Leidsdorff, for instance, a wealthy, respected pioneer and a mulatto, served on San Francisco's first board of education in 1847 and oversaw California's first public school. Reverend Jeremiah Sanderson, perhaps California's most important black educator, had been active in eastern abolition circles and a friend of Frederick Douglass's before opening Sacramento's first permanent black school in 1855. Reverend Sanderson was active in virtually every civil rights cause in California, and he opened Stockton's first school for black children in 1868. Not all teachers devoted to black education were black. In the town of Red Bluff, Sarah Brown, daughter of martyred abolitionist John Brown, ran a school for local black children that survived many years.[31]

In San Francisco, black Californians left out by the city's refusal to admit them set about educating their children through private efforts. The first such school was established May 22, 1854, by Rev. J. J. Moore in the basement of the A.M.E. Church on Jackson, between Powell and Stockton Streets. The basement was perhaps not the best location, and the children apparently suffered mightily through their lessons. Some years later the city superintendent described the basement as "squalid, dark, and unhealthy," and periodically San Francisco's black community attempted to secure better quarters, but only the A.M.E. Church managed any permanence.[32]

While hardly ideal, the quarters for the city's black children were not much different from those for white children around the state. In cities and towns strapped for cash, classes were often conducted in rude surroundings and in rented spaces. In Sacramento, the city school board was forced to move a school when they discovered that the building owner had rented the school's basement to a "beer vendor." District administrators around the state routinely complained to the state superintendent of the difficult conditions under which children, black and white, labored. In Los Angeles, the furnishings were "of a very unique and antique pattern . . . admirably adjusted to twist the spines of growing girls, and break the backs and weary the legs of the sturdier boys." The school set aside for the city's black children was far less furnished, with only a "line of rough board seats without backs, around the walls."[33]

In spite of such surroundings, Reverend Moore's school operated for ten years before the city's school board finally built a school for the city's black children. Unlike the "colored school" in Los Angeles, the Broadway school had furnishings "of improved style," and was "well-lighted and ventilated," with "separate halls and clothes rooms" for girls and boys. It was a school that, the city superintendent wrote, "the colored children richly deserve."[34]

At the school, the children received the same curriculum as that offered in the white schools, and their parents were determined to teach the very same values. Admonishing his fellow "Anglo-Africans" to participate in educating the community's children, one writer commented on the value of education for blacks. "Education brings with it all those principles, which will elevate and enable us to stand upon the same footing with other nations on the globe." "The present generation, has a great responsibility resting upon it," he wrote, "for the great Corner Stone has to be laid, that those who come after, may have nothing to do but lay the stones one upon another." Education, he opined, would finally win entrance to American society for African Americans, because "it evangelizes, civilizes, and raises a nation upon the great basis of equality."[35]

Black San Franciscans' shock at the closure of their school quickly turned to outrage as the reasons for the closure became clear. Not long after the board voted to close the school, they voted to reopen it for "the use of classes from the adjoining school, composed of white children." In fact, there had been rumblings about the black school for some time before the board finally acted. A year earlier, the city superintendent had published a report in which he suggested that "a new location and new building should be secured for the Colored School." "The present location," he insisted, was "unsuitable" because it was not central to the city's black population, and "besides, its proximity to the Broadway Primary is found objectionable."[36]

Black San Franciscans' ire soon settled on one board member in particular, one General Cobb, whose suggestion to close the school had been quietly accepted by the rest of the board. Cobb, according to *Elevator* editor Phillip Bell, had been a slaveholder and slave "speculator" in Texas before his arrival in California, and his questionable reputation as a gentleman was generally held beyond salvage. Cobb had been elected to the school board on a promise to close the Broadway "colored school," and once in office he made good on his promise. That large numbers of white San Franciscans approved of his action, there can be no doubt. Following the closure, the *San Francisco Morning Call*, a Democratic newspaper known for taking pleasure in baiting the city's black residents, began publishing a series of columns titled "The Negro's Natural Place." The *Call* made the link between black education and good government explicit when its columns described the chaos and anarchy that gripped nations such as "Hayti" and Liberia under black guidance. These examples convinced the editors of the *Call*, and those of the *San Francisco Examiner*, who piled on a few days later, of the unfitness of black Californians for civic life and therefore of unfitness for admission to state schools.[37]

Elevator editor Bell was especially incensed by the *Call's* invidious "comparisons between the Negro and other races, to wit—the American Indian, the Arab and the Moor." Their contention that blacks were inferior to all the others was clearly wrong, claimed Bell, and he took the opportunity to contend that black Americans were closer to whites than the *Call* suggested. "The African suffers and endures, but is progressing to a higher destiny." Meanwhile, "The American Indian is fast disappearing from the family of mankind; civilization but deteriorates him. . . . The Arab and the Moor, as separate races, are also nearly extinct; another century will only know the Indian, Arab and Moor as relicts of history."[38]

Sympathetic whites counseled patience, with one newspaper suggesting that black San Franciscans "trust to the sense of justice of the Board of Education." "'Sense of justice' forsooth!" responded the *Elevator*. "The Board showed their sense of justice by closing our school." Black San Franciscans recognized in the board's actions and in the *Call's* editorials whites' determination to defend the "aristocracy of color" that barred their full inclusion in California society. They vowed to respond with the same dedication.[39]

At a grim meeting on May 17, community leaders met at San Francisco's Bethel Church and discussed action. They met with State Superintendent Fitzgerald, who offered sympathy but little else.

Phillip A. Bell (1808–1889). As editor of one of San
Francisco's two black newspapers, the *Elevator*,
Bell worked tirelessly to advance the cause of black
civil rights. His fiery denunciations of General Cobb
helped whip up support for the lawsuit that became
Ward v. Flood. (Courtesy of the New York Public
Library, image 1219247.)

Then they settled on a petition to the city school board. The petition
made next to no impression upon the board, and over the next several
months, repeated petitions were met with silence.

By August, no action had been taken by the board, and outrage
had been replaced by bitterness. One writer, calling himself "Osce-
ola," noted that the state's prison, like the schools, was segregated.

"This is said to be the case in h—l," he wrote, where "the negroes shovel the coals to keep the white folks warm." Phillip Bell was every bit as bitter, and after a string of white accusations about "social equality," let fly with the most honest appraisal of the term ever published in California. "The highest condition of social equality," he wrote, "is sexual intercourse." And pointing to the obvious offspring of slavery, he accused the Democrats of being the true supporters of "social equality." "They are willing that licentious white men should seduce our females, but they are struck with horror at the mere possibility of niggers marrying their daughters." Looking forward to the extension of the franchise, and believing that the vote would finally help black Californians achieve equality, Bell insisted that "we have never made any claim to social equality."[40]

By November 1868, bitterness had turned to despair. Repeated entreaties to the board had finally yielded a promise to build another school, this time at the top of Russian Hill. But that promise had been broken, and the board had fixed up an abandoned schoolhouse in North Beach, on Greenwich Street, which made no one happy. The Greenwich school, complained the *Elevator*, "is in a neighborhood where our children are liable to be molested," and is "an old, dilapidated building . . . almost in marsh," that was originally abandoned because it "was pronounced unhealthy." Community leaders advised parents to keep their children home. The reason this had come to pass was clear. It had happened "because we are negroes, and having no votes, we have no political rights which the white man is bound to respect. If we had votes, these same men . . . would solicit our favor at the polls."[41]

After nearly a year without a decent school, black community leaders finally managed a meeting with city Superintendent James Denman, and extracted a promise to move the Broadway school for "colored children" and set it at the top of Russian Hill at the corner of Taylor and Vallejo Streets. The task was completed by the end of the summer of 1869, and the school opened with two white teachers teaching ungraded classes. Black San Franciscans remained unhappy, however, and continued to look for alternatives.[42]

On February 3, 1870, the Fifteenth Amendment was ratified, without the help of California, whose legislature had refused to accept it. Black Californians rejoiced and celebrated what they interpreted as the final key to their freedom across the state. Soon after, the tone of black Californian protests changed as despair turned to action. Stories began appearing relating an unwillingness to simply accept poor schools, and many black Californians began calling for the close questioning of candidates concerning their stances on schooling. The *Pacific Appeal* explicitly called for bloc voting in favor of candidates who "will be in favor of improving the present mean school facilities."[43]

Black Californians clearly accepted the commonly held notion that citizens' rights were best protected through exercise of the franchise and that social standing was determined by proper political behavior and internalization of the very values taught in the state's public schools. Social change, in other words, would follow political change in a process they had been taught was a time-honored American tradition. Their expectation that the franchise would finally bring equality and better schools revived flagging spirits and brought a renewed sense of purpose. But their faith in these precepts was sorely tested as, across the state, intransigent election officials blocked their attempts to vote or even to register to vote.[44]

After two election cycles had passed, and despite the best efforts of black Californians, the schools remained "under the control of bigoted Southerners, narrow-minded Yankees and illiberal, ignorant foreigners." The events of the past year had shown that the Fifteenth Amendment would not live up to their hopes. "We who have grown old in the country," wrote *Pacific Appeal* editor Peter Anderson, "can scarcely hope to derive much from that long delayed, yet magnanimous act of justice, the Fifteenth Amendment." "It is for our children to reap the full harvest of its benefits by being educated up to a knowledge of their rights and privileges under the law." While the Fifteenth Amendment might offer the vote, he wrote, "unless our children can be permitted to acquire an education to fit them to enjoy the increased political and social rights accorded them, the Amendment will be virtually defeated and shorn of all practical and lasting benefit to our race."[45]

The failure of the Fifteenth Amendment to ameliorate their exclusion led black Californians to, in a sense, turn their backs on the limited goals of congressional Reconstruction. Anderson's column signaled that black Californians would no longer follow the political channels laid down for them by an American political system geared solely toward the benefit of whites. Social change, it appeared, would not follow political change, and so other means would have to be found. Black Californians turned to the only instrument of social engineering available to them and began calling not for a decent school of their own but for admission to white schools. In the process, they sought to push Reconstruction beyond even what many of their white supporters felt Congress had intended, and they redefined the meaning of Reconstruction legislation to fit a more expansive version of freedom than postwar white Californians were willing to accept.

In November 1871, black delegates from around the state assembled in Stockton for an event dubbed the "Education Convention." Arguing that "education is a natural consequence of freedom," the convention declared that "proscriptive schools are contrary to the pure principles of Democracy." Delegates claimed that "the Amended Constitution . . . and the Civil Rights Bill give us full educational privileges which we cannot obtain in the caste schools as now organized," and resolved to pursue legislation desegregating the schools. More important, they resolved to "bring a test case before the United States Court and to make collections throughout the State to defray the expenses thereof."[46]

Over the next several months, as the State Legislature began its session, which ran from December to April, there was a flurry of activity around the state as black Californians sent petitions to sympathetic legislators and followed the progress of a bill introduced by Assemblyman J. F. Cowdery designed to open all schools to black Californians. In their petitions and in editorials and open letters published in newspapers around the state, black Californians argued for a broader interpretation of Reconstruction. The Fourteenth and Fifteenth Amendments, argued one writer, were not simply limited, sterile expressions of legal equality; they were also about dignity and justice. "The prime object of the Fourteenth and Fifteenth Amendments," he said, "was to prohibit all degrading distinctions made against citizens of African descent on the ground of color." The amendments, in other words, finally demolished the last dividing line between white and black; color could no longer be considered a legitimate reason for legal, political, or even social exclusion.[47]

This did not mean, however, that exclusions on other bases were prohibited. As before, black Californians vigorously resisted white attempts to link them with other nonwhites and thus deny them full inclusion. When black Californians offered their more expansive interpretations of federal Reconstruction legislation, they repeatedly and specifically limited Reconstruction's beneficence to themselves. Cowdery's bill, which had been written to suit the black Californian community, proposed to alter the law only in reference to black Californians. The Chinese, as pagans and foreigners unschooled in American government, and the Indians, as savages, might still be excluded.

In part, this was a strategy of political expedience, as they often pointed out. "Heretofore," wrote Peter Anderson, "it has been the policy of our opponents to couple the claims of colored American citizens with the most objectionable classes, such as Mongolians." The strategy, he believed, made "any just measure obnoxious enough to ensure its defeat." It was also a matter of racial standing. Attempts by whites to link black Californians with "objectionable classes" could often prompt hysterical responses, as when Peter Anderson made the outrageous claim that "the educational privileges of Mongolians in this State, at present, are superior to those of African descent."[48]

As the bills moved through the legislature, events outside the state began to make a test case more and more likely. In March 1872, the Nevada State Supreme Court struck down an exclusionary school law nearly identical to California's on the grounds that it violated the Fourteenth Amendment. At the national level, Senator Charles Sumner was busily pushing for a new civil rights bill that would include a national mandate for school desegregation. Sumner's bill and the rhetoric he employed to secure its passage generated a great deal of anger in California and around the country, and made the passage of Cowdery's bill, or any similar law, virtually impossible.[49]

Ward v. Flood

The failure of Cowdery's bill was the signal to black Californians to initiate their test case. At a meeting at San Francisco's Bethel Church on

April 23, 1872, black community leaders decried the legislature's perfidy and dedicated themselves to the courts. The test case they finally chose became *Ward v. Flood* and was argued before the state supreme court in September 1872. The court, however, withheld its decision in the case for more than a year, and while the justices dithered, school districts across the state found themselves in limbo. Arguments broke out over the racial integration of the state's public schools in San Francisco, Oakland, Stockton, and Sacramento. In Sacramento, especially, the debate threatened to tear the city apart.[50]

An argument between members of the Sacramento City School Board, mostly Republicans, and the people of the city quickly engulfed the entire city government. Throughout 1873, the board debated the question of admitting black Californians into the city's white schools. The debate so alarmed the city's parents that when the city elections were held in the fall, the Republicans were turned out and replaced by Democratic majorities, again demonstrating the potential for Reconstruction's racial politics to trump party loyalty. After the election, the lame-duck board decided not to wait for the court and moved, out of a sense of justice or perhaps spite, to admit two black girls into a city grammar school. The new Democratic city superintendent attempted to reverse the ruling, but by then one of the unseated board members, A. H. McDonald, had taken a position as principal of the very grammar school in question, and had admitted the two girls anyway. The superintendent, A. C. Hinkson, fired McDonald and precipitated a revolt in the schools. In the end, the Democrats won out by suggesting that the city wait for the court's decision.[51]

When it was finally handed down in January 1874, the court's decision revealed a fundamental clash between two very different conceptions of freedom and Reconstruction held by black Californians and white Californians. The attorney for the Wards, John W. Dwinelle, echoing earlier pronouncements tendered by black Californian writers, had argued more than a year earlier that "persons of African descent have been degraded by an odious hatred of caste, and that the Constitution of the United States has provided that this social repugnance shall no longer be crystallized into a political disability." "This," he argued, "was the object of the Fourteenth Amendment."

Dwinelle, speaking for the black Californian community, argued, in effect, that because the state school law derived from prejudice, it was in violation of the federal Constitution. The fact that both white and black children could attend state-sponsored schools and so, as the defense argued, were treated equally before the law, was irrelevant. The intent of Reconstruction, as construed by black Californians, was the abolition of prejudice, not merely equal protection, and if white Californians refused to accept that intent at the polls or in the legislature, then black Californians would use the courts and the schools to fulfill that intent.

The argument reflected the belief held by black Americans all over the United States that the events of the 1860s had granted them full freedom and license to move to the center of American life, occupying the very same civic space as white Americans. It meant, in effect, a seat on the omnibus and in the theater, a room in any hotel, and, especially, participation in the boisterous form of politics they had watched whites perform before the war. Black Californians arrived at this expansive definition of freedom at exactly the same moment that whites articulated a version of freedom narrowed by the horrors of civil war and national disorder. Black Californians were, then, asking for admission to the schools and the creation of a more diverse, inclusive polity even as whites were using the schools to create a more homogenous nation.

The justices refused to accept a vision of expanded freedom and even refused to entertain any question of prejudice. Reducing the exclusionary law to "mere policy," the court scoffed at Dwinelle's claim that the law proceeded from prejudice and insisted that, in any event, prejudice was not a proper issue for the court. They accepted the defense argument that the Fourteenth Amendment's equal protection clause was not violated because black Californians had access to the schools, even to the point of endorsing the outrageous defense claim that white children suffered from the same disability as black children because the law prevented them from attending black schools. The court further argued, quoting from a famous 1849 case in Massachusetts, that the "broad general principle" of equality before the law simply could not hold up in practice. The law in general clearly and rightly drew distinctions between men and women, and adults and children, and the school law was no different. "Equality before the law" really meant, in practice, "only that the rights of all" are "entitled to the paternal consideration and protection of the law, for their maintenance and security." The state had a right, according to the court, to separate black from white just as they might separate older children from younger, and boys from girls if such a decision was determined to improve their education. With that, the court established the principle of "separate but equal" in California twenty-two years before *Plessy v. Ferguson* made Jim Crow segregation the law of the land.[52]

The court's decision echoed the deep hostility toward Reconstruction harbored by many white Californians. In rejecting the Wards' petition, the justices sought to preserve as much white privilege as possible by narrowly, and separately, interpreting the Fourteenth and Fifteenth Amendments to sharply limit the rights those amendments offered to blacks. One of the more potent tools available to the justices for maintaining the stability of racial categories was the traditional distinction between civil and political rights. Normally, as they had several years before in *People v. Washington*, California judges were able to locate their cases in one or the other category and thus remove a whole host of rights from consideration. In other words, cases that fell under the category of civil rights did not admit discussion of political rights, and so, regardless of what such cases might do for black civil rights, limits on black political rights might be preserved. But in *Ward v. Flood*, the question of access to schools appeared to firmly link civil and political rights together. Given the arguments advanced by both sides throughout the controversy, no one could plausibly deny that schools were widely viewed as workshops producing proper American citizens, and as training grounds for virtuous political actors. Without the civil equality needed to gain the same civic training as whites, blacks might never fully achieve the political equality promised by the Fifteenth Amendment.

As their protests in newspaper editorials showed, black Californians had long recognized this. Their argument in *Ward v. Flood* effectively treated the Thirteenth, Fourteenth, and Fifteenth Amendments as three interlocking pieces expressing a single idea: the end of caste prejudice in America. The justices of California's Supreme Court, on the other hand, labored mightily to deny that link. By transforming the federal government's mandate for "equal protection" into a degrading and demoralizing "paternal consideration," the court both narrowed the range of civil rights available to black Californians and at the same time limited blacks' ability to fully participate in the democratic polity on an equal footing with whites. In a few short passages, and by cribbing a twenty-five-year-old case drawn from the days of slavery, the court linked black Californians to the status of children and managed to maintain, even in the face of federal law, "an intermediate class of people standing half-way between citizens, and aliens-born in this country, and yet not of the country."[53]

White Californians reacted to the court's decision in *Ward v. Flood* with restrained enthusiasm. Most generally approved of the decision, particularly those whose years of education in California schools had taught them that nonwhites simply could not be absorbed into the polity. Most were especially pleased by the denial of blacks' interpretation of the meaning of Reconstruction, a denial that checked the reach of the federal government in California by upholding a line between white and black that had been threatened by the Fourteenth Amendment. Most white Californians recognized that that line had clearly moved, but by 1874 most white Californians had also come to recognize that they lived in a changed world. The Civil War and the congressional program of Reconstruction had combined to irreversibly topple the regime that had governed the state's race relations during the 1850s. Given the changed nature of California's racial context, the middle distance to which the court's decision had banished blacks seemed entirely satisfactory.

Surprisingly, black Californians also hailed the court's decision and indeed considered it something of a victory, in part because even as the court upheld the principle of segregated schooling, the decision contained within it the seeds of its own destruction. True, the court had fallen short of ratifying the black vision of freedom, but by insisting that blacks were not being denied equal protection under the law, the case still represented a major step forward. The justices had been able to defend segregation only by acknowledging blacks' right to equal protection and hence the power of the Fourteenth Amendment in state affairs. This acknowledgment was given concrete form in the final paragraph of the decision in *Ward v. Flood*. While the court upheld separate schools for white and black, the justices also insisted that those schools be equal and, more, that where such schools could not be maintained, black children had a right to attend white schools. The decision put pressure on school boards around the state, including San Francisco and Sacramento, to open more schools and expend more money for their maintenance.[54]

In the end, black Californians were right to pin their hopes on the court's closing comments in *Ward v. Flood*. As had happened so many times before, events outside California intruded upon white Californians' efforts to maintain their regime of white supremacy, this time in the form of economic depression. Californians had long chafed at the difficulties that isolation from national centers of politics and economy had imposed upon trade and communication. The completion of the transcontinental railroad in 1869 had been hailed as a momentous event for the state's future, but easier connections with eastern markets meant easier connections with eastern market collapses. When the eastern economy foundered following the Panic of 1873, eastern misery flowed west along the rails and quickly engulfed the state. By 1875, cities and towns all over California smothered beneath the weight of national depression.[55]

Amid widespread economic misery and a sharp rise in new arrivals to the state, local government officials, starved of funds and desperately in search of ways to remain solvent, found it increasingly difficult to justify the expense of separate and equal school systems. Some moved beyond justification and began to openly reconsider segregation. In the summer of 1875, a committee of the San Francisco School Board recommended desegregation and sparked a sharp but brief round of debate. On August 3, 1875, the white-controlled San Francisco school district admitted black children into white schools and effectively discarded the "separate but equal" doctrine they had fought so hard to establish only a little more than a year earlier. Other districts, equally fallen on hard times, soon followed suit. By the end of 1875, Oakland, Sacramento, and Vallejo had joined San Francisco in desegregating their schools, and in the following year most of the rest of the districts in the state quietly admitted black children into white classrooms. Poverty deprived white school boards of the luxury of their racial principles, and where law had failed, economy succeeded.[56]

Reconstruction and Changing Racial Contexts

School desegregation in California took place within a national context that saw a waning of interest in Reconstruction and in black civil rights among white Americans. By the mid-1870s, most white Americans considered the labor of Reconstruction largely complete. The list of accomplishments was, at least on paper, impressive: all of the states that had taken part in the rebellion had rejoined the Union; the Thirteenth Amendment had abolished slavery; under the Fourteenth Amendment, black civil rights were protected; and the Fifteenth Amendment had extended the franchise to black Americans. In the North, a dramatic increase in immigration from southern and eastern Europe, economic turmoil, and mounting tensions between capital and labor combined to distract white northerners away from southern affairs. In the South, Redemption restored political and economic control to Democrats intent on reestablishing white supremacy, and relations between the races slowly settled into the tragedy of Jim Crow. Across the country, the issue of black civil rights, of Reconstruction, seemed to all intents closed, and everywhere, white Americans turned to what they considered more pressing problems.[57]

In one sense, California appeared to be following this national trend. School desegregation appeared to take place in an atmosphere more redolent of resignation and acquiescence than defiance. Moreover, the speed and the ease with which white Californians dismantled their regime of segregated schools raises obvious questions about the strength of the racial ideas and beliefs that justified that regime. How closely held could those ideas really have been? Did white Californians really believe in the racial ideas they espoused, or were they merely cover for the more ordinary sins of greed and envy? Had white Californians finally wearied of the struggle against Radical Reconstruction? Such questions can make sense, however, only if they are divorced from the state's peculiar racial context. The truth is that while white

Californians were most certainly influenced by crises at the national level, they also began to turn to what they considered a potentially greater demographic threat than blacks: the Chinese.

Throughout the nineteenth century, California's black population never numbered more than six thousand, and that in a state whose population topped 854,000 in 1880. The number of black children who entered white schools after 1875, therefore, was very small relative to the number of white children. In San Francisco, for instance, where most of the state's black families lived, City Superintendent of Public Instruction James Denman reported only 145 black students registered for school in 1870. In the former state capital of Benicia, whose experience more closely matched that of the rest of the state, the school census of 1880 showed just two black children. The Chinese were another matter entirely. The Burlingame Treaty of 1868 had specifically encouraged the immigration of Chinese laborers, and during the 1870s California's Chinese population rose rapidly. In 1876, a Presbyterian missionary who ran a school for the Chinese in San Francisco estimated his total enrollment at fifty-five hundred. Many, if not most, were young men, sons of Chinese merchants learning English as part of their business training. To white Californians worried about the eroding edifice of white privilege, this appeared to be the greater threat. Simply put, in the middle of the 1870s, white Californians did not discard their racial ideology or quell their concerns over the racial implications of Reconstruction. Instead, in the face of changing racial patterns they redeployed that ideology against Chinese children, and over time, their racial ideas gained in strength and coherence. The continued discrimination against Chinese children, in other words, should be understood first within the wider context of racial adjustment under Reconstruction, and second as an effort to limit the power of Reconstruction in California.[58]

The Chinese struggle for access to California's public schools closely paralleled that of black Californians. The first school for Chinese children in California opened in San Francisco in 1859 and throughout the next decade flickered in and out of existence as it struggled to secure funding. Classes were held in a room in Reverend William Speer's chapel at Stockton and Sacramento Streets. The teacher, a

Mr. Lanctot, earned $75 a month and drew his salary directly from the city school board, which had, in a fit of generosity, agreed to pay the salary after hearing a petition from a group of wealthy Chinese merchants. The school quickly ran afoul of State Superintendent Moulder's 1860 law barring local districts from using public funds for the education of nonwhites, and the school closed after only a few months. The school later reopened as a night school with private funding and was dedicated largely to teaching English to young men. The school's fortunes revived during the tenure of John Swett, and for several years enjoyed regular funding at state expense. But the school again suffered a reversal of fortune following the Democratic victory in the elections of 1867. State Superintendent Fitzgerald amended the state's school law in 1870 by dropping the word "Mongolian" from the section mandating separate schools for nonwhites. Under this new formulation, local school officials would be free to pretend the law did not require the education of Chinese children. Fitzgerald then took the further step of specifically excluding Chinese children from the school census. This had the effect of allowing the state to continue collecting taxes from Chinese immigrants to fund schools from which their children were barred. In San Francisco, where the struggle over the Broadway school continued to command the city's attention, City Superintendent Denman quietly moved to strip the Chinese school of funding, and on March 1, 1871, the school closed its doors.[59]

Excluded entirely from access to California's system of public education, the Chinese watched from the racial margins as black Californians fought their battle over the Broadway school. The decision in *Ward v. Flood* clearly held out the promise of access to public education for black Californians, and so too, perhaps, for Chinese. When, in 1875, San Francisco opened its schools to black children, the Chinese may have had reason to hope for similar treatment. But first the state laws that blocked their access would have to be challenged.

As a first step, California's Chinese relied on the traditional method of petition. In 1877, thirteen hundred Chinese residents, including many of the "principle Chinese Merchants of San Francisco, Sacramento, &c.," sent a petition to the State Legislature asking for "the establishment of separate schools for Chinese children." The choice of separate schools over full integration was the stated preference of the Chinese themselves, and given the full integration achieved by the black community, this "half-measure" reveals much about the space occupied by the Chinese in California's racial hierarchy. On a purely personal level, the Chinese may have feared for the safety of their children in integrated schools in white neighborhoods, given rising hostility to Chinese immigration. But their preference also speaks to the relatively weak influence Reconstruction had so far had in their lives. To this point, the Chinese had had limited success in turning the Fourteenth Amendment to their advantage, and many whites in California continued to insist that the amendment did not apply to them. While the Chinese had finally gained access to the courts, that access had been more the result of white resignation than Chinese victory. While black Californians had vigorously drawn Reconstruction west in defense of their civil and political rights, the position occupied by the Chinese had remained static. The focus on black civil rights at the national level had enabled black Americans to begin articulating a new conception of freedom and equality, but few, black or white, were willing to extend this vision to the Chinese. In this sense, the request for separate schools simply reflected a recognition of harsh reality rather than dreams of racial harmony and equality.[60]

In their petition, the Chinese presented themselves as honest, hardworking members of California society whose labors contributed a great deal to the wealth of the state. They complained that while they had contributed more than $42,000 in taxes specifically for the support of public schools, they had received no benefit in return. "This money," they wrote, "has been used for the support of Schools for the education of the children of negroes and white people, many of the latter being foreigners from European countries, while our youth have been excluded from any participation in the benefit. This we hold to be unjust." They asked that the school law be changed to allow the three thousand Chinese children between the ages of five and seventeen then in California the same opportunities as "the children of other foreigners."[61]

The timing of the petition could not have been worse. The economic recession that had gripped California in 1875 deepened with time, and by 1877 California's laboring classes were in desperate straits. Many white Californians blamed their predicament on the large number of Chinese laborers in the state, whose willingness to work for low wages supposedly undermined whites' standard of living. By the summer of 1877, large crowds of workingmen were gathering at San Francisco's "sandlots" to hear fiery speeches by men like Denis Kearney, who demanded an end to Chinese immigration. Under such circumstances the State Legislature was unlikely to be in a generous mood. In spite of the humility of its tone and its mild request, the petition was received by the legislature in silence and quietly tabled.[62]

The question of Chinese in California's public schools appeared settled for several years, until the fall of 1884 when a Chinese couple named Joseph and Mary Tape attempted to place their daughter Mamie at the Spring Valley School in San Francisco. In the fifteen years that he had lived in the city, Joseph Tape had worked steadily as a drayman and was known for his honesty and industry. This alone hardly made him unique among Chinese immigrants, but he had also enthusiastically embraced American life in ways that set him apart. Some time during the early 1870s, Tape had cut off his queue, converted to Christianity, and married a woman of Chinese descent named Mary McGladery in San Francisco's First Presbyterian Church. Nine months after their wedding, on August 28, 1876, their first child, Mamie, was born. Mamie had been raised in a thoroughly "American" household. According to court documents, the Tapes lived on Green Street outside of Chinatown, and had "established a Christian home in which the habits and customs peculiar to Americans have been adopted, and the English language [was] spoken by the family." Mamie, it was said, was "more proficient in English, than she [was] in Chinese." Now, after so many years living as Americans, the Tapes wanted their daughter educated in an American school.[63]

For Jenny Hurley, principal of the Spring Valley School, Mary Tape's request that her daughter be placed in a classroom was a novel one, and, seeking guidance, Hurley asked the city's school board for instructions. Her confusion stemmed in part from the fact that in the 1880 the state's school law had again been amended. Under the current law, public schools were to be "open for the admission of *all* children between the ages of six and twenty-one years of age." Chinese children were still not counted in the school census, and so ostensibly could still be excluded, but the laws appeared to conflict, so Hurley asked for help. Unfortunately for Tape, the recent municipal elections had given San Francisco a new superintendent of public instruction: a now ancient Andrew Jackson Moulder. Moulder's racial animus toward nonwhites had not diminished with age, and he instructed Principal Hurley to deny Tape's request. With the avenues of civil government closed to him, Tape appealed for help from the Chinese consul in San Francisco, an American attorney named Frederick Bee.[64]

Bee weighed in with a letter addressed to Moulder and, by extension, to the entire school board, that provoked a flurry of debate and activity. Bee declared the denial of Tape's request "so inconsistent with the treaties, constitution, and laws of the United States, especially so in this case, as the child is native born, that I consider it my duty to renew the request to admit the child." To this point, Bee was only addressing the situation faced by Mamie Tape, but then he took a further step and requested that Moulder admit "all other Chinese children resident here who desire to enter the public schools under your charge." Bee's letter signaled a change in tactics for the Chinese. In 1877, they had merely asked for the creation of separate schools. Now, seven years later, the Chinese were asking for the same privileges accorded black and white children. As later chapters will show, in the years between, the Chinese had scored a number of important legal victories in cases involving the Fourteenth Amendment, and they were now ready to use Reconstruction legislation to refashion California's racial hierarchy.[65]

Moulder, in turn, sought counsel from State Superintendent of Public Instruction William T. Welcker. Welcker, whose hostility to the Chinese matched Moulder's, instructed the San Francisco Board of Education to deny entrance to Mamie Tape and all Chinese children. The instructions suited board member Isidor Danielwitz, who declared during the ensuing debate that he would "rather go to jail than allow a Chinese child to be admitted to the schools." A majority of the board agreed and promptly passed a resolution threatening principals and teachers who admitted Chinese children with immediate termination.[66]

Tape sought the help of San Francisco attorney William Gibson, who as the son of Reverend Otis Gibson had been born in China and had a long history of friendly dealings with the Chinese. With Gibson's help and the financial backing of the Chinese consul's office, Tape filed suit in San Francisco's Superior Court to force the schools to admit his daughter. In his decision, rendered on January 9, 1885, Superior Court Judge James Maguire flatly declared that the rules barring Chinese children from the schools violated the Fourteenth Amendment. State law declared the schools open to all children, and Mamie Tape was entitled to equal protection. Maguire went on to echo the original Chinese petition submitted to the State Legislature in 1877 by adding that the rules were unjust in that they caused the Chinese to pay taxes in support of schools from which their children were excluded. Maguire softened the blow by reminding white San Franciscans that such a decision did not automatically "open our public schools to the slums of the Chinese quarter. The city's Board of Education, he said, "have ample power to keep out all children who are blighted by filth, infection, or contagion." "But," he went on, "any such objection must be personal . . . without regard to [the child's] race or color." Mamie Tape was clearly clean and healthy, and so "her application for admission to the Spring Valley school is proper and lawful, and must be granted."[67]

The superior court decision, while hardly the last word on the subject, alarmed city and state school officials. At the next board meeting, A. J. Moulder launched into a lengthy tirade in which "the notorious vices of the Chinese were reviewed," and in which he claimed that the Chinese were "a nation of liars . . . filthy and impure." He then presented a letter from State Superintendent Welcker on the matter. Welcker, in a profound state of denial, claimed that "there is not an intelligent man or woman in the United States . . . who does not know perfectly well that the Fourteenth Amendment was intended for people of African descent. No thought was had of the Chinese in the matter." Following a vituperative canvass of supposed Chinese mendacity, Welcker told the San Francisco Board of Education that "a terrible disaster is threatening our institutions" and counseled them to immediately appeal Judge Maguire's decision to the California Supreme Court.[68]

The board of education followed Welcker's instructions and filed an appeal with the state supreme court. Maguire's decision, however, in spite of Welcker's peculiar interpretation of constitutional law, had been reached on solid ground, and in March 1885 the California Supreme Court unanimously upheld the lower court's ruling in a tersely worded decision. As a result, the white men who administered California's public schools found themselves in an awkward position. The school law was quite unambiguous about their responsibilities to all children in California, regardless of race, and they were now faced with what one school official described as "an ignominious political death" if they dared to comply with the law, and jail if they did not. Superintendent Moulder solved their dilemma by noting that the court's decision had in no way undermined the "separate but equal" principle established under *Ward v. Flood*. All that was required was the passage of a new law establishing separate schools for Chinese children. California's economy had by then fully recovered from the depression of the 1870s and could easily bear the added burden. Within weeks of the decision in *Tape v. Hurley*, Moulder managed to push Assembly bill 268 through the legislature, effectively resegregating California's public schools and leaving Chinese children at California's racial margins.[69]

San Francisco's new school for Chinese children opened its doors April 13, 1885, at the corner of Stone and Jackson Streets. The rooms sat above a grocery store and rented for $10 per month. The first pupils to arrive that day were Mamie Tape and her six-year-old brother, Frank, "dressed neatly in clothes like those worn by American children," with "none of the Chinese peculiarities in regard to the manner of wearing the hair." They were joined by a boisterous and intelligent group of Chinese boys and girls, all of whom were American citizens and who could speak, read, and write in English. Their teacher, Miss Rose Thayer, according to favorable reports that day, had "already

Chinese Public School Children, ca. 1890. The Tape family's suit against the San Francisco public school district guaranteed access to public education for the city's Chinese children. Mamie Tape is seated in the second row, center. Her brother Frank is seated to her right. Photograph by I. W. Taber (Courtesy, California Historical Society, CHS2011.749. tif.)

found reason to believe that she will have no trouble in causing her class to take a high rank as to attainments." At recess, Mamie and Frank played on their roller skates.[70]

Conclusion

For white Californians, the fight over California's schools was always, at bottom, a fight to ensure a future for white children that looked much like the present. That meant ensuring a future in which white supremacy was firmly entrenched, and the state's nonwhite minorities were excluded from much of public life. One obvious requirement for ensuring that future involved barring nonwhite children from California's public schools, but it also required training California's future citizens, white and black, in the belief that a segregated world was right and just. For more than two decades, white Californians vigorously pursued that goal through a political and legal process that was slowly being reshaped by the influence of federal Reconstruction legislation. Time and again, their labors were blocked, or at least blunted, by the efforts of black and Chinese Californians to put Reconstruction to work in the West.

For black Californians, the struggle over schools was also a struggle over the future. But unlike whites, black Californians were uninterested in maintaining a status quo that banished them to California's racial margins. Instead, through their struggle to desegregate the schools, black Californians articulated a radically different vision of freedom that challenged whites' cramped vision of the state's racial destiny. While much of their struggle had only limited success, black Californians were, finally, able to see their children educated alongside white children at state expense.

After *Ward v. Flood*, the nineteenth-century struggle for black civil rights in California faded into the political and legal background, as both white and black Californians turned their attention to what both perceived as a greater threat. Between the mid-1870s and mid-1880s, Chinese immigrants lay at the center of the struggle over the shape of California's racial hierarchy as white Californians in particular sought to limit Chinese influence over California's society and especially over California's economy.

In the meantime, the "separate but equal" principle survived, and so too did the legal structure that relegated black Californians to a status inferior to that of whites. The racialized curriculum that had long supported that status also survived and continued to be taught in California schools. In the white schools, black Californian children could no longer, if they ever had, escape an education that taught them and their white schoolmates that blacks could never fully participate in a properly constituted civil society. Chinese children, by their very absence from those classrooms, were defined as even less capable. And in the interests of civic homogeneity, the law continued to say so.

Chapter 4
"Wa Shing and His Tireless Fellows"
Chinese Laundries and the Reconstruction
of the Chinese Race

WHEN THEY WERE ARRESTED in August 1885, Chinese laundrymen
Yick Wo and Wo Lee were not surprised; in fact, they had counted
on it. For five years, San Francisco's Board of Supervisors had waged
a war against Chinese laundries. Using the police powers delegated
to incorporated cities by the state constitution, the city's municipal
authorities had passed a series of ordinances regulating laundries for
hire. Yick Wo and Wo Lee had run afoul of two such ordinances that
together required operators of laundries housed in wooden structures
to pass inspections by the city fire marshal and health department,
and then to seek the consent of the board of supervisors to conduct
business. Each man's laundry business had easily passed the inspections and secured the required certificates, but the board had denied
consent nonetheless. The board regularly denied consent to Chinese
laundrymen but approved virtually all white applicants. Both men
were arrested because they continued to take in laundry without licenses. By the end of the month, they would be joined by nearly 250
other Chinese laundrymen as the unwilling guests of San Francisco's
sheriff.[1]

Almost from the moment of their arrival in California, the Chinese had been subject to legal harassment of one form or another.
Exclusion from the witness box and the public schools ranked among
the starkest examples, but lesser nuisances were visited upon them
as well. In the halcyon days of the Gold Rush during the 1850s and
1860s, civic harassment—as opposed to often more dangerous forms
of social harassment at the hands of private citizens—was largely limited to taxes like the Foreign Miners Tax and the Head Tax charged to

each Chinese immigrant upon arrival at one of California's ports. But in the 1870s, deteriorating economic conditions and changes in the nature of Chinese immigration combined to push the terms of civic harassment in a more vicious direction.[2]

By the late 1860s, the placers in California's gold fields had largely given out, and the freewheeling ways of Gold Rush individualism had given way to large-scale, capital intensive mining interests. Californians searching for new routes to prosperity pinned their hopes on the transcontinental railroad, which when finished would finally link the state with larger national and international markets. Instead, the railroad imported the eastern boom-and-bust business cycle just in time to transmit the effects of the Panic of 1873 and its financial collapse west. Along with economic misery, the railroad also brought a tidal wave of immigration: between 1870 and 1880, California's population increased by more than 50 percent. At the same time, the now complete railroad was discharging thousands of workers. Worse still, the railroad also carried cheap eastern goods west, forcing many of California's once-isolated industries to close their doors, making work difficult to find.[3]

As the state absorbed these blows, the Comstock Lode experienced its second boom in as many decades. The Comstock, seated along the California-Nevada border, was the richest deposit of silver in the world and should have pumped much needed cash into California's ailing economy. Instead, rampant speculation in mining stocks drained capital away from local industries, worsening the depression. When the Consolidated Virginia Mine opened in 1874, speculation boosted its aggregate value by $1 million a day for two straight months. The ensuing craze induced wild fluctuations on San Francisco's three stock exchanges, varying the aggregate value by as much as $139 million in a single month in a market never valued at more than $240 million. In such an atmosphere, panics were inevitable. In 1875, a run on the Bank of California, the state's most trusted financial institution, temporarily closed the stock exchanges and impoverished thousands. The final crash came in 1877 when the stock of the two largest Comstock mines suffered a combined loss of $140 million, or $1,000 for every adult male in San Francisco. The shock of these crashes rippled through the state's economy, causing twelve bank failures in the second half of the decade and 451 business failures in 1877 alone.[4]

Even as California's economy stalled, the rate of Chinese immigration to the state increased. In 1868, federal officials seeking better trade relations with China negotiated a new treaty that encouraged immigration and enlisted the powers of the federal government in defense of the rights of Chinese laborers in the United States. Under the influence and protections built into what came to be known as the Burlingame Treaty, the Chinese population of California jumped by 50 percent in the 1870s, rising from 49,310 to 75,218, or nearly 9 percent of the total population. Because the vast majority of these new immigrants were young men of working age, their impact on labor markets was magnified well beyond their actual numbers. While Chinese immigrants may never have amounted to more than 10 percent of the total population in nineteenth-century California, they could amount to as much as a third of the adult male workforce, and to white workers desperately seeking employment in a collapsing economy, rising numbers of Chinese laborers willing to work for lower wages seemed a real threat. For frustrated white workers, Chinese immigrants also made obvious targets as scapegoats.[5]

The combination of economic distress and rising immigration led labor organizations and even some business owners to pressure government officials at all levels for some kind of relief. At the state level, their agitation meant success for a long-simmering movement that sought to deal with California's mounting social and economic complexity by rewriting the state's constitution. At the constitutional convention in 1878, members of the virulently anti-Chinese Workingmen's Party of California successfully lobbied for the inclusion of some of the harshest measures ever enacted against Chinese immigrants, including one passage prohibiting corporations chartered in California from employing Chinese. White workers who hoped that these measures would finally end their misery by removing Chinese laborers from the state's economy saw their hopes dashed when federal courts quickly struck down the new measures.[6]

The failure to contain Chinese economic and social influence at the state level convinced many white Californians that only federal legislation could once and for all rid the state of the Chinese "menace." Both the Democratic and Republican state parties exhorted their national representatives to redouble their efforts against Chinese immigration by passing a Chinese exclusion act. At the same time, white Californians also recognized that federal legislation was often slow in coming, particularly when it came to issues in western states, and even more so when it was supported largely by the working classes. A general lack of faith in the federal government led white Californians to supplement their national efforts with more intensely vigorous harassment of the Chinese locally.

In San Francisco, where fully one-quarter of the state's Chinese were crowded into the city's Chinatown, officials initiated a campaign of civic harassment that would last for two decades. Throughout the 1870s and into the 1880s, city ordinances designed to make life difficult for San Francisco's Chinese imposed onerous regulations on Chinese labor activities such as fishing and vegetable peddling, leisure activities such as gambling and opium smoking, and even Chinese burial practices. Regulations such as the Cubic Air Ordinance, which required 500 cubic feet of space for each occupant of a residential building, and the notorious Queue Ordinance, which required shaving the heads of inmates in the City Jail, added humiliation to the harassment. Across the state, city governments wielded their vaguely defined police powers to strictly limit the ability, and even the right, of Chinese immigrants to earn a living in any capacity, with the intention of driving them from the state.[7]

The laundry ordinances that led to the arrests of Yick Wo and Wo Lee were key components in the regime of legal harassment initiated against the Chinese in San Francisco. Like other forms of anti-Chinese harassment, the attack on laundries drew a great deal of its energy from working-class misery and agitation. But beyond this most basic similarity, the campaign waged against Chinese laundries differed markedly from other forms of harassment in both scale and in substance. Perhaps most important, the war on the Chinese laundries drew its real strength from San Francisco's middle and upper classes. Before the 1880s, these two groups had largely scorned the rhetoric and tactics of traditional anti-Chinese agitators. During the 1880s, however, their relationship to the "Chinese Question" changed. This change coincided with the spread of Chinese laundries into the exclusive suburban neighborhoods to which San Francisco's more affluent citizens had retired over the previous decade.[8]

The movement of Chinese laundries into white residential neighborhoods panicked white residents who had been largely isolated from contact with people of other races. In the 1880s, many of those who had disdained the coarse politics of the Workingmen's Party now demanded that the city government move to contain the spread of Chinese laundries. In this, San Francisco was hardly alone. Sacramento, Oakland, Alameda, Stockton, Modesto, Napa, San Jose, and other towns engaged in similar efforts to harass Chinese laundries out of existence. In each case, these efforts were tied to the movement of Chinese laundries out of central business districts and into the white residential neighborhoods they served.

The crisis over Chinese laundries invigorated a simmering ethnological debate over the proper place of Chinese in California society. The debate was rooted in California's extended project of racial definition and ranking. While the reconstruction of black and Indian status in California had been mostly settled by the mid-1870s, the role to be played by the Chinese remained an open question, not least because of some remarkable successes the Chinese had in the courts using Reconstruction legislation to defend themselves. In articles, pamphlets, tracts, and scholarly treatises, opponents and supporters of the Chinese discussed in detail the nature of Chinese civilization and Chinese character, and the implications both had for California's future.

The war over Chinese laundries was a profoundly local one, involving questions concerning race, the use of urban space, and the reach and proper application of municipal police powers. Yet it was a local conflict with national implications. Both Yick Wo, Wo Lee, and others tested the laundry ordinances in cases that eventually reached the highest court in the land. Chinese legal challenges to local laundry ordinances eventually forced the U.S. Supreme Court to reinterpret municipal police powers in light of the Fourteenth Amendment and as a result played an important role in shaping national Reconstruction. At the same time, the racial ideas that had informed the laundry war in the first place ultimately helped to define the status of Chinese in California, a status laden with ominous implications for future immigrants from Asia.

The Social World of Chinese Laundries

The Chinese have so long been associated with laundries for hire that many Americans have come to see the laundry business as a traditional occupation rooted in Chinese civilization and imported from China. The Chinese laundry is, however, an American invention. In fact, Chinese laundrymen in Gold Rush California reported having learned their trade from American women. The Chinese, after all, made the difficult crossing to California in search of wealth, first in the gold fields and later in railroad construction, agriculture, and the mercantile trades. It is safe to say that none traveled to California with a burning desire to wash the linens of strangers.[9]

And yet, forty years after the arrival of the first Chinese immigrants, the Chinese dominated the laundry trade in California. Their movement into the laundries was precipitated in part by the changing nature of the state's economy. Chinese laundries began appearing in large numbers in California only when the placers gave out in the state's gold fields. In the late 1850s and early 1860s, as mining in California moved from an enterprise dominated by individual producers to one dominated by large-scale operations backed by vast reserves of capital, Chinese miners began looking elsewhere for their livelihoods. At first, the number of laundrymen remained small because railroad construction and later an agricultural boom offered opportunities for employment. But with the completion of the transcontinental railroad, thousands of Chinese laborers found themselves discharged and without work. Agriculture continued to absorb Chinese labor—in some counties Chinese immigrants accounted for as much as 86 percent of agricultural labor—but farming was never able to sustain the entire population. Chinese laborers moved into cities like San Francisco, Stockton, and Sacramento, taking jobs most commonly in cigar and shoe factories and laundries.[10]

Racial hostility also played an important role in the development of the Chinese laundry trade. Throughout the period, Chinese workers were routinely pushed from occupations coveted by white Californians. Successful Chinese miners were driven from their diggings by unscrupulous white miners jealous of their success. In California's growing cities, white laborers and the unemployed agitating against the employment of Chinese often successfully persuaded white employers to discharge their Chinese workers. Even city governments were not immune. In 1867, thirty Chinese laborers employed on a street grading project in San Francisco were attacked by nearly one hundred white San Franciscans and driven off the work site. By 1870, official city policy barred Chinese from employment on public works projects. The most egregious example was, of course, the constitutional attempt to bar California corporations from employing Chinese in any capacity. Although that element of the new constitution was quickly struck down, other elements survived and played a role in the laundry wars of the 1880s.[11]

In a volatile economy and a hostile racial environment, laundries may well have seemed like a safe and comfortable refuge. Some Chinese immigrants found work as domestics, but that occupation was less than desirable. Housekeeping meant a life ordered by the whims of the housemistress and required an uncomfortable intimacy with the *bok kwei*, Chinese for "white devil." In any event, in the housekeeping trade, Chinese men competed with Irish and black women for positions. Laundries for hire were one occupation in which there was little, if any, white competition. California's rapid transformation from an isolated frontier economy to a modern, industrial one during the first two decades of statehood offered white workers enough economic opportunities to leave that niche open. Moreover, in California's overwhelmingly male society, demand for laundries for hire was high.[12]

The laundry trade offered the opportunity for self-employment, and starting a business was relatively simple. The initial investment was low compared to other enterprises. Investments in Chinese laundries ranged from $400 to $1,600; the average start-up cost was just over $800. Entrepreneurs devoted most of this initial investment to rent. Beyond this, all that was needed was a large tub for washing, a kettle for hot water, and wooden racks for drying. Running a laundry required no special skills and minimal facility with the English language.

Finally, the laundry trade was almost totally unregulated, so Chinese laundrymen were, at least at first, free from municipal harassment.[13]

Chinese domination of the laundry business proceeded rapidly. By 1870, there were nearly three thousand Chinese laundries in the state, spread through every major city, most towns, and the mining areas. In San Francisco, where sheer numbers make the development of the trade easier to trace, there were thirteen hundred Chinese laundrymen. Over the decade of the 1870s the concentration continued and by the dawn of the new decade three of every four laundries for hire was owned by a Chinese immigrant. The 5,435 Chinese launderers represented 79.6 percent of all launderers in California in 1880, and by 1890 that number had risen to 6,400. In smaller towns like Napa, where six of seven laundries were Chinese-owned, the domination could be especially stark. In the 1880s, white Californians, often French immigrants, began moving into the laundry trade by starting huge, heavily capitalized operations that employed as many as two hundred workers. But even as their size dwarfed individual Chinese laundries, there was never enough white interest to overcome Chinese domination. "Madame La Lingerie . . . has no chance," claimed one observer, "of successfully competing with Wa Shing and his tireless fellows." In 1880, 10 percent of the entire Chinese population in California was engaged in the laundry trade, and one-third of all Chinese-owned businesses were laundries. By 1900, the percentage of Chinese laundrymen relative to the entire Chinese population had risen to 25 percent.[14]

In spite of the vast numbers of Chinese immigrants engaged in the laundry business in California and their geographical dispersion across the state, Chinese laundries were remarkably uniform in appearance and operation. The nature of the work itself imposed similarities from one laundry to another; washing clothes is not an occupation that admits of much variety. The common economic circumstances shared by Chinese laundrymen also ensured a kind of homogeneity. At the same time, however, factors totally unrelated to the trade itself, and instead related to Chinese culture and white racial hostility, significantly affected the evolution of the Chinese laundry trade.[15]

Chinese laundries were normally housed in buildings that were little more than shacks. In 1880, the city of San Francisco estimated that 310 of the city's 320 laundries were constructed of wood. They were often cheaply constructed and were widely viewed by whites as rickety fire traps. There was some truth to this, given the fact that with little start-up capital, Chinese laundrymen likely sought out work sites that offered the lowest possible rents. The buildings were often cramped. Chinese laundries were rarely more than twelve or fifteen feet wide, with just enough room at the front for a door and window. In the window, billboards listed prices for various services. Outside, all Chinese laundries were marked by a red sign with white lettering; the colors signified good luck and prosperity. Most Chinese laundries saved space in the interior by erecting scaffolds on the roofs of their shops for drying. White San Franciscans regularly complained about the appearance of Chinese laundries and especially about the rooftop scaffolding, claiming that the businesses were a blight and an eyesore in otherwise tidy neighborhoods.[16]

While the exterior appearance of a Chinese laundry was tied to capital investment, the interior was shaped by both investment and the racial hostility laundrymen faced in California. The large numbers of laundries and laundrymen made them an obvious target for both angry mobs and smaller bands of hoodlums. Over time, such assaults fashioned a sharp division between public and private spaces within the laundry. Inside, at the front of the washhouse, the proprietor dealt with his clients from behind an L-shaped counter. The counter limited and confined the laundry's public space and closed off the back from the front of the shop. Access to the rear could be had only through a hinged door latched from the inside. Fences often extended the height of the counter, offering further protection. The need for such precautions grew out of regular attacks on laundries. In one such incident in San Francisco, a correspondent to the *Daily Alta California* described an afternoon's amusement for "a dozen of more aspirants for San Quentin's classic honors." A group of boys ranging in age from six to sixteen took apart a laundry at the corner of Bryant and Fourth Streets in the South of Market district using wood they had cadged from a nearby lumber seller. "They were indulging in the mystic rites, and making day hideous with a sort of song and dance, *a la* Modoc, and keeping time by a lively pounding on the windows and doors of a

Chinese washhouse located there. The place had been visited before, apparently, for but very few windows were left to demolish." Interestingly, what upset the writer was the supposed Indian-like behavior of the boys and the absence of more constructive activities in the neighborhood. The damage to the Chinese laundry was incidental.[17]

Behind the counter of a Chinese laundry, every inch of space was put to use. Both owners and workers lived in the laundries, and washhouse layouts reflected the mixed use. First came the ironing room, often the only part of the shop in public view. Chinese laundrymen created a unique form of ironing board not found in white-owned laundries. The board was normally four or more feet long and two and one-half to three feet wide. It was attached to the wall by hinges that allowed it to swing up into the wall. When lowered, it was supported by legs at the outer corners. The board was covered with a felt pad and a muslin cloth that hung over the front masking storage beneath. The Chinese name for these boards translates as "ironing beds," which explains their peculiar construction and their secondary use when time permitted. A narrow hallway normally led back to living quarters and a drying room, if space allowed. At the back of the shop were the washroom, with kettles of hot water, and a kitchen.[18]

Laundry work was tedious and tiring. Most Chinese laundries were small operations, typically employing from five to ten workers. Laundrymen normally worked six days a week with free days staggered among the workers so that the laundry could run without rest. A typical workday began before 7 A.M. and often lasted until after midnight, or until the day's work was done. Work was performed in cramped, overheated, steam-filled rooms. Pick-ups and deliveries were undertaken on foot by laundrymen who, at least at first, carried clothing in baskets suspended from poles that rested on their shoulders. This form of portage was common in China and so also common in Chinatown. Complaints from white San Franciscans about being jostled by basket-carrying laborers in several trades spawned one of the earliest ordinances aimed at harassing Chinese laundrymen. A San Francisco ordinance approved in 1870 banned the use of the poles on city sidewalks. The laundrymen simply switched to using canvass bags slung over their shoulders and continued their deliveries on foot.[19]

A Chinese laundryman enjoys a rare moment of rest in a San Francisco laundry, ca. 1890. Chinese laundrymen worked long hours in tight quarters for very little money. Even so, the independence offered by the laundry business tempted thousands of Chinese immigrants. Note the hinged gate dividing public space from private, and the ironing beds along the right-hand wall. (Courtesy of the Asian American Studies Collections, Ethnic Studies Library, University of California, Berkeley, AAS ARC 2000/41: fol. 27: laundry).

Laundrymen, like most Chinese immigrants, mostly came from small villages in the rural Guangdong province of China. Such villages were most often controlled by a single clan, and villagers were known by a surname that identified them as members of that clan. In America, clan affiliations formed the most basic social unit around which the lives of family-less laundrymen revolved. Laundrymen in California sought work in shops owned and staffed by their clansmen. In this way, the thicket of familial and social relationships that governed life in China was transferred, root and branch, to the United States. Chinese systems of reciprocal obligation, hierarchies of deference and authority, and local loyalties were mirrored in each and every Chinese laundry in California. Further still, Chinese laundrymen normally conducted business within their clans, purchasing supplies, food, and leisure goods and services through, for all intents and purposes, the family. Clan membership eased the uncertainty and loneliness of life in California by making the strange familiar. At the same time, however, the presence of clan organizations tended to isolate Chinese laborers by retarding contact with the larger society. Social contact and even, to some extent, economic contact could be stronger between Chinese laundrymen and family in China than that between laundrymen and their fellow Californians.[20]

Clans that hearkened from the same district in China and that spoke the same dialect, were embraced by larger and more powerful district associations known as *hui kuans*. The *hui kuans* dominated life in Chinatown and were, for most whites, the public face of the Chinese in California. *Hui kuans* facilitated Chinese immigration to the United States and regulated the labor of immigrants once they arrived. In a nation where Chinese were for decades barred from offering testimony in courts, the *hui kuans* settled disputes between immigrants and even, some claimed, meted out punishments. The most famous of the *hui kuans*, known as the Six Companies, were also politically active. Before the Chinese government established a consulate in San Francisco in 1878, the Six Companies essentially acted as a diplomatic corps, defending Chinese immigrants against discriminatory legislation and racial violence. Throughout the first three decades of statehood, the Six Companies repeatedly sent petitions and letters to the State Legislature, hired white attorneys to defend their accused members, and pursued business relationships with the state's elites. Where local government was at best unresponsive and at worst hostile to Chinese needs, the *hui kuans* took the place of the state.[21]

A third prominent form of social organization in the Chinese community was the *tong*. Most *tongs* earned a sanguinary reputation as territorial criminal organizations that controlled gambling, prostitution, and the opium trade. *Tongs* were also accused by white Californians of providing murderers for hire to anyone willing to pay. Such men were known as "highbinders" in the white press and were widely believed to be behind much of the violence that whites associated with Chinatowns all over the state. But *tongs* were more than mere criminal organizations. They also acted as guilds and benevolent societies. Because they were not necessarily affiliated with clans or districts, *tongs* offered a counterweight to the power of those larger organizations. As guilds, *tongs* operated as a regulatory force, reducing competition and providing stability within various industries, notably the laundry trade. Whites often resented the power of the *tongs* and accused them of being little more than monopolies, but for the Chinese their role in stabilizing economic activity was indispensable.[22]

Success or failure for Chinese laundries was closely tied to location, and that in two ways. First, the pressure of numbers threatened everyone's livelihood. In the wake of the economic upheavals already described, legions of Chinese miners, factory workers, and farmers transformed themselves into laundrymen. In such towns as San Francisco and Stockton they opened one laundry after another, saturating business districts and driving down prices. The saturation could often be exacerbated by the cycles of anti-Chinese violence that gripped California towns throughout the era. When attacks on Chinese labor in other occupations increased, Chinese laborers sought refuge in the one business whites appeared to countenance. Whites' fight against Chinese competition, in other words, always led to increased competition within the Chinese community.[23]

In such an uncertain and chaotic environment, the regulatory powers of the *tongs* proved invaluable. In San Francisco, the Tung Hing Tong controlled the laundry trade. Tung Hing Tong set upper and lower limits for prices, dispensed licenses to laundry operators, and settled disputes between laundrymen. Most important, *tong* rules provided stability by channeling the spatial growth of the trade. No laundry was allowed to locate within ten houses of another, on either side of a street. Laundries located on corner lots controlled a ten-house area in all four directions running from the intersection, effectively giving the laundry an eighty-house potential market, or several blocks. Spreading the laundries out offered a simple solution to market saturation.[24]

The Tung Hing Tong first came to the notice of white San Franciscans in the aftermath of a major riot in Chinatown in May 1870. Each Sunday, the Tung Hing Tong met in a joss house, or religious shrine, over a gambling house on Sacramento Street between Kearny and Dupont. At these meetings, *tong* leaders dispensed licenses and heard disputes between laundrymen. On May 22, 1870, a dispute between the Wah Yeup Company and several other laundries exploded into violence. Wah Yeup had moved into the territory of another laundry and was waging a price war in violation of *tong* rules. Laundrymen "armed with iron bars, cleavers, pistols, knives, hatchets and clubs," crowded into the joss house, and when the decision went against Wah Yeup, "the Chinamen shouted and yelled like demons, and the Bloody Work of shooting, stabbing and clubbing commenced." By the time police arrived, the battle had spilled onto the streets below, and hysterical witnesses claimed that as many as three thousand Chinese men had joined the riot. For the first time, the inner workings of Chinese society were on public display, and the riot and its causes confirmed in the minds of many whites the belief that the Chinese operated by rules different from those of the rest of San Francisco society. The tone of haughty amusement registered in the newspaper reports of the riot commonly appeared in descriptions of Chinese behavior, but it could be maintained only so long as such occurrences were limited to the Chinese quarter. The policies of the Tung Hing Tong, and the *tong*'s ability to enforce them, guaranteed that in time that would no longer be the case.[25]

In spite of occasional disagreements, the Tung Hing Tong was very successful in muting competition, channeling growth, and stabilizing the laundry trade. Both Yick Wo and Wo Lee are testaments to that fact. When he was arrested, Yick Wo had been running his laundry business at 349 Third Street for twenty-two years. Wo Lee, at the time of his arrest, had owned a laundry at 318 Dupont Street for twenty-five years. The location of Yick Wo's laundry also testified to the ability of Tung Hing Tong to channel growth. While Wo Lee's laundry sat in the very center of Chinatown, Yick Wo's was in the heavily Irish neighborhood south of Market Street.[26]

In channeling the spread of Chinese laundries, Tung Hing Tong also served the laundries' second intimate connection with location. Because Chinese laundries were small operations with relatively low capital investments, few could afford the horse-drawn wagons that the giant, white-owned laundry operations employed. Even into the 1890s, pick-ups and deliveries continued on foot. Success, in other words, required Chinese laundries to locate in the neighborhoods they served. As the city spread across the peninsula, so too did the Chinese laundries. Tung Hing Tong regulated the growth outside Chinatown as well as inside, and by 1880 nine out of every ten Chinese laundries in San Francisco were located beyond the limits of Chinatown.[27]

Movement into the tonier neighborhoods diminished competition and guaranteed income, but it also imposed some important changes on the laundry business. Suburbs in San Francisco and across the nation were created by developers who achieved class and racial segregation by dividing neighborhoods into larger than usual lot sizes. Land in the new neighborhoods was obviously more expensive, prohibitively so for Chinese laundrymen. In San Francisco, the Chinese laundrymen surmounted this difficulty by forming partnerships. Two companies would agree to pay for and work in one suburban shop: one company would work during the day, the other would work through the night. The practice allowed Chinese laundrymen to move out with their client base. At the same time, these partnerships doubled the number of Chinese men living in a given suburban neighborhood, rendering them doubly threatening and objectionable to white suburbanites.[28]

The Contamination of a White Refuge

Chinese laundries moved out of San Francisco's central business district at the same moment that transportation innovations and rising affluence produced the city's first streetcar suburbs. Like middle- and upper-class Americans across the country, San Franciscans of means left the nineteenth-century walking city behind in favor of wide, tree-lined streets and spacious houses. Suburbs in the new Western Addition and the Mission District offered an escape from the turbulence that wracked central San Francisco in the 1870s. In the countryside at the city's edge, a burgeoning white-collar class enjoyed a lifestyle that shunned the grime, noise, and unwashed masses of newly industrial San Francisco.[29]

Most obviously, suburbs divided the affluent from the working classes, and white from nonwhite. But geographical separation spawned an ultimately more important cultural separation. As Frederick Law Olmsted pointed out in 1868, "the essential qualification of a suburb is domesticity." Suburban residents self-consciously developed a kind of hyper-domesticity that contrasted sharply with that which reigned at the city center. Larger homes, lawns, backyards, and open spaces spoke to lives of peaceful comfort. In moving to the suburbs, San Francisco's managerial class achieved a new level of separation between work and home life. The economic activity that dominated downtown held no sway at the city's edges. In the suburbs, work was limited to family and home, and, at least for male homeowners, an atmosphere of leisure prevailed. Even in the female world of child rearing and housework, a deep gulf separated the suburbs from town. Suburban housewives could afford domestics, and periodicals of the day were filled with advice to housewives struggling to choose between Irish and Chinese "help." In the suburbs, mothers raised children safely in an atmosphere free from the poisonous influences that bred crime, dissipation, and prostitution.[30]

The hyper-domesticity of the suburbs, however, had invidious implications for those left behind. San Francisco's residential stratification matched the hierarchy that reigned in the factory. The larger suburban housing lot, in fact homeownership itself, and the comfort level and geographical separation all served as spatial reminders of the growing economic distance between the working classes and city elites. Suburban separation for the wealthy stood as a rebuke and a judgment upon the spatial familiarity between white workers and Chinese, further elevating and rarifying suburban life. Suburbs in effect were sanctuaries walled off from more urban neighborhoods, and within them the affluent fashioned a new and exclusive lifestyle.

To white residents, Chinese laundries violated these sanctuaries in every conceivable way. The run-down, cheaply constructed shantytown look of the typical Chinese laundry, with its rooftop scaffolds, steam, and alien smells, disfigured otherwise tidy neighborhoods. The laundrymen themselves, sometimes as many as a dozen in each laundry, were also a visible violation of the strict separation between races the suburbs were meant to achieve. And the leisure activities of the laundrymen, which included opium smoking and gambling, were reminders of the iniquitous urban influences that suburbanites had hoped to escape. Chinese laundries were effectively Chinese "outposts," in the words of one writer: little Chinatowns embedded in white sanctuaries.[31]

Local papers fed whites' fears with reports that Chinatown itself was spilling over its boundaries. "Chinatown has extended its borders," screamed the *San Francisco Chronicle*, "and with the same crafty insidiousness that marked the first moves of the invasion, John has been creeping eastward and northward until what has been looked upon as the best part of the city for wholesale business is slowly but surely becoming a Mongolian annex." "But it is not alone eastward," they continued, "that the bedragoned flag has taken its way: its saffron-colored folds have jaundiced the westerly parts adjacent to old Chinatown. Time was when Stockton street was a boundary of and was not included in Chinatown; now it has been swallowed up by the Asiatic and another slice of the city has gone over to Peking." As the rising number of complaints these neighborhoods sent to the city's board of supervisors attests, for white residents the Chinese Question was once again a vital one. Who the Chinese were, how they lived in China, and what that meant for the future of California became singularly important.[32]

During the panic over Chinese laundries, white Californians reached for familiar rhetoric to describe the Chinese. But California's racial context had changed radically in the decades between *People v. Hall* and the laundry wars. In the 1850s, Chinese racial status had been formed in relation to California Indians and black Californians. White Californians drew links between the three groups that ended up defining them all as equally unworthy of participation in the white polity. White Californians maintained their binary color line through powerfully circular reasoning: the Chinese were unworthy because they were like blacks and Indians, while blacks and Indians were unworthy because they were like the Chinese. Chinese racial status and definition were, in other words, constituted through Indians and black Californians.

Reconstruction, however, had fundamentally changed the racial landscape in California. Black Californians had, through the Reconstruction Amendments, been admitted to the witness box, the ballot box, and even into the state's public schools on a basis of equality with whites. Reconstruction had effectively transformed black Californians into responsible Americans, and black Californians sought to defend that status by regularly joining in the chorus against Chinese immigration. Given this fact, defining the Chinese with reference to this new black status threatened to undermine the logic by which whites justified a racial hierarchy that banished Chinese to the margins of California society. Chinese use of the Fourteenth Amendment in defense of their rights made severing the links between the races all the more urgent. Moreover, by the early 1880s, the California Indians, like black Californians, no longer offered a useful foil against which the Chinese might be defined. The state's Indian population had declined so drastically that California Indians rarely figured in public discussion. The Indians most commonly discussed by this time were the Apache and the Sioux, two groups whose legendary reputations as warriors and whose current rebellions against the U.S. government made them wholly unsuited to comparison with the supposedly enervated and degraded Chinese.[33]

Given California's new racial environment, many whites struggled to develop new metaphors of racial difference to explain the role and status of the Chinese. Amid the controversy of the laundry wars, white Californians pushed their racial rhetoric in a subtly different direction. Where Chinese immigrants had once suffered by connection with black Californians and Indians, they were increasingly compared not with other human beings but with disease. In the course of the laundry wars, white Californians harnessed an elaborately articulated body of ethnological studies to metaphors of contamination meant to define the Chinese out of the human family and ultimately out of California.[34]

During the era of the laundry wars, life in China was a central concern. Everyone who participated in the ensuing ethnological discussion was aware, for instance, of the technological and artistic achievements of Chinese civilization. But opponents of the Chinese universally pointed out, as had opponents in the testimony controversy twenty-years earlier, that those achievements had been accomplished long ago. Since then, they argued, Chinese civilization had grown moribund. This, they hastened to add, was not a matter of uninformed opinion, but the rational judgment of science. "'Caucasian' science has pronounced its edict against the 'Mongolian,'" wrote H. N. Clement, an attorney in San Francisco, "classing him with those races afflicted with that most fatal of diseases, *'arrested development.'*" For some time, Chinese civilization had remained stagnant, producing nothing new of note. "With the sudden arresting of his progress," wrote historian Hubert Howe Bancroft, "his mind likewise seems to have become fossilized." Some, unable to completely abandon the old rhetoric, even argued that the stagnation had rendered Chinese society retrograde to the point where they would inevitably shrink from Western civilization. Echoing the link between Indians and Chinese that anti-Chinese forces had trotted out for decades, Clement suggested that it would be cruelty to continue contact with them. "Like the North American Indian . . . 'The Chinaman must *die.*'"[35]

Generations of stagnation had, moreover, doomed all future generations to the same fate. In a speech before Congress pleading for passage of a Chinese exclusion bill, Romualdo Pacheco, a California congressman and former state governor, attempted to educate his fellow legislators about the dangers represented by Chinese stagnation. "By the laws of heredity," he claimed, "the habits of his ancestors live in his character and are incorporated into his blood and brain." Little had changed, he argued, in thousands of years. "With the Chinaman of to-day," he continued, "the great question is of mere subsistence. The same fierce struggle which has engaged his ancestors for centuries engages him now." Hubert Howe Bancroft voiced similar sentiments. Describing "these queer little specimens of petrified progress," Bancroft seemed almost saddened by their fate. Chinese children, he wrote, were "really attractive and intelligent," but "with increasing years they retain a certain simplicity of expression, a childlike innocence." Even that rather benign nature did not last, however, because as they aged "a characteristic and repulsive stolidity and unconcern settle upon them, as if the bright, unsophisticated mind had been rudely cramped within the narrow compass of bigoted custom and hopeless bondage before it had gained time to develop."[36]

Charles Loring Brace, a well-known civil leader, amateur ethnologist, and observer of California society, pegged language as the
engine behind the supposed Chinese failure to advance. Brace likened
the Chinese language to "the first utterances of children," in which
"each word or each syllable is a sentence." Describing this as a "petrified" kind of language, Brace determined that it was "a fearful barrier
to advance in learning, or science, or general knowledge." "Oratory,"
he claimed, "could scarcely exist with it, or poetry, or any popular
literature."[37]

Such descriptions conveniently placed proper self-government
beyond the reach of the Chinese people. In place of self-government,
the Chinese, according to Bancroft and others, had become inured
to, and even comfortable under, "bondage" and tyranny. "They stand
before us now," wrote Bancroft, "a mixture of the child, the slave, and
the Sphinx. The eye in particular is cold, meaningless, yet cunning in
expression." Political, moral, and social stagnation had deprived the
Chinese, according to Bancroft, even of honest feeling. Describing
the reaction of Chinese whose queues were cut off while in jail in
accordance with San Francisco's queue ordinance, he wrote, "The
victims shrieked with horror at the sacrilege, and never recovered
their self-respect—in this displaying the quality of a manufactured
conscience."[38]

Stagnation had wiped away all semblance of humanity, leaving
behind a society mired in degraded morals and animal behavior. Congressman Pacheco said of the Chinese that "his ancestors have . . .
bequeathed to him the most hideous immoralities. They are as natural
to him as the yellow hue of his skin, and are so shocking and horrible
that their character cannot even be hinted." But where the congressman shrank from detailing the depths of Chinese degradation, others
appeared to relish it. One ethnological polemicist, William B. Farnell
of San Francisco, published a lengthy treatise for his fellow San Franciscans with the express purpose of showing "so far as reference to
recognized authorities will permit, the vices, low grade of morality,
cruelties, and all the general evil qualities which the race possess." In
colorful detail, Farnell described the horrors of Chinese slavery, the

"satanic cruelty" of their barbarous tortures, and the filth he claimed gripped their cities. Infanticide was widely practiced in China, he informed his readers. According to Farnell, Chinese parents typically sacrificed their daughters by drowning them in a tub, throwing them into a stream, or burying them alive in the belief that doing so might guarantee that the next child would be a boy. In the end, Farnell pronounced the Chinese "a race unfit in every aspect of life to mingle with and exist among a Christian community."[39]

The supposed evils of Chinese civilization were by no means confined to the borders of the Celestial Kingdom. Each Chinese immigrant carried a piece of that degraded society with him on his travels. "The Chinaman is the Chinaman still, whether upon his native soil or transplanted to other lands," cautioned Farnell, "and should excite no other feeling but that of horror and disgust in the breasts of all civilized people." No good could come of their arrival in California. He insisted that "their presence on our shores results alone in sowing the seeds of immorality, vice and disease among our people."[40]

Once in California, Chinese immigrants were said to reproduce the horrors of their homeland. Chinatown was described in terms that repeated and magnified the themes of disease and infestation. Periodically, various government authorities would tour Chinatown and report their findings to the general public. "We went into places so filthy and dirty," reported one congressman, "that I cannot see how these people live there. The fumes of opium, mingled with the odor arising from filth and dirt, made rather a sickening feeling creep over us. I would not go in that quarter again for anything in the world." Any city could be expected to have its less savory quarters, reported one committee, "where filth, disease, crime and misery abound." "But in every aspect which 'Chinatown' can be made to present, it must stand apart," the committee insisted, "conspicuous and beyond them all in the extreme degree of all these horrible attributes, the rankest outgrowth of human degradation that can be found upon this continent." Another commentator warned wealthier San Franciscans not to be fooled by the apparent cleanliness of their Chinese house servants. "Individually John Chinaman is a clean human; collectively he is a beast. Ah Stue, the cook, keeps his coppers clean and bright, washes his hands in going from dish to dish . . . and [is] ever arrayed in spotless white and blue. Follow him home, and you will find this cleanly unit become one of a herd of animals living in a state of squalor and filth." "John," the correspondent concluded, "as a domestic is invaluable and a nuisance, a perfect treasure and a horror."[41]

Whereas white Americans could hardly be expected to survive in such an environment, the Chinese were said to thrive in it. In this they were aided by a curious and hideous strength they mysteriously derived from their very degradation. "The long course of training which has gone on for so many generations," claimed Congressman Pacheco, "has made of the Chinaman a lithe, sinewy creature, with muscles like iron, and almost devoid of sensibilities." White Californians were fascinated by this strength and the various ways it manifested itself. In 1880, a Chinese man named Wing was shot by a highbinder. The bullet entered the left side of his chest and then angled downward, slicing though several organs before exiting near the base of his spine. Incredibly, he survived. "He," claimed the *San Francisco Chronicle*, "is one of many instances of the remarkable tenacity of life characteristic of the Chinese." The paper went on to describe other such instances, including a woman who had survived having a hatchet sunk into her head all the way to the handle.[42]

The specter of such a people planting a colony in California frightened many whites. For them, Chinese immigration was indistinguishable from colonization. "The history of Chinese immigration and colonization," wrote William Farnell, "is a history of antagonism of races that is marked with massacre and bloodshed." Former governor and now senator Newton Booth claimed that "Chinese immigration simply plants a foreign colony in this country." Speaking of Chinatown, one committee of inspectors claimed that "the advance guard of the Mongolian army saw that the location was good, and they advanced upon it and captured it." In their eyes the section had quickly grown to mirror the hollowed-out moral shell they believed Chinese civilization had become, and to the metaphor of disease the writers added a metaphor of rape. "Its capture was but a work of form, for civilization retreats instinctively from contact with the race with the same feeling of horror that the fair and innocent maiden would exhibit in shrinking from the proffered embrace of an unclean leper."[43]

The power and ubiquity of the Six Companies did little to convince white Californians that Chinese immigration could be anything other than colonization. The Six Companies had long been accused of representing an *imperium in imperio*, governing their Chinese charges according to their own lights rather than by American standards. Applying their own laws, complained a State Senate special committee, the Six Companies "exercise a despotic sway over one-seventh of the population of the State of California" and "constitute a foreign government within the boundaries of the Republic." Another commentator reported simply that if "any question of importance arises, such as the date at which San Francisco is to be declared a Chinese colony, delegates from the six companies meet in solemn council."[44]

In the minds of white Californians, the filth, the degradation, and the strange power all added up to an overwhelming force threatening to boil out of Chinatown. Chinatown was slowly spreading block by block, and descriptions of the spread always followed the new script of disease and infestation. "In two or three cases while the houses that bound the blocks are still inhabited by whites, the pigtailed rat has burrowed within, and made himself a home with only a thin shell to hide his nest. The outer shell will soon fall in, for Chinatown grows daily, and is the centralization of an extraordinary power." Chinatown was a "hive" swarming with agents of degraded colonization who spread like "devil-fish." "Call this crowded?" whined one white merchant on Washington Street. "Why they're all above us and around us, like mites in a cheese."[45]

In 1880, such talk, and a smallpox epidemic, led to hysteria and a municipal assault on San Francisco's Chinatown. Citing the "willful and diabolical disregard of our sanitary laws by this infamous race," the city's chief health officer, J. L. Meares, M.D., condemned the entire district as a public nuisance and directed city authorities to "abate" it. On February 24, 1880, Dr. Meares published a public notice warning that in thirty days the authorities would "empty this great reservoir of moral, social, and physical pollution." The order caused no small consternation in the Chinese community. The Six Companies published notices in Chinese warning the people of the district of the "strong feeling against" them and exhorting them to comply with the health department as best they could. "You are earnestly requested to . . . place your houses in a cleanly condition," they begged, "and keep them so, so as to avoid all complaint." They also, through the Chinese consul, San Francisco attorney Frederick Bee, published open letters to Dr. Meares decrying their treatment at his hands. In them, Bee accused Meares of a dereliction of duty in allowing the problems in Chinatown to fall to such a state when he had the power all along to deal with them. Ultimately it was decided that Chinatown, with its nearly twenty thousand inhabitants, was far too big to simply "abate." The matter was dropped, but the rhetoric continued.[46]

The rhetoric of disease was just as readily distilled into descriptions of Chinese laundries. In 1885, city inspectors described the interior of a laundry in terms that matched descriptions of Chinatown at large. "The frequent custom with this people," the inspectors sniffed, "is to have the brick and mortar bench where cooking is carried on, the sink, always more or less filthy, and an open, filthy, bad-smelling water closet, all adjoining each other in the same room." "Frequently," they continued, "a space at the end of this cooking range—if we may call it so—is used as a urinal, the only outlet from which is the absorption of and seepage through some earth placed there for that purpose." Laundries were described as agents of epidemic. "Over and over again," opined the *San Francisco Chronicle*, "laundries have been known to be used as private hospitals and the dirty clothes doing duty as a sick bed." Medical science claimed that syphilis, which was believed to be widespread among the Chinese, was spread through saliva. This disturbing discovery doubly damned the laundrymen because of their use of the "sprayer," a brass tube through which a mist of water was blown onto clothes for ironing. Given this, claimed the *Chronicle*, it "is obvious that the glistening linen that comes home from the laundries may be so many shirts of Nessus."[47]

Laundries, as little colonies, threatened to spread the Chinese contagion to suburban sanctuaries. Here the rhetoric took another subtle turn as the metaphor shifted away from the biological to the cultural. The Chinese virus threatened to undo everything that suburban domesticity was meant to protect. The mere proximity of the Chinese threatened to undermine the bonds of family and race and represented not merely an invasion of the neighborhood but of the home as well. Working-class white women closed ranks with their suburban sisters to battle the spread of Chinese laundries and domestics. In 1882, the Women's Protective League labored to open laundries staffed by white women and to place white women and girls as domestics in the city's better homes. "The household," they claimed, "which man had ever admitted to be the domain of woman, had been usurped by the Chinese." This could, in the eyes of whites, have dire consequences.[48]

The presence of Chinese men in the household and laundrymen in the neighborhood was held to undermine the moral purity of white women and tore at the very fabric of white privilege. The story of local girl Sarah Brown was instructive. Sarah had once been "a neat, buxom girl of hardly twenty, strong and healthy," but then, for unfathomable reasons, she married a laundryman named Ah Joe. The two opened a restaurant in Chinatown and at first did very well. Ah Joe cooked while Sarah waited tables, and Chinese patrons flocked to the restaurant, apparently "in order to be waited upon by a white woman." Eventually the novelty wore off, and the restaurant failed. Shortly thereafter, Sarah was living in "one of the numerous allies of filthy Chinatown . . . as low a wreck as opium and whiskey can produce." Her fate, a local storekeeper said, was common to all such women who "seek to drown their consciences in Oriental vices." City inspectors were horrified at the number of white female prostitutes in Chinatown and even more scandalized by the number of white women who married Chinese men.[49]

Worst of all, the invasion of Chinese laundrymen and their terrible habits threatened children. City inspectors reported that Chinese prostitution was "the source of the most terrible pollution of the blood of the younger and rising generations among us." They claimed that "boys eight and ten years old" were appearing in clinics with "some of the worst cases of syphilis." In 1880, a bill in the State Senate took notice of such poisonous influences around the state by seeking to ban opium. The problem, its supporters claimed, was not just in the cities. The *San Francisco Chronicle* reported: "From small towns in nearly every portion of the state where the Chinese have obtained a foothold come loud complaints that boys and girls of tender years are being demoralized and ruined by indulgence in the deadly habit."[50]

To white, suburban San Franciscans, it seemed as if nothing was safe. The Chinese contagion had crossed an ocean, destroyed some of the best land in the city of San Francisco, and ruined the neighborhoods and even homes of the city's best citizens. Almost every day, stories in local papers and from around the state described a swarm of disease-infested humanity that was poised to wrest control of the state from white citizens, and to many the vanguard of the movement seemed to be laundries.

The Laundry Wars

White Californians translated their panic into restrictive municipal ordinances designed to contain the contagion. All over the state, towns and cities saw Chinese laundries spread into previously white enclaves just as they had in San Francisco, and they passed laws that restricted where, when, and how laundries for hire could operate. In most cases, the laws were designed or operated in such a way as to encourage the growth of white-owned businesses and to smother the Chinese laundry trade. San Francisco's municipal government pursued this strategy most vigorously, and it was there that the Chinese fought back. In the process, they reshaped Reconstruction and, particularly, the Fourteenth Amendment.[51]

The laundry wars opened in February 1880 at the same moment that the San Francisco Health Department was seeking to "abate" Chinatown. Eleven Chinese laundrymen perished in a fire that destroyed their washhouse along with another home. For some time, white citizens of the city had complained that the Chinese washhouses were fire traps that represented a danger to the entire city. San Francisco, after all, had burned to the ground more than once and would do so again. The white man who owned the building in which the laundry was housed lived in a building in back of the shop and lost his home as well. He and his family narrowly escaped the flames by tearing a hole in a fence. Two white women who lived on either side of the laundry also managed to escape, but barely, as the papers breathlessly reported. Authorities suspected that the laundrymen who died had been "under the stupefying influences of opium at the time the fire broke out," and so failed to make their escape. The episode contained all the elements of the Chinese infection: a laundry packed with sleeping, single Chinese men, surrounded by white-owned homes; opium; and families and white women endangered. The board of supervisors seized the opportunity to strike at the Chinese from a different direction. Under the guise of "fire safety," the board passed two measures couched in racially neutral language but clearly designed to drive Chinese laundrymen in San Francisco out of business. The first, passed just days after the fire, sought to make the opening of new laundries prohibitively expensive by requiring that all laundries built after March 1, 1880, be made of brick. The second, passed three months later, dealt with existing laundries by requiring owners of laundries made of wood to obtain an operating license from the board.[52]

Since 310 of the city's 320 laundries, and virtually all Chinese laundries, were made of wood, the target was obvious, and it was under this ordinance that Yick Wo and Wo Lee were arrested five years later. In the meantime, however, the city of San Francisco experimented with variously worded laundry ordinances designed to harass Chinese laundries out of business. Between 1873 and 1884, the city of San Francisco passed fourteen ordinances related to licensing and construction of laundries alone. Most of these laws were passed after 1880 and reflected frustration with failures to curb Chinese immigration at both the state and federal levels. In most cases, these ordinances were carefully worded in race-neutral language to avoid running afoul of the equal protection clause of the Fourteenth Amendment and thus pass constitutional muster.[53]

The strongest and most obviously discriminatory of the ordinances was passed May 8, 1882. The ordinance described boundaries within which laundry operators were required to be licensed by the board of supervisors. The boundaries contained the entire central business district of the city and most of the city's residential neighborhoods. Licenses would only be granted to those laundry operators "upon the recommendation of not less than 12 citizens and tax-payers in the block in which the laundry" was located. This law, by requiring Chinese laundry operators to gain the permission of twelve white citizens effectively enlisted nearly every resident of the city of San Francisco as agents of the state in the effort to eliminate the Chinese from their midst. Local papers regularly reported the names of whites who received licenses, but Chinese names never appeared. At one point, a protest submitted to the Board asking that Chinese licenses be summarily refused was tabled until the board actually received such a request. One Chinese laundryman, Wong Poo Ling, managed to secure the necessary signatures, but the League of Deliverance, an ardently anti-Chinese vigilance club, pressured the whites who had signed to remove their signatures, and he went without a license.[54]

The Chinese for their part worked up an organized resistance to the ordinance. In the summer of 1882, the Six Companies retained attorneys and prepared to defend test cases in the hope that the courts would strike down the law. In *In re Quong Woo*, they succeeded, but not in the way they had hoped. The federal circuit court took no notice of racial discrimination and instead decided the case solely in terms of the legitimate use of municipal police powers. The law was unconstitutional, the court declared, because the provision concerning the twelve citizens amounted to an unwarranted delegation of municipal police powers. In other words, the board was the only entity empowered to refuse licenses, but the board lacked the authority to pass that power on to another entity.[55]

The court thus embarked on a pattern of avoiding race at all costs when deciding the many laundry cases that would come before it. Because the equal protection clause of the Fourteenth Amendment refers to "persons" as opposed to "citizens," the Chinese were ostensibly entitled to such protection. And yet, to this point, no legal case that might firmly establish that protection and compel a federal defense of Chinese rights had come before the court. Again and again, the Chinese brought suits on grounds of racial discrimination, which, after all, had prompted Reconstruction legislation in the first place. Yet judges at nearly all levels repeatedly and self-consciously based their decisions on distinctly nonracial foundations. To have done so would have been to invoke federal Reconstruction legislation in a manner that would firmly define Chinese immigrants as worthy of federal protection and thus put them explicitly within the reach of the Fourteenth Amendment. In many cases in the 1870s and 1880s, U.S. Supreme Court jurists, including Justice Stephen J. Field of California, located legal controversies on the narrow field of municipal police powers, just as in *Quong Woo*, apparently for this very reason. When the cases are taken as a body of work, it is difficult to avoid the judgment, aided by hindsight, that the justices were coaching white Californians toward Chinese restrictions that would pass constitutional muster. In fact, in two cases in the 1870s, Justice Field had specifically pointed to police powers as potentially useful tools in abating nuisances. His coaching ultimately appeared in later ordinances and in the infamous corporations article of California's Constitution of 1879.[56]

In spite of his helpfulness, Field was widely vilified in California for voiding the ordinance in *Quong Woo*. White Californians took offense most strongly to his assertion in the decision that "the business of a laundry . . . is not itself against good morals, or contrary to public order or decency." His words flew in the face of everything whites in California believed to be true. The editors at the *San Francisco Chronicle* sarcastically suggested that on this point "a few facts would have been of immense benefit to Justice Field." To that end they repeated the charges that Chinese laundries were fire traps and dens of iniquity.[57]

In any event, the board of supervisors tried again. The following year, it passed an ordinance that expanded the district covered to include all residential areas; it also barred laundries from operating between the hours of 10 P.M. and 6 A.M. weekdays and Saturdays and all day on Sundays. Clearly, this amounted to an attack on laundries operated by partnerships in suburban neighborhoods. It was designed to squeeze the Chinese out of the trade by limiting their profits and to run them out of the state by limiting their ability to work. This time, the Supreme Court, under Field's influence, upheld the law, arguing that limiting hours of operation was a legitimate use of police powers. Race could not be made an issue "unless in its enforcement it is made

Hon. Stephen J. Field (1816–1899). As a U.S. Supreme Court justice, Field heard dozens of cases alleging racial discrimination against the Chinese. Field played an important role in the development of the Court's interpretation of the Fourteenth Amendment, and he had a significant influence on the Court's decision in *Yick Wo v. Hopkins*. (Courtesy of the Bancroft Library, University of California, Berkeley, California Faces: Selections from the Bancroft Library Portrait Collection.)

to operate only against" one group. No evidence of this was offered, so race did not figure in the case.[58]

But just as whites had taken notice of hints offered by the justices, so too did the Chinese. If they were to end municipal harassment, the Chinese would have to force the issue of race on the Supreme Court in a way that left the justices no room to maneuver. A new wave of arrests in the summer of 1885 enabled the laundrymen to go to court with proof of racial discrimination. In *Yick Wo v. Hopkins*, decided the following year, the laundrymen were finally able to show that even though ordinances 1569 and 1581 were written in race-neutral language, their operation left whites untouched while Chinese were made wards of the San Francisco sheriff. This left the Court with little choice, and the justices were at last forced to find that the statute was in direct violation of the Fourteenth Amendment. Justice Stanley Matthews, writing for the majority, was very clear. "Though the law itself be fair on its face and impartial in appearance, yet, if it is applied and administered by public authority with an evil eye and an unequal hand, so as practically to make unjust and illegal discriminations between persons in similar circumstances . . . the denial of equal justice is still within the prohibition of the Constitution." For the first, but not the last, time, the Court argued that the due process and equal protection clauses of the Fourteenth Amendment applied to aliens as well as citizens. For the first time, the Fourteenth Amendment was explicitly tied to the fates of Chinese immigrants, and Chinese immigrants were firmly tied within the web of rights guaranteed by the civil rights acts that gave that amendment life.[59]

Conclusion

In *Yick Wo v. Hopkins*, the Chinese finally found the key legal strategy they needed to defend themselves from municipal efforts to deprive them of the right to work, and so dealt a death blow to laundry legislation and other forms of municipal harassment across California. Most important, they established a legal principle through which they could compel the federal government to defend their rights in California and thus drew Reconstruction ever further west. In this sense, *Yick Wo v. Hopkins* obviously represented a major step forward in the

Chinese struggle to win space for themselves in the United States. And yet, for all that, their legal status in the United States, and in California in particular, remained ill defined. The passage of the federal Chinese Exclusion Act even as the laundry wars raged testified to the ambiguous position of Chinese immigrants. Further, while Chinese protection under the Fourteenth Amendment was firmly established, as the next chapter notes, the extent to which the various federal civil rights acts would touch the Chinese was still in doubt.

As important as *Yick Wo v. Hopkins* was in the Chinese struggle for federal protection, we should not lose sight of the importance of earlier cases that were not as successful. The cycle of legislation and legal testing during the laundry wars ended by refining both the Fourteenth Amendment and the arena of municipal police powers. In their efforts to prevent the Chinese from availing themselves of the Fourteenth Amendment's equal protection clause, judges at all levels effectively allowed the Chinese to engage in a project that was potentially even more subversive of white political power. By focusing their legal decisions on municipal police powers, the nation's judicial guardians of racial purity gave Chinese immigrants nearly free reign to shape the ability of local governments to control their own affairs. In a sense, the laundry wars in California offer a particularly striking example of the ways in which immigrants shaped urban growth in the United States.

Both of these legal developments were the outgrowth of a changed racial context in California that was intrinsically related to Reconstruction. The movement of black Californians into the white polity undermined older racial formulations and led directly to the development of new metaphors of disease and contamination to describe the Chinese and their role in California. Both the new rhetoric and the agitation over Chinese laundries drew their strength from the participation of California's middle and upper classes in anti-Chinese agitation.

By defining the Chinese as disease and pestilence as opposed to simply human beings racially unworthy of participation in American society, white Californians wrote the Chinese outside of the human race and so justified any and all arguments for their total exclusion from the United States. Traditionally, blame for exclusion has been laid at the feet of the working class. More recently, Andrew Gyory has sought to absolve workers at the expense of eastern politicians who cynically seized upon the Chinese issue as a way of marshaling western votes. In each of these explanations, wealthier Americans have remained unstained by the racial travesty of exclusion. That exclusion finally succeeded at precisely the moment that California's more affluent white citizens joined their voices to the chorus of anti-Chinese agitation raises serious questions about traditional interpretations that ignore their role.[60]

In the years immediately following passage of the Chinese Exclusion Act however, many Californians who had celebrated its passage came to see it as a monumental failure. In the mid-1880s, frustration over those perceived failures and over the failure of the program of municipal harassment reached a fever pitch. In this highly charged atmosphere, the new racial metaphors developed during the laundry wars served as the primary catalyst as legal attacks on the Chinese became physical attacks.

Chapter 5
"The Chinese Must Go!"
The Twin Careers of Exclusion and Expulsion

BY THE MID-1880s, the long project of racial reconstruction in California was mostly completed. The rhetorical and legal links that had, during the 1850s, defined the state's Indian, black, and Chinese populations as equally unworthy of inclusion in the white polity no longer governed race relations in the state. The clear line that had marked white racial dominance in California had been broken apart. Where once virtually all civic and social privileges had been reserved for whites, new laws and new federal oversight opened what had traditionally been white privileges to other races. Now a more complicated racial regime governed by federal Reconstruction legislation shaped the daily lives of all Californians, white and nonwhite.

California Indians, once the common denominator that had yoked all three groups in a common image of degraded humanity, lay trapped in their original status as the weakest and most marginalized people in the state. After decades of cultural destruction and pogroms masquerading as warfare, barely seventeen thousand California Indians survived. The remnants of the world's most linguistically diverse population were now wards of the federal government on a handful of miserable reservations. California's Indians were so sharply segregated from white society, both physically and ideologically, that they hardly registered in the state's racial discussions. They had, in effect, become little more than ideological foils against which other groups might be negatively defined.[1]

The movement of California's tiny black population into the white polity, by contrast, had worked a profound transformation upon the state's racial hierarchy. The Civil War and Reconstruction, along with the civil rights activities of California's nonwhites, severed the connections white Californians had drawn between the state's black, Chinese, and Indian populations, effectively elevating the racial status of black Californians. The Thirteenth, Fourteenth, and most especially the Fifteenth Amendments had opened the state's civil institutions to black participation. Black Californians were, if hardly welcomed, at least tolerated in California's courts, voting booths, and schools. But while Reconstruction had dismantled the legal barriers to black inclusion, the rhetorical barriers that whites had erected over the years endured. Under the influence of racial ideas developed over decades and more, white Californians continued to hold their black neighbors at a middle distance; blacks were neither as fully degraded as Indians nor as fully included as white European immigrants.

The Chinese, however, remained an unsettled element within the state's increasingly complicated racial hierarchy. Their fight against municipal laundry regulations had led the U.S. Supreme Court to embrace a more capacious Fourteenth Amendment, one that extended equal protection beyond citizens to all *persons*, including the Chinese. But while securing constitutional protections bolstered Chinese efforts to fend off legal harassment, those protections could not guarantee success. Nor could they arrest the rhetorical processes through which Chinese immigrants were defined as racially inferior. Those processes persisted. By defining the Chinese as subhuman, the metaphors of contagion developed during the laundry wars effectively marked the rhetorical end of racial reconstruction in California. These metaphors justified laws that sought to inoculate the state's urban landscapes against the spread of Chinese settlement, and at the same time helped to justify the survival of legal barriers to the full participation of Chinese in California society. They had even strengthened justifications for the prohibition of Chinese immigration at the federal level. Yet, in spite of such laws, the Chinese, and Chinatowns, with all of their perceived problems, continued in whites' eyes to plague California. Racial rhetoric, in other words, had not yet been translated into physical reality. In fact, Chinese migrants continued to land at San Francisco by the thousands even after passage of the Chinese Exclusion Act, leading many white Californians to conclude that the act was a failure.

By the mid-1880s, relief over the passage of the Exclusion Act turned to frustration over the inability of the political system to confront the Chinese Question once and for all. In late 1885, a scandal involving corruption and Chinese immigration in the San Francisco Customs House confirmed whites' worst fears, and frustration turned to outrage. Under the influence of the metaphors of contagion, white Californians performed a simple syllogism whose conclusion had dire consequences for Chinese immigrants. From the perception that the Chinese were a disease against which America needed protection, it was but a short step to the assertion that Chinatowns were an infection that required excision. Movements devoted to the expulsion of the Chinese sprang up in towns and cities across the state and throughout the West. In contrast to earlier, organized efforts aimed at ridding California of the Chinese, these movements explicitly avoided legislative halls and courts. Instead, these were extralegal movements in the tradition of San Francisco's infamous Vigilance Committees. Chinese laborers had been subject to violent, extralegal attacks almost from the moment of their arrival in California, and the fiercest of those attacks had occasionally driven them from their homes and businesses. But in the mid-1880s, the violence and frequency of the attacks on Chinese communities represented something new and grew directly out of recent events associated with the racial reconstruction of California. The expulsions of the 1880s differed too in terms of sheer numbers. Between February 1885 and February 1886, dozens of towns from one end of the state to the other and across the West forcibly expelled their Chinese residents in acts best described as ethnic cleansing.[2]

The Chinese responded, as they always had, through the courts. But while the form of their response was familiar, the substance spoke to a Chinese community gripped by despair and exhausted by years of constant attacks. In case after case leading to this moment, the Chinese had turned to the courts seeking equality of access and opportunity, asking only that they be treated the same as everyone else in California. Now, for the first time, they abandoned their efforts to be included in California society and instead embraced their status as aliens in an attempt to win privileges unavailable to other Americans.

The strategy, although in one sense a vigorous defense of Chinese rights, in another sense represented a capitulation, an acceptance of permanent alien status and a permanently marginalized existence in America.

The Failure of Exclusion

White Californians greeted the passage of the Chinese Exclusion Act in 1882 with an odd mixture of relief and disappointment. Passage of the act vindicated more than a decade of debate, pleading, and threats with respect to the Chinese community, and many white Californians praised the federal government for finally coming around to their evaluation of the Chinese. The state's Republicans offered unhesitating praise, if only because a Republican president had signed the act into law. Declaring itself "unalterably opposed to Chinese immigration," the Republican Party deemed the act a "cause for congratulation" and considered the matter closed. California Democrats were less effusive in their praise but were grateful nonetheless, and they applauded party representatives in Washington, D.C., for their efforts. "Such action," wrote the state Democratic leadership, "again illustrates the fidelity of the party to its pledges . . . to preserve the heritage we have a right to enjoy from the merciless ravages of the Asiatic hosts."[3]

Yet at the same time, Californians were disappointed by limitations built into the Chinese Exclusion Act. The most glaring limitation concerned time. The act expired after ten years, raising the possibility that in the absence of strong political will, Chinese immigration might begin anew in the next decade. Less obvious, but perhaps more alarming, were the loopholes built into the legislation that allowed some immigration to continue. The act applied only to those Chinese immigrants classified as laborers. Those whose credentials marked them as merchants, students, diplomats, and tourists could enter and travel about the country at will. Laborers outside the country when the law went into force could enter if they could prove prior residency. Laborers already residing in the United States before the act passed were free to come and go as they pleased using "return certificates" issued by customs officials. Perhaps most frightening to diehard foes of Chinese immigration, children of Chinese residing in the United States had the right to join their parents. This last loophole threatened to plant another generation of Chinese immigrants in California and to extend the crisis well into the future.[4]

Some white Californians, then, viewed the Chinese Exclusion Act as a dubious victory and continued to press for stronger measures. The Democrats, partly for partisan advantage and partly out of real disappointment, gently chided Congress for its "partially successful" efforts "against Chinese immigration," and pledged not to rest in pursuit of "the early and perfect accomplishment of this great work." Others were more blunt. The editors of the *Truth*, a labor sheet published in San Francisco, derided the Chinese Exclusion Act as "practically worthless." Voicing an opinion apparently held by many in San Francisco, the *Truth* decided that "whatever California wants done, she must do herself."[5]

While prevailing opinion held that the Chinese Exclusion Act was weakened by these loopholes, the state's most hardened anti-Chinese activists saw a more fundamental, and ultimately fatal, flaw. The act, simply put, did nothing about the Chinese already in the United States. Days before the act was signed into law by President Chester Alan Arthur on May 6, 1882, a coalition of labor unions met in San Francisco and founded an organization devoted to driving the Chinese not merely from San Francisco but from the entire Pacific Slope. The League of Deliverance, as it was called, proposed to accomplish this goal by, first, boycotting all Chinese businesses and labor and all white-owned businesses that patronized or employed Chinese. Second, and more ominous, the league divided the Pacific Slope into districts and directed district officers to demand of all Chinese in their midst that they leave immediately. Those who refused would be declared a menace. At that point, in language that echoed San Francisco's chief health inspector, the league authorized its members to "abate such danger by force." In the end, their efforts were more hope than reality. The league, riven by class issues and financing scandals, fell apart several months later. Perhaps most important, in the months immediately following passage of the Chinese Exclusion Act, the loopholes seemed less important than passage of the act itself, and the league failed to generate much enthusiasm. But its tactics and goals set a pattern of attack when the time was ripe. That time would come once white Californians had an opportunity to see the act in operation.[6]

The Chinese inadvertently helped change public perception by seizing every opportunity to thwart the act. Following its passage, Chinese immigrants rushed to enter the United States before the gates closed. In the three months between the passage of the Chinese Exclusion Act and its enforcement, 39,579 Chinese immigrants passed through U.S. customs houses. Once the act went into effect, customs officials in San Francisco vigorously enforced it. Even so, Chinese immigrants hoping for better lives in California continued to arrive. To blunt the enthusiasm of customs officials, the Chinese pursued a legal strategy that exhausted the courts by endlessly testing the act and tenaciously exploiting every loophole available.[7]

The most useful legal maneuver available to Chinese trying to enter the United States was the writ of habeas corpus. When a would-be immigrant's right to disembark on American soil was challenged by a customs official, the Chinese detainee, with help from white lawyers retained by the Six Companies, filed a writ in either the federal district court or the federal circuit court in San Francisco. Throughout the 1880s and 1890s, both courts were choked by petitions and pleadings offered by Chinese immigrants, almost to the exclusion of all other court business. Between 1882 and 1890, for instance, the district court alone heard more than seven thousand Chinese habeas corpus cases. By September 1882, only one month after enforcement began, local newspapers were snidely referring to both courts as "habeas corpus mill[s]," and the two justices who administered the two courts soon took to using the term themselves.[8]

The two judges, Ogden Hoffman of U.S. district court and Lorenzo Sawyer of U.S. circuit court, both played important roles in the legal battles over race in California, and their response to the Chinese habeas corpus petitions presents some intriguing questions concerning the intersection of race, politics, and law. Both men felt overwhelmed by the number of Chinese habeas corpus cases that came their way, and despaired of ever being free of them. Yet both men's strict adherence to Republican Party principles lent them a more disinterested disposition with regard to race than that possessed by their Democratic counterparts in California's state courts. The two men had been instrumental in striking down the more odious anti-Chinese elements of the new state constitution ratified in 1879, and both had stood at the center of the controversy surrounding Chinese laundries. In several laundry cases, Justice Sawyer in particular had shown a generous legal disposition toward the Chinese. When it came to the Chinese habeas corpus cases, both men were scrupulously fair. Between 1882 and 1890, 86 percent of the Chinese habeas corpus petitioners successfully entered the United States via the federal district or circuit courts, a record that earned Hoffman and Sawyer the enmity of many white Californians.[9]

And yet, outside the context of the judiciary, both men harbored hostile opinions concerning Chinese immigration and the Chinese themselves. Lorenzo Sawyer, in particular, regarded the presence of Chinese as a menace to the morals and good order of California society. "I do not think it at all desirable that the Chinese should come here permanently," he told Hubert Howe Bancroft in 1890. "They are a race entirely different from ours and can never assimilate." Sawyer favored laws designed to prevent the permanent settlement of Chinese in California, especially laws that struck at the formation of family ties. "If they would never bring their women here," he told Bancroft, "and never multiply . . . their presence would always be an advantage to the state." He praised "their industry, their economy, their frugality, and perseverance," but he also felt that those virtues made Chinese immigrants more machine than human. This line of Sawyer's thinking had a chilling end. "When the Chinaman comes here and can't bring his wife here," he claimed, "sooner or later he dies like a worn out steam engine, he is simply a machine."[10]

The justices, in other words, allowed entry to hundreds and even thousands of Chinese immigrants despite popular opinion, despite legal options to do otherwise, and despite their own racial prejudices. That they did so is testament to an abiding faith in the rule of law prevalent in nineteenth-century American jurisprudence. Both judges muted their racial antagonism toward the Chinese while seated at the bench. They did so, as Hoffman's biographer Christian G. Fritz points out, not so much out of sympathy for the Chinese as out of a desire to defend legal and personal principles. The writ of habeas corpus, wrote Hoffman, was not some whimsical legal nicety. It was, instead "among English-speaking peoples the most sacred monument of personal freedom." The writ, he argued, would have to be specifically limited by Congress "before any court could venture to withhold its benefits from any human being, no matter what his race or color." Diluting the power of the writ without congressional imprimatur was out of the question. Protecting the Chinese in their right to the writ of habeas corpus, moreover, was as much a question of national honor as it was a question of defending legal principle. Thus for men like Justices Sawyer and Hoffman, who were in their professional lives cloaked with the authority of the United States government, personal honor might easily be conflated with national honor. In at least two international treaties, the U.S. government had pledged to protect Chinese subjects living and working in its jurisdiction. To deny the Chinese the right of habeas corpus would be to break a promise and bring national as well as personal disgrace.[11]

Even so, for most white Californians, the two justices were far too accommodating toward the Chinese. Both Hoffman and Sawyer were widely maligned in California newspapers and pamphlets, where they were alternately cast as either corrupted by Chinese money or hapless dupes of the Six Companies. The editors of the *San Francisco Chronicle*, for instance, argued that the writ of habeas corpus was reserved for jailed citizens, not for aliens detained aboard a ship. Since nothing limited their freedom to return to China, the proceedings in both federal courts amounted to a "prostitution of a valuable legal remedy." Members of the local press who observed the court proceedings often sarcastically cast them as a circus, further inflaming public opinion. "The United States District Court yesterday assumed the appearance of a Chinese playhouse," scoffed the *Chronicle*. "Those present seemed to enjoy the performance quite as well as a first-class Chinese farce, for they smiled incessantly at the tales told by the petitioners on the stand." In the end, the writer concluded, Judge Hoffman was fooled again as he "allowed five Chinese to land and took two cases under consideration."[12]

Judge Hoffman occasionally sought to defend his public reputation through his written decisions. The huge number of habeas corpus cases made it impossible to render written decisions in each case, and, as a result, Hoffman believed, "the rulings of the court have been very imperfectly reported by the press." Arguing that it was his duty to uphold both treaty obligations and the exclusion law as written, Hoffman pointed out that the evidence presented in case after case, often "corroborated by testimony of white persons," left him no choice. The fault lay with loopholes built into a law he was bound to uphold, in spite of "cases [that] proved exceedingly embarrassing to the court."[13]

Hoffman's self-defense fell on deaf ears. The very vocal and public vilification continued, and even increased when San Francisco newspapers began reporting on the numbers of Chinese immigrants who successfully petitioned the courts on writs of habeas corpus. In October 1885, the *San Francisco Chronicle* reported that, since August 9, 1882, the day the exclusion act went into effect, 9,524 Chinese had landed at San Francisco and passed through Judge Hoffman's court. Customs records also showed that 28,294 Chinese had left San Francisco during the same period, but that fact made little impression on frustrated white Californians. And perhaps rightly so since, as events would soon show, those numbers were highly suspect.[14]

Much of the public outcry stemmed from a growing suspicion that the Chinese were fraudulently exploiting loopholes in the exclusion act. Public scrutiny at first centered on what were known as "Canton Certificates." Chinese arrivals at the San Francisco Customs House who claimed "merchant" status carried with them certificates attesting to that status printed by Chinese authorities in Canton. Under the obligations imposed by treaties with China and by the exclusion act, Canton Certificates were to be considered "*prima facie* evidence of a right to land" in the United States. According to Justice Hoffman, a petitioner often simply "presented a Canton certificate to the court and rested his case." The judge had little or no authority to challenge the validity of the certificates. Moreover, the issue was not the immigrant's status in China, but the occupation that immigrant would pursue in the United States. A man who had been a laborer in China could claim that he had arrived to work in a brother's or uncle's mercantile concern, thus guaranteeing merchant status. Worse still, there was no American control over the distribution of certificates in Canton. White Californians were especially incensed over the spectacle presented by U.S. government offices blindly following the lead of unaccountable foreign officials.[15]

Whites' frustrations only increased when a series of strikes by Chinese workers revealed one of the more perverse results of the Chinese Exclusion Act. Chinese laborers in California quickly recognized that the exclusion act increased their bargaining powers simply by shutting off the flow of cheap labor from China. The abrupt constriction in the labor market allowed Chinese laborers to push for higher wages and better working conditions in all manner of occupations, particularly in the cigar and laundry trades. Suddenly, Chinese laborers were acting like white laborers and bending industrial interests to their will.[16]

Suspicion and frustration exploded into full-throated outrage in the fall of 1885 when a smuggling ring was discovered in the San Francisco Customs House. Investigations quickly centered on what were known as "red certificates." Chinese laborers living in the United States who wished to visit China and then return home could acquire a "return certificate" from customs officials. Upon return to San Francisco, the traveler could simply present the certificate and reenter the country. The certificates were red in color and were printed with the laborer's name and a physical description. For some time, controversy had surrounded the potential for abuse of the right of return. Commentators, for instance, often ridiculed the generic descriptions that customs officials printed on the red certificates. The certificate presented by an immigrant named Yet You offers a case in point. "Complexion, brown; physical marks, none; height, five feet six inches." "That," exclaimed the incredulous *San Francisco Chronicle*, "is the remarkable description by which it is supposed the customs officer can identify the Chinese." "The description given," continued the writer, "is almost as comprehensive as the old woman's who described a lost canine as 'a brown dog with two ears.'" The fraud uncovered in October 1885, however, went much deeper than lazy description. Investigative reporters for the *San Francisco Chronicle* discovered that several customs officials were trafficking in the red certificates, selling them in Chinatown, and undermining the Chinese Exclusion Act.[17]

The scam was a simple one. Normally, a few days before a ship was scheduled to set sail for China, a Chinese traveler would go down to the Customs House and apply for a certificate. The traveler's name was written down, he or she was measured, and a brief description was taken. The traveler was then handed a white ticket and told to bring it on the day of departure. On that day, the traveler was met aboard ship by a customs official who exchanged the white ticket for a red certificate. The officer then returned the white ticket to the customs office and recorded the transfer. A Chinese "syndicate" hoping to cadge red certificates need only send "fifty or a hundred dummies . . . have them measured, take out the white tags and carry them up to Chinatown." When the customs officer, who was in on the scam, boarded the ship a few days later, "he finds fifty or a hundred red certificates in his possession uncalled for." The extra red certificates were exchanged in Chinatown later that day for the dummy white tickets, which were then recorded. The red certificates were later secretly shipped to Hong Kong and sold, allowing new immigrants to enter the United States as "returns."[18]

With the Customs House under intense scrutiny, other scams were soon discovered. "Every day there is some new system of fraud developed in the Chinese attempts to evade the Restriction Act," complained the *San Francisco Chronicle*. A favorite "new system" was to smuggle Chinese women ashore dressed as men, a practice that outraged respectable San Franciscans. Another was the practice of bringing Chinese children into the United States using phony documentation. These "paper sons" were coached on how to answer customs inspectors' questions upon arrival and armed with detailed information about "relatives" already in the United States. Sometimes, as in the case of Mrs. Tung Yueng, the stories told in court were less than satisfactory. Mrs. Tung Yueng had left the United States for a visit to China with two young girls. Several years later, she returned with two girls, but both girls were far too old to be the same girls with

This political cartoon from the *Wasp*, a satirical magazine, depicts the red ticket scandal that unfolded at the San Francisco Customs House in 1885, and it skewers both Justice Ogden Hoffman and U.S. Congressman William S. Rosecrans, whom many Californians blamed for passage of a weak Chinese Exclusion bill. (*Wasp* [back cover], 1/26/84, Courtesy of the Bancroft Library, University of California, Berkeley.)

whom she had left. Such cases were reported more and more often in California newspapers as the investigation into the Customs House frauds unfolded.[19]

The constant frauds made a mockery of the exclusion act and threatened the continued spread of the Chinese contagion into the United States. Many wondered whether, in spite of exclusion, the state's Chinatowns were growing. An investigation by the *San Francisco Chronicle* during October 1885 combed through county poll tax records to find out. In the end, the results were inconclusive, but many white Californians, including Justice Ogden Hoffman, believed that the state's Chinese population was on the rise. Newspaper editorials quickly called for an official investigation into the allegations of fraud and abuse. The *San Francisco Chronicle* demanded that Customs Collector John S. Hager, chief of the San Francisco Customs House, pursue his own investigation. Hager's reputation as a staunch defender of white privilege had been won more than a decade earlier when, as a state senator, he had played a prominent role in California's rejection of the Fifteenth Amendment. Now, though, even he could not escape the public's wrath. The paper's editors charged that Chinese money controlled the Customs House, and that Chinese officials were running U.S. immigration policy.[20]

Justice Hoffman leapt at the opportunity to repair his damaged reputation and relieve the pressure placed on his court by the multitudes of habeas corpus cases. On October 19, 1885, he convened a federal grand jury to investigate the allegations of fraud in the San Francisco Customs House. Some worried that, given Judge Hoffman's record with regard to the Chinese and the closed nature of grand jury proceedings, the scandal would be buried. Hoffman's instructions to the grand jury quickly dispelled any objections. "You have no doubt been startled, perhaps surprised, at the recent publication . . . relative to extensive frauds," he began. "If it astonished you, it did not me. I have long been convinced that those practices prevailed." Hoffman claimed that he had brought allegations of fraud before Collector Hager in times past, but because his evidence was only hearsay, little had come of it. He read them a letter from the American Consul in Hong Kong, dated the previous July, alleging that a lively traffic in red certificates had been conducted there for some time. Now, he was determined to root out the corruption that had tormented his courtroom for so many years. Arguing that a grand jury had broader investigative powers than did the district attorney, Hoffman directed the grand jury to avoid investigating "a charge against any particular person" but to instead determine whether "a system has prevailed here for years." He empowered them to question anyone they chose, especially Chinese immigrants who might have relevant information. Finally, Hoffman questioned the accuracy of customs records that showed more Chinese had left California than had arrived since the exclusion act went into effect. He charged the grand jury with finding a definitive answer to the question.[21]

As more and more subpoenas were sent out by the grand jury, and the investigation widened further still, white Californians grew increasingly agitated. Reports that Chinese officials feared for the safety of Chinese in America grew increasingly common. "It is well known," reported the *Chronicle*, "that the almond-eyed heathen are becoming uneasy." Chinese living in isolated small towns began flocking to the relative safety of San Francisco's Chinatown, raising the specter of an internal invasion. "The number of Chinese here at present is estimated at between 30,000 and 40,000," claimed the *San Francisco Chronicle*. "The sleeping accommodations in the Chinese quarter are insufficient, and the result is, at all hours of the day and night, the heathen are to be found prowling around the streets." With daily revelations about the ongoing investigations into fraud and the failure of the Chinese Exclusion Act, racial turmoil between white Californians and Chinese immigrants reached an all-time high.[22]

Expulsion

Meanwhile, rising concerns over the continued presence of the Chinese and frustration over the failure of the exclusion act to remedy the situation generated violent reactions all over California and the West. In the northern coastal town of Eureka, California, the era of expulsion opened with a vengeance when white residents violently purged their town of Chinese residents in February 1886. Tensions between working-class whites and Chinese laborers in Eureka had been simmering for more than a decade. Job opportunities in Eureka's lucrative timber industry had lured both groups to the region in the 1860s and 1870s, but the hard times that followed the Panic of 1873 undermined both groups' hopes for prosperity. As they had in San Francisco and elsewhere in California, working-class white men fastened blame for their predicament on the Chinese, and calls for ridding Eureka of the Chinese "curse" boiled out of one mass meeting after another. In 1875, a mob of white men disrupted Eureka's Chinese New Year celebration, assaulting revelers and damaging property. By the late 1870s, white workers had organized themselves into one of the state's most powerful chapters of the virulently anti-Chinese Workingmen's Party of California, and Eureka experienced a wave of strikes designed to force local employers into discharging all of their Chinese laborers. Eureka's white community lent its vocal support to the drive for passage of the Chinese Exclusion Act in the hope that federal action might finally satisfy their desire for racial purity.[23]

Instead, much to the dismay of white residents, Eureka's Chinese population actually increased after passage of the act. The city's Chinese quarter rapidly gained a reputation for violence and iniquity, with reports of shootings and assaults dominating local news. Complaints of foul odors, sewage, and piles of unattended refuse regularly appeared in local newspapers, convincing Eureka's white community that Chinatown was a source of disease. Together, these reports gave rise to the suspicion that the presence of Chinese in Eureka represented a danger not merely to the economic livelihoods of white workers but to the very survival of the town.[24]

On February 6, 1886, that suspicion turned to certainty when a dispute between two Chinese men escalated into a gunfight and a wild shot struck down a local city councilman. At a mass meeting held within hours of the shooting, whites determined that the Chinese would have to go. Throughout the night, mobs of white men stormed through Eureka's Chinatown, destroying property and dragging Chinese men and women to the waterfront, where it had been decided they would be placed on two ships then anchored in the harbor for transport to points south. Mobs scoured the countryside around the town in search of Chinese laborers who had fled, forcing them back into town and onto the docks. In all, more than three hundred Chinese men and women were loaded onto the ships and sent south to San Francisco and an uncertain fate.[25]

The expulsion in Eureka was just the first in a long and ugly string of attacks on Chinese communities in which frustration over the failures of the exclusion act and the rhetoric of disease combined to form essential catalysts. As always, economic considerations played an important role in the attacks, but now they were also heavily inflected with the consequences of Reconstruction in California and throughout the West. In September 1885, Chinese miners in Rock Springs, Wyoming, refused to join the Knights of Labor union in a strike over wages. Resentful Irish miners responded by attacking the Chinatown at Rock Springs, leading to the worst anti-Chinese violence in American history and claiming the lives of twenty-eight Chinese laborers. The editors of *Harper's Weekly* explicitly recognized the connections between the violence at Rock Springs and Reconstruction when they likened the actions of the Irish miners to "the Ku-Klux outrages in the Southern States." Not long after the attack in Rock Springs, the violence spread to Washington Territory, where three Chinese miners were killed by a mob in Squak Valley twenty miles east of Seattle. And in Seattle a month later, Washingtonians moved noisily toward evicting the city's Chinese residents.[26]

Washington Territory's troubles really began in the port city of Tacoma, fifty miles south of Seattle. California newspapers reported that on November 3, 1885, a mob of white Tacomans "forcibly removed" the town's Chinese residents "beyond the city limits." Rumblings of a similar sort were heard in Seattle, and the territorial governor, Watson C. Squire, warned that he would call in federal troops at the first sign of mob action there. Californians followed these events closely, and as they unfolded, the spirit of the old League of Deliverance began to rise in all quarters of the state.[27]

In Seattle, public meetings continued in spite of the governor's warnings, and "the anti-Chinese fever . . . gained ground." On November 5, representatives of the Knights of Labor met with leaders of Seattle's Chinese community and offered to pay for the transportation of seventy-five Chinese residents to San Francisco. The Chinese agreed to leave as soon as they could sell their property, but whites in Seattle were not mollified. That night, Tacoma's now-empty Chinatown was burned to the ground, and calls for similar action rang through Seattle. The mayor, fearing that "the city [was] in danger of falling into the hands of the mob," demanded that Governor Squire send in federal troops.[28]

The following day, Squire did just that. President Grover Cleveland also weighed in, condemning certain "evil disposed persons" and "admonishing all good citizens" to refrain from unlawful acts against the Chinese. On November 8, ten companies of the Fourteenth Infantry arrived in Seattle. If Seattle's Chinese residents harbored any hopes that the troops would offer protection, such hopes quickly evaporated. The Sacramento *Daily Record-Union* reported that the "half-intoxicated soldiers" were even less disposed toward the Chinese than local whites. "Several times today," reported the *Daily Record-Union's* correspondent, "parties of soldiers have attacked Chinamen, as they consider them to blame for their having been ordered here." The soldiers publicly voiced their disdain for the Chinese and let it be known that "they would not protect the Chinese in case of trouble."[29]

At first, California newspapers followed the editorial lead of Seattle's newspaper editors in emphasizing the role of workingmen in the agitation. This was, after all, the pattern they had seen with the rise of the Workingmen's Party in the late 1870s, and in more recent reports—erroneous as it turned out—of events in Eureka. But thirty-two indictments handed down against the conspirators in the Tacoma eviction suddenly revealed a very different sort of anti-Chinese movement. The movement crossed class lines, involving union organizations like the Knights of Labor and "gentlemen of property and standing." Indicted were not only three merchants, two butchers, an attorney, a civil engineer, six carpenters, and a photographer, but also Tacoma's mayor, police judge, and two of the city's newspaper editors. In this, the agitation in Washington Territory matched the class cooperation seen in California's laundry wars. And just as in California, calls to rid Washington Territory of the "Chinese pest" were redolent with the rhetoric of disease and infection. Once again, the new rhetoric offered common ground for workingmen, businessmen, and officials alike.[30]

The events in Washington Territory were especially relevant to California. As previously mentioned, Californians followed these events closely through daily reports in local newspapers. Given the uproar over the Customs House frauds, and over the failure of the Exclusion Act to stem the tide of Chinese immigration, the agitation in the Pacific Northwest was obviously of great interest. But the relevance of those events goes much deeper. While California newspapers had initially claimed that workingmen had instigated the expulsion at Eureka, it soon became clear that the mob had included some of the town's leading citizens. The cooperation between middle- and working-class residents in both Tacoma and Eureka lent the move toward expulsion an air of legitimacy despite the moral qualms some may have had over the use of violence. As towns along the Puget Sound expelled their Chinese residents, more and more white Californians called for similar expulsions closer to home. White Californians were especially emboldened after the arrival of federal troops failed to quell the disturbances in Seattle.

When the dam finally broke, and whites across California began to act, their expulsions followed exactly the patterns set in Eureka and Washington Territory. Local citizens first met with Chinese leaders and warned them to leave for their own safety. Community groups offered to pay for transportation and even for property. If the Chinese left peacefully, so much the better, but violence always lurked beneath the surface. Finally, in town after town, spontaneous anti-Chinese movements were composed of a cross-section of California society; workingmen and businessmen, under the influence of "anti-Chinese fever," acted together to rid their towns of the Chinese "infection."

Alongside the racial ideas driving the alliance between businessmen and workingmen, economic considerations played a significant role. Small businessmen in California also found common cause with workingmen on the Chinese issue because they were experiencing increased competition from large companies that employed cheaper Chinese labor. Owners of smaller, local concerns were less able to weather extended boycotts than were larger ones, and they relied much more on the goodwill of the community for their survival. Because of this, they tended to hire only white labor, and thus were often driven to the brink of bankruptcy by competition with those larger businesses. Expelling the Chinese, then, was in their economic interests as well as their racial interests.[31]

After the events at Eureka, white Californians watched and waited anxiously to see what consequences might flow from the expulsion. While authorities in Washington Territory had quickly responded to the anti-Chinese "fever" with federal troops and indictments, California authorities remained silent. No intimation came from Sacramento that troops would be called. In fact, many of the state's authorities whose responsibility it was to protect the Chinese joined the expulsion movement. When it became clear that there would be few if any consequences, the California expulsion movement reignited into a full-throated conflagration. The renewed activity began in Pasadena. On November 6, a fire broke out in a Chinese laundry on Fair Oaks Avenue. Before it could be extinguished, the fire had destroyed the laundry, a meat market owned by William Buttner, and a restaurant run by a man named John Clapp. The fire was attributed to "the carelessness of the Chinese" and provided all the excuse white townspeople needed to get rid of them. One hundred white men marched to Pasadena's Chinese quarter, where a committee headed by Thomas Banbury, son of State Assemblyman Jabez Banbury, met with the Chinese and demanded their immediate departure. The Chinese were given twenty-four hours to leave and warned that if they did not comply, "the crowd would be summoned by the school bell and the expulsion [would be] made forcibly." A committee of businessmen offered to pay the outstanding rents owed by the Chinese. Curiously, the same committee issued a statement to the effect that "no mob law [would] be allowed in Pasadena," implying that their action to expel the Chinese was in keeping with the law and good order of the community. The Chinese quickly packed their belongings and moved beyond the city limits.[32]

Over the next two weeks, calls for the formation of anti-Chinese leagues were issued in Santa Cruz and neighboring towns Lorenzo and Boulder, Sacramento, Stockton, and Hollister. Lorenzo's "Anti-Chinese Club" warned local business owners to discharge their Chinese employees, and by November 14 it had expelled all of the Chinese living in the town. Boulder soon followed suit. Stockton's "property-owners" promised $10,000 for the purchase of Chinese properties in anticipation of an expulsion movement, and they formed a "Citizens' Protective Organization" for the purpose. The group was led by a city councilman, a county supervisor, a former congressman, two newspaper editors, and the city attorney. "There is little doubt," reported the Sacramento *Daily Record-Union*, that "the Chinese will be removed from the city limits, as the best class of citizens lead the movement."[33]

In San Francisco, Judge Ogden Hoffman took note of the spontaneous movements cropping up around the state and grew apprehensive. He summoned the grand jury and pushed them to hasten their investigations into irregularities associated with Chinese immigration. In doing so, Hoffman accurately located the source of the trouble. He "reminded them of the general opinion that, so far from excluding Chinese immigrants, the Exclusion Act really works the other way, that under it Chinese immigrants have been pouring into the country." Hoffman hoped to avoid any more "acts of violence which disgrace our people," and instructed the jury to "let the public know what the facts are." Sensing the urgency of the situation, Hoffman pressed the grand jury for an immediate release of information. "If," he told them, "you have not time to make a full report, let the public have a partial report . . . and the present feeling of irritation in the public mind shall be calmed."[34]

In spite of Justice Hoffman's efforts, what little information the grand jury offered only further inflamed the "feeling of irritation in the public mind." Public focus shifted to the Sierra-Nevada mountain town of Truckee, where for more than two months Californians followed a tense confrontation between Chinese and white residents. In Truckee, anti-Chinese feeling had long been a force in the local community. Several years earlier, a fire destroyed the Chinese quarter of town and nearly burned all of Truckee. Following the fire, a "Safety Committee" composed of local whites demanded that the Chinese leave town and gave them a week to do so. When the Chinese refused and began rebuilding their homes, several hundred white citizens marched on the Chinese quarter and calmly tore the houses down. Then the mob acted in a remarkably orderly fashion. Each "house was taken down and the lumber was carefully piled in the streets." "Aside from the cheering and the somewhat disorderly crash of falling buildings," reported one correspondent, "everything was done quietly and without any riotous words." In 1885, the tone was markedly different.[35]

On November 25, 1885, Charles F. McGlashan, noted attorney, state assemblyman, and editor of the Truckee *Republican*, published an editorial that best captures the new tone. Titled "The Cue Klux Klan," the editorial self-consciously linked the racial turmoil and terrorism inherent in both southern and western Reconstruction, while at the same time explicitly acknowledging the unique conditions presented by western racial diversity. The editorial encouraged white citizens in Truckee and around the state to assault Chinese immigrants and shave their heads. McGlashan claimed to have "seen Chinamen take fifty lashes without quivering a muscle, but pray as men seldom pray, that their throats might be cut in preference to losing their cues." He argued that "cue cutting [is] merely a misdemeanor" and so hardly a dangerous matter. The editor even went so far as to suggest that rewards be offered, "as is the case with pelts of wolves, coyotes, and like vermin when they become a pest," once again marshaling the rhetoric of disease and infestation to degrade the Chinese.[36]

In spite of such heated rhetoric, McGlashan actually hoped to avoid violence, which he feared might provoke a strong official reaction and criminal and civil penalties. As a prosperous member of Truckee's business community, McGlashan had a great deal to lose. Instead of encouraging the Chinese to leave through threats of violence, McGlashan suggested a strategy that would encourage them to leave of their own accord. Under his direction as self-appointed leader of Truckee's expulsion movement, the Safety Committee was revived, and whites in Truckee fashioned one of the most powerfully disciplined boycotts ever seen in California. Following the pattern set by the less successful League of Deliverance three years earlier, Truckee's white citizens sought to squeeze the Chinese out of town. White men of substance offered to purchase Chinese properties in exchange for a promise to leave immediately. White patronage of Chinese businesses in and around Truckee ceased before the end of November 1885. White-owned businesses came under intense pressure to discharge all of their Chinese employees. Those who refused saw their businesses dry up as they too fell victim to the boycott. One after another, Truckee's white-owned businesses fell in line and the boycott began to strangle Chinese livelihoods.[37]

At first, the Chinese in Truckee resisted. They continued to work their jobs and run their shops, and they refused to sell their property. They also showed a willingness to defend themselves if need be. In one incident, two lengths of fire hose claimed by the city were "appropriated by the Chinese," ostensibly in case another fire endangered Chinese property. When the city demanded that the hoses be returned, the Chinese made it known that they were armed and "threatened to shoot if an attempt was made to recover" them. Although the Chinese avoided bloodshed in that incident, as the boycott wore on they suffered mightily. By mid-December, many of the town's Chinese-owned businesses had either failed or were on the brink of bankruptcy. Discharged Chinese workers were out of money and facing a lean winter just a few miles from infamous Donner Pass, where forty years earlier American pioneers trapped by winter snows had resorted to cannibalism to survive. Fear of starvation sapped their resistance, and by December 16, ninety-eight Chinese had left Truckee. Frederick Bee, the Chinese consul in San Francisco, urged them to stay and fight, but the boycott was too strong. By mid-February 1886, seven hundred Chinese laborers in and around Truckee were "idle and destitute," and the Chinese began leaving in large numbers.[38]

Truckee's boycott was supported and strengthened by constant public displays organized by the town's Safety Committee. Regular mass meetings in public spaces, replete with incendiary speeches and "mammoth bonfires," helped to maintain a high level of enthusiasm and involvement. Torchlight processions through the Chinese quarter at night served the same purpose and also served as a constant reminder to the Chinese of their powerlessness and the precariousness of their predicament. The Safety Committee also created a "secret league" whose purpose was to resort to force in the event the Chinese refused to leave. The existence of the secret league helped to contain the violent tendencies of the Truckee mob by fostering the impression that violence was already being planned. But the league served

This cartoon from *The Wasp*, published in 1878, previews arguments made throughout the 1880s that the Chinese were a menace whose presence was sustained by white patronage of their businesses. Note the panel at center left showing a Chinese laundryman blowing water on a client's clothes, a practice many whites believed was responsible for spreading disease. (*Wasp*, no. 93, pp. 648–649, Courtesy of the Bancroft Library, University of California, Berkeley.)

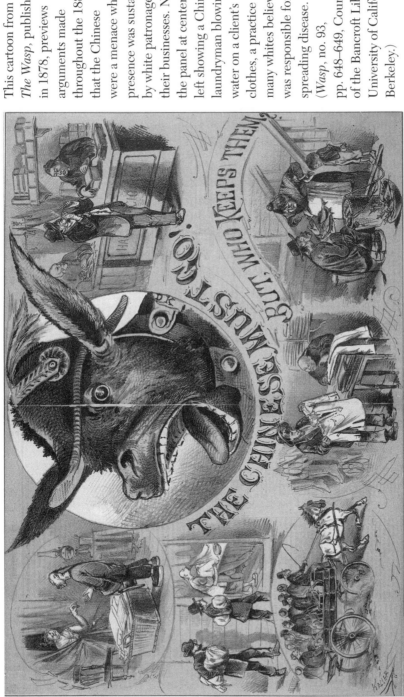

as a further reminder to the Chinese of what might lie ahead. All of this—the mass meetings, the bonfires, the constant warnings, the secret league, and the ever-present threat of violence—were strongly reminiscent of the behavior of the Ku Klux Klan in the South a decade earlier. In Truckee, just as in Alabama and elsewhere, displays of power, threats of terror, and racial animosity worked together to cow a racial minority into submission.[39]

Outside Truckee, life for the Chinese continued to deteriorate. On January 18, 1886, Captain Jesse Wickersham and his wife were murdered at their Sonoma ranch. A Chinese man named Ang Tai Duck, who had worked for the Wickershams as a cook, was widely believed to be the murderer. He fled the country, and for several weeks newspapers treated Californians to an international manhunt and endless recapitulations of the dreadful crime. Meanwhile, Californians read regular reports of continued Chinese immigration using the now-suspect red certificates. Such publicity kept the expulsion movement alive, and towns all over the state followed the example set in Truckee by forming expulsion committees. In February, the towns of Galt, Livermore, Napa, Santa Rosa, San Jose, Placerville, Traver, Yreka, Red Bluff, and Los Angeles all followed suit. In all, at least thirty-five California towns moved toward expelling their Chinese residents during the crisis. California's racial Reconstruction was being matched by a physical reconstruction.[40]

While each of these movements took notice of other, similar activities around the state, each was spontaneous; there was no central entity organizing a Chinese Expulsion Movement. Some Californians saw the lack of central arrangement as a weakness and called for a state convention for the purpose of coordinating the disparate activities of each local movement. In early February 1886, one hundred delegates from around the state met at San Jose to discuss the issue. Charles McGlashan, whose success in leading the Truckee movement had earned him statewide fame as "hero of Truckee," capitalized on his success by winning election as the convention president. Calling themselves the "Non-Partisan Anti-Chinese Association," the delegates decided to meet again as an even larger group in Sacramento the following month. At that meeting, delegates addressed a lengthy and rambling tract to President Grover Cleveland and the U.S. Congress calling for official approval of their movement. In it, the delegates offered justifications for their movement and rededicated themselves to their course of orderly expulsions, which they described as free of mob action and violence. Even as the delegates made this pledge, however, events moved beyond them and out of their control, and the movement shifted back to the chaos and violence that had characterized events in Eureka and Tacoma.[41]

Nicolaus and Baldwin v. Franks

On February 6, 1886, the Anti-Chinese Club of the small town of Nicolaus, just north of Sacramento in Sutter County, "formed itself in solemn procession and waited on the Chinese" living in and around the town. Those Chinese who owned no property were ordered to leave town within ten days. Chinese property owners were given thirty days to settle their affairs and get out. In the mid-1880s, many of the Chinese living in Nicolaus worked on the hop farms surrounding the town. The owners of five of these farms received letters threatening them with death if they did not immediately discharge their Chinese workers. To this point, events in Nicolaus followed the established pattern of boycott, intimidation, and threats of violence. But twelve days later, whites in Nicolaus broke with that pattern and resorted to actual violence.[42]

In the early morning hours of February 18, 1886, masked white men charged through Nicolaus's Chinese quarter, firing revolvers and sending "terror through all Chinatown." Some of the masked men raided five hop farms near the town whose owners had refused to discharge their Chinese employees. The mob rounded up the local Chinese laborers "barely giving time to pack up their blankets, and being careful that they did not pack up their money," and hustled them down to the bank of the Feather River. In all, forty-six Chinese laborers were herded aboard a barge tied up to the steamer *Knight* and held there until morning. The townspeople took up a collection and offered the steamer's master, Captain Hunter, $125 to transport the Chinese to Sacramento. Hunter declined the payment, but he accepted the Nicolaus refugees, and at noon, as the barge pushed off downriver, crowds lined the levee, cheering wildly and toasting David Redfield, the prime mover behind the Nicolaus expulsion.[43]

Later that same afternoon, the Nicolaus refugees arrived in Sacramento and disappeared into the city's Chinatown. Local newspapers reported that "their advent seemed to create a very depressed feeling among the residents." Depressed did not mean defeated, however. Three days later, Ching-Ping, the Chinese vice consul based in San Francisco, arrived in Nicolaus to investigate the expulsion. He had been very active in recent weeks, traveling about the state and gathering evidence on the expulsion movement in preparation for a formal protest to the U.S. government. He had been on his way to Red Bluff when the events at Nicolaus unfolded. In Nicolaus, Ching-Ping met with the seven Chinese merchants who had managed to escape the purge and was apparently greatly distressed by the change in tone implied by the Nicolaus expulsion. The Chinese response to the expulsion movement rapidly shifted from piecemeal resistance to a coordinated legal defense of Chinese rights. The Chinese vice consul encouraged two of the Chinese expelled from Nicolaus, John Sing and Sing Lee, to file formal complaints with the local U.S. marshal.[44]

On March 12, 1886, Deputy Marshal J. C. Franks arrested twenty-one white men on charges of "conspiracy to violate the laws and treaties of the United States." The Nicolaus conspirators offered no resistance when Marshal Franks arrested them, and Franks returned the favor by treating them gently. In sharp contrast to the harsh treatment the Chinese had received in Nicolaus, the white conspirators enjoyed a rather sumptuous incarceration. The prisoners were saved from the damp of a river barge and instead made the trip to Sacramento in "road vehicles." Once in town, they were treated to "supper at a restaurant," and then taken to the Windsor Hotel where they were "made as comfortable as possible." Their case had generated no small amount of interest, and judging by their reception at Sacramento and the legal talent that quickly descended upon the town, their cause was widely supported.[45]

The strength of the Chinese case was bolstered by the cooperation of two hop farmers, Julius Orth and Patrick Carroll, whose farms had been raided on February 18. According to local papers, it was upon their "instigation" that warrants had been sworn out against the Nicolaus conspirators. The two men had received death threats, and their public alliance with the Chinese legation did not endear them to the local anti-Chinese club. Their reputations were repeatedly savaged in the press and in public meetings. This confrontation between the hop farmers and the anti-Chinese club was much more than a local feud. It was, instead, emblematic of a larger rift developing in the expulsion movement. The cooperation between hop farmers and the Chinese legation marked the limits of the alliance between workers and businessmen, and so marked the beginning of the end of the expulsion movement as a whole.

Of the two farmers, Patrick Carroll was the more vocal in defending his actions. Several days after the Nicolaus expulsion, Carroll traveled to Sacramento, where he spoke with a representative of the *Daily Record-Union*. Carroll professed himself in close agreement with the racial ideals that motivated the expulsion movement. He was careful to voice his wish to see "all Chinese labor replaced with white labor as fast as it can possibly be brought about," but he saw real danger in the events at Nicolaus. The sudden departure of the Chinese, he told the reporter, meant "that hop-raising will probably have to be given up" in Nicolaus, and that most likely fruit growers would have to suspend operations as well. Chinese labor was crucial to the survival of local farmers, "as there cannot, at once, be found white laborers sufficient who are experienced." And, he added, it would not be just farmers who suffered. If the farms failed, argued Carroll, a ripple effect would "create a shock to many prominent industries in the State," throwing many more out of work. The shift from Chinese to white labor, insisted Carroll, must be made slowly "without injury to our industries, and our people."[46]

The expulsion movement had been successful in California's cities and larger towns because of the presence of surplus white labor. In other words, white Californians in cities and larger towns were for the most part insulated from labor shortages and so had the luxury of acting upon their racial ideas. White workingmen facing direct competition from Chinese laborers easily found common ground with small, local businessmen facing competition from larger corporations that employed Chinese labor. When the expulsion movement reached rural California, however, the Chinese Exclusion Act again worked to increase the power of Chinese workers by artificially restricting the labor supply. Farmers who relied on Chinese labor simply could not afford to indulge a movement that might strip an entire region of all farmworkers, however much they might agree with the racial principles behind the movement. In 1886, as winter turned to spring, the momentum of the expulsion movement simply disappeared into California's sparsely populated farm regions.

Yet even as the power of the movement dissipated in the hinterland, expulsion remained a potent force for reconstructing California. Many towns across the state were now a physical reflection of the racial rhetoric that had come to define the Chinese as an alien infection. For those few Chinese in the larger towns yet to be alienated, the diffusion of the expulsion movement in other parts of the state offered little comfort; for those whose homes had been lost, it offered none at all. In the more populated areas of the state, the potential for violence was no less diminished, and the need for a vigorous defense of Chinese lives, rights, and property was no less urgent. As the struggle over expulsion moved into the courts, Californians once again readied for a loud and difficult argument over the extent to which federal Reconstruction would reach into their state.

The Nicolaus conspirators were represented by former state Attorney General Augustus L. Hart and Grover Johnson, a major figure in the anti-Chinese movement. The Chinese plaintiffs were nominally represented by an apparently reluctant U.S. attorney with political aspirations named Samuel Hilborn. Perhaps sensing his reluctance, the Chinese retained private counsel, first through the Sacramento law firm of Armstrong and Hinkson and later through Hall McAllister, who had long defended Chinese interests while on retainer with the Chinese Six Companies. Throughout the case, U.S. Attorney Hilborn assumed a wholly passive role and essentially ceded control of the case to McAllister, most likely in an effort to protect his political future. Neither the state of California nor the federal government played a prominent role in arguing what would become *Baldwin v. Franks* once the case reached the U.S. Supreme Court. From the beginning, the case really belonged to the Chinese consulate, and the strategy pursued in the case reflected Chinese desires.[47]

The Chinese revealed their strategy at a March 16 preliminary hearing when vague charges of conspiracy listed in the warrants were exchanged for the more specific charge of having violated Section 5519 of the Civil Rights Act of 1871. Congress had enacted that section to curb the terror visited upon blacks in the South by the Ku Klux Klan, making it illegal to "conspire, or go in disguise on the highway or on the premises of another, for the purposes of depriving, either directly or indirectly, any person or class of persons of the equal protection of the laws." The statute appeared to fit the events at Nicolaus perfectly, but there was one problem: the statute had been declared unconstitutional in a Tennessee case three years earlier. In *United States v. Harris*, a group of whites had been convicted of assaulting a group of blacks. The U.S. Supreme Court had overturned the statute on the ground that criminal acts of this sort, between private citizens, violated state laws and were properly under the jurisdiction of the states and not the federal government. The Chinese, however, argued that their status as subjects of Imperial China, as opposed to citizens of the United States, presented a very different set of circumstances and might revive the statute. The federal government, as a signatory of treaties with China, was obligated to protect Chinese subjects in its jurisdiction, and that obligation, they argued, trumped the barriers erected by federalism.[48]

This argument represented a departure from the traditional Chinese legal strategy. While Chinese legal arguments had often made reference to treaty rights and protections, such considerations had always played a secondary role in their struggle against racially discriminatory laws. Those laws supported and perpetuated a set of racial ideas that had for decades defined the Chinese as unworthy of participation in the white American polity and, later, as an alien contamination. Chinese opposition to the laws had been shaped by their opposition to the ideas the laws supported. Undermining those ideas required a legal strategy that emphasized the similarities between Chinese immigrants and white Americans while brushing aside their differences. This goal lay at the heart of the invidious distinctions that the Chinese had drawn between themselves and black and Indian Californians during the 1850s, as well as more generous comparisons between the Chinese and American civilizations. The strategy had grown increasingly important as the metaphors of contagion that defined the Chinese not only outside the white polity but beyond the human race gained in strength. Now, however, facing expulsion from California, the Chinese suddenly embraced their status as political aliens.

Rather than try each of the twenty-one Nicolaus conspirators, lawyers on both sides agreed to allow one to stand for all of them. On March 30, 1886, Thomas Baldwin appeared before Circuit Judge Lorenzo Sawyer and Nevada District Judge George M. Sabin, who occasionally traveled to California to help Justices Sawyer and Hoffman with their caseloads. Before the court, Hall McAllister pressed the Chinese argument that international treaties concluded between the United States and China required the intervention of the federal government in the event that the rights of Chinese subjects were impaired. National honor demanded that Section 5519 be revived to protect the Chinese and end the expulsions. Baldwin's lawyers countered by staking out a standard states' rights position. The Chinese argument, they insisted, struck directly at state sovereignty. Siding with the Chinese in this instance would effectively remove all cases involving the Chinese from state jurisdiction and hinder the state's ability to police its own people.[49]

Judge Sawyer was convinced by the Chinese argument. The Chinese argument rested, in part, on questions of national honor and so fit neatly with the reasoning California's federal judges had long employed in the Chinese habeas corpus cases. The Nicolaus conspiracy, he said, "is a matter not merely of State but international concern . . . and may well involve the question of peace or war." "The United States government," he continued, "has imposed upon itself . . . an express obligation to exert all its powers . . . to protect Chinese residents." Of this much, Sawyer was certain, but the statute as written posed a constitutional problem, and that problem led Sabin to dissent. While Sawyer held that Section 5519 applied to the Chinese, it also clearly encompassed people other than the Chinese—namely, American citizens—and it was on these grounds that the Supreme Court had struck it down. The question that remained before the court was whether the constitutional part dealing with the Chinese could be separated from the unconstitutional part dealing with citizens. On this point, both Sawyer and Sabin were uncertain. Saying that "the questions now presented are of too great consequence to be finally decided by a subordinate court," Sawyer encouraged the defendant to appeal his decision to the U.S Supreme Court. Baldwin did just that in less than a month.[50]

In spite of the urgency felt in California over the expulsion movement, the U.S. Supreme Court took a full year to decide the case. The Court was in the awkward position of potentially offering legal remedies to Chinese immigrants that were unavailable to American citizens. Once again the West's racial diversity offered a bizarre twist to Reconstruction. The discriminatory laws that barred Chinese from naturalization might very well press the federal government into a defense of their rights and property. Meanwhile, the citizenship so highly prized by black Americans actually limited the ability of the federal government to protect them. Writing for the majority, Chief Justice Morrison Waite declined to be caught in such a dilemma. While conceding that treaty obligations required the federal government to protect the Chinese, Waite declined to read Section 5519 in a way that rendered it constitutional with regard to them. "A single provision," he wrote, "which makes up the whole section, embraces those who conspire against citizens as well as those who conspire against aliens." Because, in other words, the statute was all of a piece, "the limitation which is sought," insisted Waite, "must be made, if at all, by construction, not by separation." This would amount to making new law, which the Court was loath to do. With that, the prosecution of the Nicolaus conspirators came to an end, and the expulsion movement came to a close.[51]

Conclusion

Reactions to the decision in *Baldwin v. Franks* were mixed. The Court's decision effectively exonerated Thomas Baldwin and his compatriots. Moreover, the decision allowed the expulsions in California to stand. In that sense at least, the decision was a victory for the expulsion movement, and anti-Chinese activists were elated. On the other side, the decision worried some white Californians. Former Californian Justice Stephen J. Field filed an alarmed dissent that took the majority to task for failing to uphold national obligations. "The result of this decision," wrote Field, "is, that there is no national law which can be invoked for the protection of the subjects of China." Field voiced concerns that were increasingly common in California. Some whites who had generally supported expulsions on the Truckee model had been dismayed by the events at Nicolaus. The expulsion movement had moved beyond the control of the state's more respectable citizens, and violence had resulted. Establishment newspapers like the *Daily Record-Union* and the *Daily Alta California*, hoping to avoid future vigilante violence, called upon Congress to provide for the protection of Chinese immigrants.[52]

In spite of the expulsion movement, the immigration problems that had precipitated the movement remained. A chorus arose in California demanding that Congress close the loopholes that had made a mockery of the Chinese Exclusion Act. Following the decision in *Baldwin v. Franks*, U.S. representatives tried to renegotiate the treaty with China in an effort to stem the flow of immigrants. When protests in China stalled negotiations, Congress acted on its own. In October 1888, President Cleveland signed the Scott Act permanently barring Chinese laborers from entering the United States and nullifying the right of return. Those Chinese outside the United States holding return certificates were prohibited from reentering, regardless of family or property left behind. White Californians rejoiced at the passage of an exclusion law that had every prospect of success.[53]

The Scott Act ratified and perpetuated the judgment of the Chinese embedded in the metaphors of contagion. By singling out one racial group for exclusion, the Scott Act worked to train up future generations in the belief that the Chinese were little more than an alien contagion. Over time, some Chinese returned to the towns from which they had been expelled, but the majority clung to the safety of Chinatowns in cities like San Francisco, Sacramento, Stockton, and Los Angeles. In sparsely populated rural areas where Chinese labor was still crucial to the health of California's booming agricultural economy, a small and unthreatening Chinese population persisted. But in the coming decades, an isolated and dwindling Chinese population served as a physical reminder of the ideas that defined them as utterly incompatible with white civilization. In this sense, the exclusion acts of 1882, 1888, and, later, 1892 rendered the ideas that informed them to be self-fulfilling prophecies.

Conclusion

WHILE THE EXPULSION MOVEMENT in California may have evaporated in the dry heat of the state's agricultural districts, the racial sentiments and conflicts that had informed the movement persisted, and Californians continued to harvest its bitter fruit for years to come. In 1891, two white men, neighbors in the southern California coastal town of Ventura, found their affairs poisoned by that very fruit. Five years earlier, in March 1886, just as the expulsion movement was winding down, a Mr. Steward had sold a portion of the land he owned along Ventura's Main Street to a Mr. Gandolfo. The deed by which the land was conveyed contained within it a curious agreement that had been hammered out between the two men:

> It is also understood and agreed by and between the parties hereto, their heirs and assigns, that the party of the first part shall never, without the consent of the party of the second part, his heirs or assigns, rent any of the buildings or ground owned by said party of the first, and fronting on said East Main street, to a Chinaman or Chinamen. . . . And said party of the second part agrees for himself and heirs that he will never rent any of the property hereby conveyed to a Chinaman or Chinamen.

As part of the deed to the land, their agreement amounted to a legal covenant, a restriction on the use of the land covered by the deed that would continue to bind whoever possessed the deed no matter how many times it or the land changed hands. Some time later, Mr. Steward sold the remainder of his land to a Mr. Hartman. Not long after he had purchased the land, Hartman, who was either unaware of or uninterested in the agreement between Steward and Gandolfo, proposed to lease his land to two Chinese men, Fong Yet, and Sam Choy. When Gandolfo got wind of the impending lease, he sued, and everyone concerned wound up in California's Southern District Federal Court facing Judge Erskine Ross.[1]

On numerous occasions, most recently in *Baldwin v. Franks*, the courts had made clear to white Californians that the Fourteenth Amendment barred state and local governments from enacting laws that discriminated on the basis of race. By 1891, this was supposed to be a settled matter of law. And yet at the same time, again most recently in *Baldwin v. Franks*, the courts had declared that the power of the Fourteenth Amendment did not reach the actions of private individuals. Gandolfo argued that the racial covenant that he and Steward had signed was a private agreement, a private contract, between two private individuals, and so passed constitutional muster. Furthermore, according to Gandolfo, in accepting the deed, Hartman had willingly become party to the covenant embedded in it. Judge Ross disagreed. In his brusque decision issued in January 1892, Ross argued, "It would be a very narrow construction of the constitutional amendment in question . . . to hold that, while state and municipal legislatures are forbidden to discriminate against the Chinese in their legislation, a citizen of the state may lawfully do so by contract, which the courts may enforce. Such a view is, I think, entirely inadmissible." In other words, while the state could not prosecute private individuals for acts of discrimination, neither could it support them in the commission of those acts. The covenant, therefore, according to Judge Ross, was "absolutely void, and should not be enforced in any court."[2]

The practice of expressing these sorts of private agreements in racial covenants was, in some ways, the next logical step in a long process that saw legal struggles over race slowly shift from state legislation to municipal ordinance to neighborhood convention, and from public act to private arrangement. In this sense, racial covenants might be seen as one endpoint in the legal battles that described California's long racial trajectory. Nearly half a century earlier, white Americans arriving in California had been confronted by the most racially diverse population they had ever encountered. Beginning with the state constitution of 1849, white Californians established a crude yet powerful racial hierarchy that divided the state's population into two broad racial categories: white and nonwhite. The state legislature strengthened and extended that division over the next several years through the passage of laws designed to banish nonwhites to the political, legal, and social margins of California society, reserving control over the public sphere and the trappings of power and status for the sole benefit of whites. Beginning in the 1860s, however, events outside California challenged whites' ability to maintain the stability of their racial regime, particularly when it came to the law. Loyalty to the Union during the Civil War weakened many white Californians' commitment to racial exclusion and opened significant gaps in the ideological defense of white supremacy. The legal stability of California's racial regime was threatened further by the passage of federal Reconstruction legislation following the war. Most important of all, California's nonwhite minorities mounted a sustained assault on white privilege by drawing Reconstruction west. That assault aimed first at state laws that supported racial discrimination, such as the laws barring nonwhite testimony in state courts, and later at local ordinances that sought cooperation between city governments and whole neighborhoods, such as the laundry licensing laws passed in San Francisco, Modesto, Stockton, and other towns around the state. By the time Mr. Gandolfo hauled his neighbor into court, the legal limits of racial discrimination had been drawn and redrawn so often that private agreements may have appeared as the only remaining option.

Of course, *Gandolfo v. Hartman* did not spell the end of legal discrimination in California. In spite of Judge Ross's decision in 1892 and all the decisions that had come before, white Californians continued to fashion legislation designed to maintain white supremacy. White Californians continued to write racial covenants into real estate deeds. The "separate but equal" principle established in *Ward v. Flood* survived well into the twentieth century. State and federal laws barring the naturalization of nonwhites also persisted for decades. California's Alien Land Act, passed in 1913 and aimed largely at Japanese immigrants, limited the right to own land in the state solely to those who were eligible for citizenship. Chinese exclusion laws also continued to block Chinese immigration until World War II. In 1964, Proposition 14, a statewide ballot measure designed to allow racial discrimination in housing, passed by a two-thirds majority, only to be overturned by the courts three years later. And yet, through it all, these efforts to shore up California's racial regime were shaped by the weight of the past. California's experience with Reconstruction had established limits upon the sorts of legal disabilities that might be visited upon racial minorities, and even as they sought to evade them, white Californians were forced to acknowledge those limits.[3]

As Californians articulated the legal boundaries of racial discrimination, they also reordered and refined their ideas about race. Nonwhites' assault on whites' legal regime collapsed the crude binary distinction between white and nonwhite, and in the process redefined each racial group's status as well as the qualities and characteristics popularly supposed to be associated with each racial group. By the end of the nineteenth century, whites, who had once had sole possession of the qualities necessary for proper self-government, shared political power with black citizens. Black Californians had seen a dramatic improvement in the range of rights and privileges available to them but still suffered from persistent legal disabilities and prejudices that held them back from full inclusion in California society. The Chinese, whose labor had done so much to advance California's fortunes, had been defined first as unworthy of inclusion in California society and then as unworthy even of inclusion in the ranks of humanity. California Indians, under federal protection, finally halted their precipitous decline and began a long, painful recovery. For each racial group, the broad categories that had defined their place in California in the 1850s were replaced by a much more complicated scheme.

These new racial conceptions were hardly the elements of a coherent, stable racial ideology. They were instead a slippery and uncomfortable patchwork of shoddy science, history, political ideology, and economic self-interest. And yet it was precisely this imprecision that gave California's racial hierarchy its flexibility and hence a kind of stability that allowed it to survive longer than it otherwise would have. This flexibility allowed whites to maintain and justify their dominance of the state's racial hierarchy by adjusting the basis for their justification according to the shifting sands of circumstance. At the same time, California's nonwhite minorities marshaled the spaces opened by those shifting justifications in the service of demands for greater inclusion. Those demands often spawned competition between non-white minorities for status and position, and in the process actually helped strengthen the state's racial structure by implicitly conceding the legitimacy of racial distinctions. California's racial hierarchy was, then, a hierarchy always in flux, its stability paradoxically grounded in inherent instability.

The shape of the racial hierarchy, and the meaning it gave to ideas about race and to Californians' lives varied from day to day, and from place to place, and it continued to vary as California passed through the crises and triumphs of the twentieth century. The hierarchy that Californians developed in the nineteenth century shaped the state's reaction to the waves of emigration from Mexico following the Mexican Revolution in the 1920s and throughout the twentieth century. The ideas embedded in the hierarchy developed in the nineteenth century also shaped Californians' reactions to the "Okie" migration of the 1930s, the upheavals of the war years of the 1940s, the tensions of the civil rights movements of the 1950s and 1960s, and the arrival of immigrants from Southeast Asia after 1965. As Proposition 187 in 1994 made clear, the legacy of California's nineteenth century racial past continues to press upon the present.[4]

That legacy, however, is not limited to California. Even as nineteenth-century Californians were articulating the legal boundaries of racial discrimination and spinning ever more elaborate racial fantasies, they were also playing a significant role in interpreting the meaning of Reconstruction not only for themselves but for the rest of the nation. The legal cases brought by California's nonwhite minorities, particularly in federal courts, but also in state courts, shaped life and law for all Americans. And as the consequences of the California cases reached other states, they carried with them many of the racial patterns established in California.

In the early twentieth century, rural distress and the lure of higher paying industrial jobs drew black southerners first to southern cities and then to cities in the North. Whites across the country reacted by passing municipal ordinances that sought to limit blacks' access to jobs and housing, ordinances that closely mirrored those that Californians had aimed at Chinese immigrants only a few years earlier. When both state and federal courts, drawing largely on precedents established in California cases, struck down those laws, racial discrimination in American cities turned in a more private direction, and here *Gandolfo v. Hartman* again becomes relevant. As the first recorded case involving a racial covenant in the United States, *Gandolfo v. Hartman* may very well have been the catalyst for the sudden appearance of racial covenants in every state in the Union. In spite of the fact that a federal judge had ruled such contracts unconstitutional, Americans across the nation embraced racial covenants during the first three decades of the twentieth century as a means of evading the prohibition against racial discrimination embodied in Reconstruction legislation. Black Americans regularly challenged these laws, but again and again Judge Ross's decision in the Ventura, California, case was ignored as judges in city after city, state after state, deployed the power of government in the enforcement of discriminatory contracts between private individuals. As a result, California's racial experience cast a terrible shadow eastward.[5]

When nonwhites in California drew Reconstruction west, they could hardly have anticipated the consequences that their decisions would have for the rest of the nation. Their intentions were much more immediate and local. Even so, their actions deeply influenced the future course of American history. By drawing southern Reconstruction west, California's racial minorities also made Reconstruction a national rather than a regional issue, and so they rendered the failures of Reconstruction a national rather than a regional tragedy. This is perhaps their most important contribution to the story of Reconstruction. The history of Reconstruction in California should not be seen as a lesser chapter grafted onto the "real" story that took place in the American South. The California experience was instead central to a drama that had national implications for the future of American race relations.

The traditional narrative casts southern Reconstruction as a tragic failure, a moment of great promise that ultimately went unfulfilled. In that telling, once federal troops withdrew, the South turned from Reconstruction to Redemption and slipped into the eighty-year nightmare that was Jim Crow. But when viewed through the lens of

California's experience, our understanding of the meaning of Reconstruction is shifted in an entirely new direction. Lifting Reconstruction out of its regional context recasts the southern experience as a kind of racial misdirection, and the Jim Crow South suddenly has much less to say about the nation's racial future than do the patterns established in California. While the South lay trapped in a bitterly static confrontation between black and white, the rest of the nation underwent a profound demographic transformation. By the time of the Civil Rights era of the 1950s and 1960s, the racial composition of the American population mirrored that of nineteenth-century California, and the adjustments that accompanied that transformation conformed more closely to patterns established in California than those established in the American South.

It has become a cliché to say that Americans who wish to see their future should look to California. Like all clichés, this one contains a kernel of truth, but at the same time it hides a deeper truth. California has, since Americans first took possession of it, been central to American destiny in ways few other states, or even regions, can match. While imagining the future might be an amusing diversion, understanding the present is an absolute necessity, and here California is equally important to national destiny. As California's experience with Reconstruction shows, if Americans wish to understand not merely who they will be, but who they are now, they should look to California.

Notes

Introduction

1. Charles Loring Brace, *The Life of Charles Loring Brace, Chiefly Told in His Own Letters*, edited by Emma Brace (New York: Scribner's Sons, 1894), 286; Charles Loring Brace, *The New West; Or, California in 1867–1868* (New York: G. P. Putnam and Son, 1869), 37–52. Brace had also earned fame as an advocate for New York City's poor and indigent and as the primary mover behind the infamous "orphan trains" of the mid-nineteenth century.

2. Brace, *The New West*, 81–100.

3. Ibid., 88, 367–70. See also Charles Loring Brace, *The Races of the Old World: A Manual of Ethnology* (New York: Charles Scribner, 1863), v.

4. Brace, *The New West*, 137–46, 209–17, 285.

5. Ibid., 213.

6. The literature on Southern Reconstruction is vast and far too large to treat thoroughly here. To trace the ideas that helped form the arguments presented in this book, see W. E. B. DuBois, *Black Reconstruction: An Essay toward a History of the Part Which Black Folk Played in the Attempt to Reconstruct Democracy in America, 1860–1880* (New York: Russell and Russell, 1935); Kenneth Stampp, *The Era of Reconstruction, 1865–1877* (New York: Knopf, 1965); Leon F. Litwack, *Been in the Storm So Long: The Aftermath of Slavery* (New York: Knopf, 1979); Eric Foner, *Nothing but Freedom: Emancipation and Its Legacy* (Baton Rouge: Louisiana State University Press, 1983), and *Reconstruction: America's Unfinished Revolution, 1863–1877* (New York: Harper and Row, 1988); Michael Perman, *The Road to Redemption: Southern Politics, 1869–1879* (Chapel Hill: University of North Carolina Press, 1984); Laura F. Edwards, *Gendered Strife and Confusion: The Political Culture of Reconstruction* (Urbana: University of Illinois Press, 1997); Stephen David Kantrowitz, *Ben Tillman and the Reconstruction of White Supremacy* (Chapel Hill: University of North Carolina Press, 2000); and *Reconstructions: New Perspectives on the Postbellum United States*, ed. Thomas J. Brown (New York: Oxford University Press, 2006).

7. Various approaches to the study of white supremacy may be found in Winthrop Jordan, *White over Black: American Attitudes toward the Negro, 1550–1802* (Chapel Hill: Published for the Institute of Early American History and Culture at Williamsburg, Va., by the University of North Carolina Press, 1968); Edmund Morgan, *American Slavery, American Freedom: The Ordeal of Colonial Virginia* (New York: Norton, 1975); George Frederickson, *White Supremacy: A*

Comparative Study in American and South African History (New York: Oxford University Press, 1981); Alexander Saxton, *The Rise and Fall of the White Republic: Class Politics and Mass Culture in Nineteenth-Century America* (New York: Verso, 1990); and David R. Roediger, *The Wages of Whiteness: Race and the Making of the American Working Class* (New York: Verso, 1991).

8. On the economic effects of Northern Reconstruction, see Stanley Coben, "Northeastern Business and Radical Reconstruction: A Reexamination," *Mississippi Valley Historical Review* 46 (June 1959): 67–90; David Montgomery, *Beyond Equality: Labor and the Radical Republicans, 1862–1872* (New York: Vintage, 1972), and *The Fall of the House of Labor: The Workplace, the State, and American Labor Activism, 1865–1925* (Cambridge: Cambridge University Press, 1987); Foner, *Reconstruction*, esp. chap. 10; Grace Palladino, *Another Civil War: Labor, Capital, and the State in the Anthracite Regions of Pennsylvania, 1840–1868* (Urbana: University of Illinois Press, 1990); and Sven Beckert, *The Monied Metropolis: New York City and the Consolidation of the American Bourgeoisie, 1850–1896* (Cambridge: Cambridge University Press, 2001). On the rise of the post–Civil War state, see Martin J. Sklar, *The Corporate Reconstruction of American Capitalism, 1890–1916: The Market, the Law, and Politics* (Cambridge: Cambridge University Press, 1988); and Richard Franklin Bensel, *Yankee Leviathan: The Origins of Central State Authority in America, 1859–1877* (Cambridge: Cambridge University Press, 1990). See also Williamjames Hull Hoffer, *To Enlarge the Machinery of Government: Congressional Debates and the Growth of the American State, 1858–1891* (Baltimore: Johns Hopkins University Press, 2007). On Reconstruction's effects on women, gender, and society, see Anne Firor Scott, *Natural Allies: Women's Associations in American History* (Urbana: University of Illinois Press, 1992); Joan Waugh, *Unsentimental Reformer: The Life of Josephine Shaw Lowell* (Cambridge: Cambridge University Press, 1997); Rebecca Edwards, *Angels in the Machinery: Gender in American Party Politics from the Civil War to the Progressive Era* (New York: Oxford University Press, 1997); and Barbara Young Welke, *Recasting American Liberty: Gender, Race, Law, and the Railroad Revolution, 1865–1920* (Cambridge: Cambridge University Press, 2001). For Reconstruction in the West, see Eugene Berwanger, *The West and Reconstruction* (Urbana: University of Illinois Press, 1981); Bonnie Lynn-Sherow, *Red Earth: Race and Agriculture in Oklahoma Territory* (Lawrence: University Press of Kansas, 2004); Najia Aarim-Heriot, *Chinese Immigrants, African Americans, and Racial Anxiety in the United States, 1848–1882* (Urbana: University of Illinois Press, 2003); and Heather Cox Richardson, *West from Appomattox: The Reconstruction of America after the Civil War* (New Haven, Conn.: Yale University Press, 2007). See also Elliot West, "Reconstructing Race," *Western Historical Quarterly* 34, 1 (Spring 2003): 6–26.

9. On the social construction of race, see Michael Omi and Howard Winant, *Racial Formation in the United States from the 1960s to the 1980s* (New York:

Routledge and Kegan Paul, 1986). On California Indians, see Hubert Howe Bancroft, *History of California*, Vol. 7 (San Francisco, 1890), 474–94; Alfred L. Kroeber, *Types of Indian Culture in California* (Berkeley, Calif.: University Press, 1904); J. Ross Browne, *The Indians of California* (San Francisco, Calif.: Colt Press, 1944); Sherburne F. Cook, *The Population of the California Indians, 1769–1974* (Berkeley: University of California Press, 1976); George H. Phillips, *The Enduring Struggle: Indians in California History* (San Francisco: Boyd and Fraser, 1981); James J. Rawls, *Indians of California: The Changing Image* (Norman: University of Oklahoma Press, 1984); Albert Hurtado, *Indian Survival on the California Frontier* (New Haven, Conn: Yale University Press, 1988); Douglas Monroy, *Thrown among Strangers: The Making of a Mexican Culture in Frontier California* (Berkeley: University of California Press, 1990); Lizbeth Haas, *Conquests and Historical Identities in California, 1769–1936* (Berkeley: University of California Press, 1995); and Ferdinand F. Fernandez, "Except a California Indian: A Study in Legal Discrimination," *Southern California Quarterly* 50, 2 (Spring 1968): 161–75. On black Californians, see Delilah Beasley, *The Negro Trailblazers of California* (Los Angeles: Times Mirror Printing and Binding House, 1919); Rudolph M. Lapp, *Blacks in Gold Rush California* (New Haven, Conn.: Yale University Press, 1977); Douglas Henry Daniels, *Pioneer Urbanites: A Social and Cultural History of Black San Francisco* (Philadelphia: Temple University Press, 1980); and Quintard Taylor, *In Search of the Racial Frontier: African Americans in the American West, 1528–1990* (New York: W. W. Norton, 1998). On California's nineteenth-century Mexican population, see Josiah Royce, *California: A Study of American Character* (Boston: Houghton, Mifflin, 1886); Hubert Howe Bancroft, *History of California*, Vols. 5 and 6 (San Francisco, Calif.: History Company 1888); Theodore H. Hittell, *History of California*, Vol. 3 (San Francisco, Calif.: Pacific Press Publishing House, 1898); Joseph Ellison, *California and the Nation, 1850–1869: A Study of the Relations of a Frontier Community with the Federal Government* (Berkeley: University of California Press, 1927); William H. Ellison, *A Self-Governing Dominion: California, 1849–1860* (Berkeley: University of California Press, 1950); Leonard M. Pitt, *The Decline of the Californios: A Social History of the Spanish-Speaking Californians, 1846–1890* (Berkeley: University of California Press, 1966); Richard Griswold del Castillo, *The Los Angeles Barrio, 1850–1890: A Social History* (Berkeley: University of California Press, 1979); Rodolfo Acuna, *Occupied America: A History of Chicanos* (New York: Harper and Row, 1981); David J. Langum, *Law and Community on the Mexican California Frontier: Anglo-American Expatriates and the Clash of Legal Traditions, 1821–1846* (Norman: University of Oklahoma Press, 1987); Matt S. Meier and Feliciano Ribera, *Mexican Americans/American Mexicans: From Conquistadors to Chicanos* (New York: Hill and Wang, 1993); Juan Gomez-Quinones, *The Roots of Chicano Politics, 1600–1940* (Albuquerque: University of New Mexico Press, 1994); Monroy, *Thrown among Strangers*; and Haas, *Conquests and Historical*

Identities. And on Chinese immigrants in California, see Mary Roberts Coolidge, *Chinese Immigration* (New York: H. Holt and Co., 1909); Elmer Clarence Sandmeyer, *The Anti-Chinese Movement in California* (Urbana: University of Illinois Press, 1939); Gunther Barth, *Bitter Strength: A History of the Chinese in the United States, 1850–1870* (Cambridge, Mass.: Harvard University Press, 1964); Stuart Miller, *The Unwelcome Immigrant: The American Image of the Chinese, 1785–1882* (Berkeley: University of California Press, 1970); Stanford Lyman, *The Asian in the West* (Reno: University of Nevada System, Western Studies Center, Desert Research Institute, 1970); Sucheng Chan, *This Bittersweet Soil: The Chinese in California Agriculture, 1860–1910* (Berkeley: University of California Press, 1986); Ronald Takaki, *Strangers from a Different Shore: A History of Asian Americans* (New York: Penguin, 1990); and Yong Chen, *Chinese San Francisco, 1850–1943: A Trans-Pacific Community* (Stanford, Calif.: Stanford University Press, 2000).

10. On critical legal studies, see Derrick Bell, *Race, Racism, and American Law* (Boston: Little, Brown, 1992); and Ian Haney-López, *White by Law: The Legal Construction of Race* (New York: New York University Press, 1996).

Chapter 1. *"Every Colored Man Is the Victim"*

1. *People v. Hall*, 4 Cal. 399 (1854); *People v. Hall* Case File, WPA 7158, Supreme Court of California Records, California State Archives.

2. *People v. Hall* Case File, WPA 7158, Supreme Court of California Records, California State Archives. The case file reveals that John Hall was acquitted of murder charges, but no record of the outcome of Wiseman's trial remains. *Statutes of California* 1850, ch. 99, § 14. The exclusion of black and Indian testimony against whites in criminal cases was matched in civil cases by a section in the "Act Concerning Civil Cases," *Statutes of California* 1851, ch. 5 title 11, ch. 1, § 394.

3. On the development of California's legal system, see Gordon Morris Bakken, *Practicing Law in Frontier California* (Lincoln: University of Nebraska Press, 1991), and his *The Development of Law in Frontier California: Civil Law and Society, 1850–1890* (Westport, Conn.: Greenwood, 1985); Hubert Howe Bancroft, *History of California*, Vol. 7 (San Francisco: History Company, 1890), 191–219; and Martin Ridge, "Disorder, Crime, and Punishment in the California Gold Rush," in *Riches for All: The California Gold Rush and the World*, ed. Kenneth N. Owens (Lincoln: University of Nebraska Press, 2002). On the mixing of Spanish, Mexican, and American legal traditions, see Richard R. Powell, *Compromises of Conflicting Claims: A Century of California Law, 1760–1860* (Dobbs Ferry, N.Y.: Oceans Publications, 1977); and Paul Kens, *Justice Stephen J. Field: Shaping Liberty from the Gold Rush to the Gilded Age* (Lawrence: University Press of Kansas, 1997), 74. On the development of mining law, see Howard Shinn, *Mining Camps: A Study in American Frontier Government* (New York: Charles Scribner's Son, 1885).

4. On crime and vigilantism in Gold Rush California, see Hubert Howe Bancroft, *California Inter Pocula* (San Francisco: History Company, 1888), 582–657, 763–73; William Henry Ellison, *A Self-Governing Dominion: California, 1849–1860* (Berkeley: University of California Press, 1950), 192–233; Philip Ethington, *The Public City: The Political Construction of Urban Life in San Francisco, 1850–1900* (New York: Cambridge University Press, 1994); Ridge, "Disorder, Crime, and Punishment"; and Clare V. McKanna, *Race and Homicide in Nineteenth-Century California* (Reno: University of Nevada Press, 2002), and "Enclaves of Violence in Nineteenth-Century California," *Pacific Historical Review* 73, 3 (2004): 391–423.

5. On Field's difficulties with Judge Turner, see Kens, *Justice Stephen J. Field*, 32–35; and Bancroft, *History of California*, Vol. 7, 196–98. On David S. Terry, see Kens, *Justice Stephen J. Field*, 275–83.

6. *People v. Hall* Case File, WPA 7158.

7. *People v. Hall*, 4 Cal. 402, 399.

8. Edgar Camp Whittlesly, "Hugh C. Murray: California's Youngest Chief Justice," *California Historical Society Quarterly* 20, 4 (December 1941): 366–69; quote taken from *Harry Breen Scrapbooks*, 88 (California Historical Society).

9. *People v. Hall*, 4 Cal. 399–400.

10. For the most thorough discussion of these ideas and their development, see Reginald Horsman, *Race and Manifest Destiny: The Origins of American Racial Anglo-Saxonism* (Cambridge, Mass.: Harvard University Press, 1981). See also William Stanton, *The Leopard's Spots: Scientific Attitudes toward Race in America, 1815–59* (Chicago: University of Chicago Press, 1961); John S. Haller, Jr., *Outcasts from Evolution: Scientific Attitudes of Racial Inferiority, 1859–1900* (Urbana: University of Illinois Press, 1971); and Arthur O. Lovejoy, *The Great Chain of Being: A Study of the History of an Idea* (Cambridge, Mass.: Harvard University Press, 1942).

11. *People v. Hall*, 4 Cal. 401.

12. Allan Lonnberg, "The Digger Indian Stereotype in California," *Journal of California and Great Basin Anthropology* 3, 2 (1981): 217–18.

13. Quotes taken from *Penny Magazine of the Society for the Diffusion of Useful Knowledge* 3 (1834): 55; James H. Carson, "Early Recollections of the Mines," in *Bright Gem of the Western Seas: California, 1846–1852*, ed. Peter Browning (Lafayette, Calif.: Great West Books, 1991), 41; J. Lee Humfreville, "Early Recollections of the Mines," in *Bright Gem of the Western Seas: California, 1846–1852*, ed. Peter Browning (Lafayette, Calif.: Great West Books, 1991), 290; *Daily Alta California*, June 17, 1851. On the military response to Indian "hostilities," see Albert R. Hurtado, "Clouded Legacy: California Indians and the Gold Rush," in *Riches for All: The California Gold Rush and the World*, ed. Kenneth N. Owens (Lincoln: University of Nebraska Press, 2002), 90–117, and *Indian Survival on the California Frontier* (New Haven, Conn.: Yale University Press, 1988),

125–48. On California Indians as obstacles to white progress and on racial atti-
tudes toward California Indians in general, see James J. Rawls, *Indians of California: The Changing Image* (Norman: University of Oklahoma Press, 1984): xiv, 138,
186–201 passim. For the American popular image of the Indian, see Brian Dippie,
The Vanishing American: White Attitudes and U.S. Indian Policy (Middletown,
Conn.: Wesleyan University Press, 1982); Richard Slotkin, *Regeneration through
Violence: The Mythology of the American Frontier, 1600–1860* (Middletown,
Conn.: Wesleyan University Press, 1973), and *The Fatal Environment: The Myth
of the Frontier in the Age of Industrialization, 1800–1890* (New York: Atheneum,
1985). For the California Indians in general, see Alfred L. Kroeber, *Types of In-
dian Culture in California* (Berkeley: University Press, 1904); Douglas Monroy,
Thrown among Strangers: The Making of Mexican Culture in Frontier California
(Berkeley: University of California Press, 1990); and Ferdinand F. Fernandez,
"Except a California Indian: A Study in Legal Discrimination," *Southern California Quarterly* 50, 2 (Spring 1968): 161–75.

14. On the racial ideas that led to the policy of Indian removal, see John
P. Bowes, *Exiles and Pioneers: Eastern Indians in the Trans-Mississippi West*
(Cambridge: Cambridge University Press, 2007); Dippie, *The Vanishing* Ameri-
can, 45–78; Horsman, *Race and Manifest Destiny*, 189–228; and Arrell Morgan
Gibson, *The American Indian: Prehistory to the Present* (New York: D. C. Heath,
1980), 280–360.

15. On the role of California Indians as laborers, see Rawls, *Indians of California*, xiv passim; Hurtado, *Indian Survival on the California Frontier*, 24, 70–71,
197–98 passim. On the Act for the Government and Protection of Indians, see
Statutes of California, 1850, chap. 1033; Hurtado, *Indian Survival on the California Frontier*, 129–30; and Chauncey Shafter Goodrich, "The Legal Status of
the California Indian: Introductory," *California Law Review* 14 (1926): 91–93. An
1860 amendment to the law extended the period of indenture for Indian children
to thirty for boys over fourteen, and twenty-five for girls. See Goodrich, "The Legal Status of the California Indian," 94.

16. *People v. Hall*, 4 Cal. 404–405.

17. *People v. Hall*, 4 Cal. 403. On the inheritability of cultural characteristics
and the influence of Lamarck's theories, see Charles Loring Brace, *The New West:
Or, California in 1867–1868* (New York: G. P. Putnam, 1869), esp. 367–73.

18. On the racial definition of Californios in the California Constitution of
1849, see J. Ross Browne, *Report of the Debates in the Convention of California
on the Formation of the State Constitution* (Washington, D.C.: J. T. Towers, 1850),
63. For background on the Californios, see Leonard M. Pitt, *The Decline of the
Californios: A Social History of the Spanish-Speaking Californians, 1846–1890*
(Berkeley: University of California Press, 1966); Monroy, *Thrown among Strangers*; and Lizbeth Haas, *Conquests and Historical Identities in California, 1769–
1936* (Berkeley: University of California Press, 1995). For Californio support of

the testimony exclusions, see *California Assembly Journal*, 3rd Session, 1852, 395; 4th Session, 1853, 259; and 9th Session, 1858, 164.

19. Bancroft, *History of California,* Vol. 7, 474–75. On the destruction of Indian environmental resources, cycles of retaliation, and Indian decline, see Hurtado, "Clouded Legacy," 92–103, and *Indian Survival on the California Frontier,* 100–48 passim; Rawls, *Indians of California,* 138–215.

20. Delilah Beasley, *The Negro Trailblazers of California* (Los Angeles: Times Mirror Publishing and Binding Co., 1919), 60; Rudolph M. Lapp, "Negro Rights Activities in Gold Rush California," *California Historical Society Quarterly* 45, 1 (March 1966): 7; *Pacific Appeal,* May 8, 1863, and May 30, 1863.

21. *People v. W. H. Potter,* printed in David L. Snyder, *Negro Civil Rights in California: 1850* (Sacramento: California State Library, 1969). The case file from 1850 is equally clear about Ms. Carroll's race. Next to her name are printed the letters "f.w.c." which in early California court records stood for "free woman of color."

22. Mifflin W. Gibbs, *Shadow and Light: An Autobiography, with Reminiscences of the Last and Present Century* (Lincoln: University of Nebraska Press, 1995; original printing, 1902, n.p., 45–46). Beasley, *Negro Trailblazers,* 54–60. See also *(San Francisco) Daily Evening Bulletin,* February 4, 1857, and March 20 and 27, 1862.

23. On early meetings, see the *Pacific Appeal,* April 12, 1862, and James J. Fisher, "The Struggle for Negro Testimony in California, 1851–1863," *Southern California Quarterly* 51, 4 (December 1969): 315. *Proceedings of the First State Convention of the Colored Citizens of the State of California* (Sacramento: Democratic State Journal Printer, 1855; rpt. San Francisco: R and E Research Associates, 1969). Throughout the 1830s and 1840s, abolitionists had choked congressional calendars with petitions designed to both publicize their hatred for slavery and to challenge the gag rule created by Southerners unwilling to discuss slavery. See Samuel Flagg Bemis, *John Quincy Adams and the Union* (New York: Knopf, 1956), and William Lee Miller, *Arguing about Slavery: The Great Battle in the United States Congress* (New York: Knopf, 1996).

24. Colored Citizens of California, *Proceedings of the First State Convention,* 6, and Colored Citizens of California. *Proceedings of the Second Annual Convention of the Colored Citizens of the State of California* (San Francisco: J. H. Udell and W. Randall, 1856), 5. Anger at the first convention was especially pointed in part because of the conclusion of the *Levanter* case a week earlier. In that case, Judge Matthew Hall McAllister, of the U.S. Circuit Court in San Francisco, would not accept the testimony of a black witness to a murder aboard the ship *Levanter,* thus allowing the killer to grow free, which extended the reach of state law into the federal courts. See Dorothy H. Huggins, "Continuation of the Annals of San Francisco," *California Historical Society Quarterly* 16, 3 (September 1937): 285.

25. Colored Citizens of California. *Proceedings of the First State Convention,* 4–11. Yates's remarks outraged some delegates, and the following day he

amended them, adding the words "he is unable under existing circumstances to compete," after "Caucasian race."

26. *Sacramento Daily Union*, February 2, 1858.

27. For petitions received by the state legislature, see California. *California Senate Journal*, 8th Session, 1857, 285, and 9th Session, 1858, 149, 159, 238. See *Mirror of the Times*, August 22, 1857. On the relations between Irish and African Americans, see David R. Roediger, *The Wages of Whiteness: Race and the Making of the American Working Class* (New York: Verso, 1991); Noel Ignatiev, *How the Irish Became White* (New York: Routledge, 1995); and Matthew Frye Jacobson, *Whiteness of a Different Color: European Immigrants and the Alchemy of Race* (Cambridge, Mass.: Harvard University Press, 1998).

28. Quintard Taylor, *In Search of the Racial Frontier African Americans in the American West, 1528-1990* (New York: W. W. Norton, 1998), 122.

29. *Daily Alta California*, June 4, 1853, quoted in Charles Caldwell Dobie, *San Francisco's Chinatown* (New York: D. Appleton, 1936), 58. Frank Soule, John H. Gihon, and James Nesbitt, *The Annals of San Francisco* (San Francisco: D. Appleton, 1855), 378. *Remarks of Hon. J. E. Clayton, On the Chinese Question. Delivered in the Assembly Chamber, on the 8th of April, 1855*, in Horace Davis, ed., *Chinese Immigration Pamphlets*, Bancroft Library, University of California, Berkeley.

30. Chun Chuen Lai, *Remarks of the Chinese Merchants of San Francisco upon Governor Bigler's Message, and Some Common Objections With Some Explanations of the Character of the Chinese Companies and the Laboring Class of California* (San Francisco: Office of the Oriental, 1855), in Horace Davis, ed., *Chinese Immigration Pamphlets*, Bancroft Library, University of California, Berkeley. Governor Bigler's "Annual Message" to the state legislature had called for a halt to all Chinese immigration, and had included a highly legalistic argument urging the state to ignore federal immigration laws and treaty obligations. See California. *Appendix to the Assembly Journal*, 6th Session, 1855 (Sacramento: State Printing Office, 1855).

31. William D. Speer, *The Oldest and Newest Empire: China and the United States* (Hartford, Conn.: S. S. Scranton, 1870), 3.

32. Reverend William Speer, *An Answer to Common Objections to Chinese Testimony: And an Earnest Appeal to the Legislature of California for Their Protection by Our Law* (San Francisco: Chinese Mission House, 1857), 7–8. See also Reverend William Speer, *An Humble Plea, Addressed to the Legislature of California, in Behalf of Immigrants from the Empire of China to this State* (San Francisco: Office of the Oriental, 1856).

33. For race and the Democratic Party, see Ignatiev, *How the Irish Became White*, 68–70; Roediger, *The Wages of Whiteness*; Alexander Saxton, *The Rise and Fall of the White Republic: Class Politics and Mass Culture in Nineteenth-Century America* (New York: Verso, 1990); Jean H. Baker, *Affairs of Party: The Political*

Culture of the Northern Democrats in the Mid-Nineteenth Century (Ithaca, N.Y.: Cornell University Press, 1983). For the Democratic Party in California, see William H. Ellison, *A Self-Governing Dominion*. For reaction to the black petitions, see California, *Assembly Journal*, 3rd Session, 1852, 395; 4th Session, 1853, 259. Gibbs, *Shadow and Light*, 49; *Sacramento Daily Union,* February 3, 1858.

34. On the flight of black Californians, see Gibbs, *Shadow and Light*, 59; and Douglas Henry Daniels, *Pioneer Urbanites: A Social and Cultural History of Black San Francisco* (Philadelphia: Temple University Press, 1980), 45.

35. *(San Francisco) Daily Evening Bulletin*, Dec. 21, 1857. On the growth of the Republican Party in California, see W. Ellison, *A Self-Governing Dominion*; Gerald Stanley, "Slavery and the Origins of the Republican Party in California," *Southern California Quarterly* 60, 1 (Spring 1978): 1–16, and "The Slavery Issue and Election in California," *Mid-America* 62, 1 (Spring 1980): 35–45.

36. *(San Francisco) Daily Evening Bulletin*, April 8, 1857.

37. Pitt, *Decline of the Californios*, 202.

38. William Penn Moody, "The Civil War and Reconstruction in California Politics," Ph.D. diss., University of California, Los Angeles, 1950, 153, 166, 176–77.

39. Fay had known some fame in 1850 for having purchased a slave at an auction in Stockton and immediately setting him free. See the *Winfield J. Davis Scrapbooks*, Vol. 4, 207, Huntington Library.

40. Schell is sometimes referred to as "Rodney." The trial was followed by the press throughout the state, and the account here is drawn from various newspapers. See the San Francisco *Daily Evening Bulletin*, March 20 and 27, 1862; the *Sacramento Daily Union*, March 24 and 26, 1862; and the *Pacific Appeal*, April 5, 1862. See also Beasley, *Negro Trail Blazers*, 54. *(San Francisco) Daily Evening Bulletin*, April 24, 1862.

41. *Sacramento Daily Union*, March 26, 1862. Charles Maclay, *Speech Before the California Assembly for a Bill to Permit "Inferior Races" to Testify in Court* (April 1862), Charles Maclay Papers, MC 164, Huntington Library. Assembly bill 144 was intended to amend the testimony law with regard to criminal cases, and 145 was intended to do the same for civil cases.

42. *(San Francisco) Daily Evening Bulletin*, March 15, 1862. Wright's amendment would have allowed Chinese testimony and left acceptance or rejection of such testimony up to the jury. For the rest of the legislative session, Wright vigorously advocated repeal of the testimony laws relative to all excluded groups, and he opposed any measure that left Indians and Chinese out. The following year, Wright publicly acknowledged that his purpose had been to kill both bills by tying black testimony to Chinese. Better still, had Wright's amendment succeeded, it would have fatally undermined the extension of the right of testimony. Juries were required to accept unimpeached testimony, but Wright's amendment, in leaving acceptance or rejection to the jury, would have allowed juries

to disregard nonwhite testimony, impeached or not. See the *Sacramento Daily Union*, March 6, 1863.

43. *(San Francisco) Daily Evening Bulletin* March 15, 1862.

44. *Pacific Appeal*, June 7, 1862. For the petition, see *Blacks in California Petition, 1862*, MS 169A, California Historical Society, North Baker Research Library.

45. The term "Great Chain of Being" is taken from Linnaeus. See Lovejoy, *Great Chain of Being*.

46. *Sacramento Daily Union*, March 26, 1862.

47. For the labor system regarding Indians, see *An Act for the Government and Protection of Indians, California Statutes*, 1st Session, 1849–50, ch. 133, sec. 20. For the effects of the law, see Monroy, *Thrown among Strangers*, esp. chaps. 1 and 2.

48. *(San Francisco) Daily Evening Bulletin*, March 25, 1862; Frank M. Pixley, Respondent's Brief, *Lin Sing v. Washburn* 20 Cal. 534 (1862), Huntington Library.

49. Gerritt Lansing, "Chinese Immigration: A Sociological Study," *Popular Science Monthly*, April 1882, 721.

50. *Pacific Appeal*, May 24, 1862.

51. Ibid., April 12, 1862, and May 24, 1862.

52. *Mirror of the Times*, December 12, 1857; *Pacific Appeal*, June 7, 1862.

53. *(San Francisco) Daily Evening Bulletin*, March 13, 1862.

54. On the election and its results, see Bancroft, *History of California*, Vol. 7, 291, 295–96. For the brief debates regarding Perkins's bills, see the *(San Francisco) Daily Evening Bulletin* and the *Sacramento Daily Union*, January–March 1863.

55. *Pacific Appeal*, March 7 and 21, 1863.

56. *Sacramento Daily Union*, July 27, 1867.

57. *People v. George Washington* 30 Cal. 658 (1869). *People v. George Washington Case File*, Folder 1531, Supreme Court Records, California State Archives.

58. Ibid.

59. Ibid. The two cases, cited in the court's decision in *People v. George Washington* (36 Cal. 667) were *The United States v. John Rhodes et al.*, Am. Law. Reg., February 1868, and *Smith v. Moody*, 26 Ind. 299.

60. *People v. George Washington*, 36 Cal. 658, 662.

61. Ibid.

62. *People v. James Brady*, 40 Cal. 198 (1870).

63. Ibid., 208–11.

64. *Daily Alta California*, March 4, 1872; *Antioch Ledger*, March 16, 1872. On the riot in Los Angeles, see the *Sacramento Daily Union*, October 25–28, 1871, and Nov. 2, 1871; *Daily Alta California*, Oct. 26–27, 1871.

65. In 1872, California joined a movement begun in New York and simplified

its legal system by adopting the Field Codes. In the process, many superseded, outdated, and unpopular laws were repealed, among them the testimony law. No record of the deliberations of the California Code Commission remains pertaining to the decision with regard to the testimony laws.

Chapter 2. The Apostasy of Henry Huntley Haight

1. H. Brett Melendy and Benjamin F. Gilbert, *The Governors of California: Peter H. Burnett to Edmund G. Brown* (Georgetown, Calif.: Talisman Press, 1965), 144.

2. On the national reaction to Haight's election, see, for example, the acid reaction of the *Nation*, September 19, 1867. On California and the Civil War, see Joseph Ellison, *California and the Nation, 1850–1869* (Berkeley: University of California Press, 1927), 170–207.

3. Henry H. Haight, *Inaugural Address of H. H. Haight, Governor of the State of California, at the Seventeenth Session of the Legislature* (Sacramento: D. W. Gelwicks, State Printer, 1867), 5, 7, 9–10. On the progression of black enfranchisement, see Eugene H. Berwanger, *The West and Reconstruction* (Urbana: University of Illinois Press, 1981), 130.

4. Haight, *Inaugural Address of H. H. Haight,* 9–10.

5. On the suggestion that westerners were more concerned with local issues than with Reconstruction after 1867, see Berwanger, *West and Reconstruction*, 240–55. On Reconstruction as a national experience, see Stanley Coben, "Northeastern Business and Radical Reconstruction: A Reexamination," *Mississippi Valley Historical Review* 46 (June 1959): 67–90; Berwanger, *West and Reconstruction*; Eric Foner, *Reconstruction: America's Unfinished Revolution, 1863–1877* (New York: Harper and Row, 1988), esp. chap. 10; Alexander Saxton, *The Rise and Fall of the White Republic: Class Politics and Mass Culture in Nineteenth-Century America* (New York: Verso, 1990); Najia Aarim-Heriot, *Chinese Immigrants, African Americans, and Racial Anxiety in the United States, 1848–1882* (Urbana: University of Illinois Press, 2003); and Heather Cox Richardson, *West from Appomattox: The Reconstruction of America after the Civil War* (New Haven, Conn.: Yale University Press, 2007). On Californians' reaction to congressional Reconstruction, see the *Daily Alta California* editorial of Feb. 3, 1866, under the heading "The Manner in which we are being Reconstructed," and in general Berwanger, *West and Reconstruction*.

6. On pro-Union sentiment in California, see Winfield J. Davis, *History of Political Conventions in California, 1849–1892* (Sacramento: California State Library, 1893), 193, 214; and Hubert Howe Bancroft, *History of California*, Vol. 7 (San Francisco: History Company, 1890), 320.

7. On the Union Party in California, see Bancroft, *History of California*, Vol. 7, 291–327 passim. On Democratic bolters, see Davis, *Political Conventions*, 214.

8. Davis, *Political Conventions*, 216. The "short hairs" were so called because their political operatives were generally street toughs who kept their hair short for obvious reasons. Before the war, they had been the faithful and effective minions of Senator David C. Broderick, who had earned his political chops as a bare-knuckle politician in New York's Tammany Hall. It was against these toughs, and their head-knocking, ballot-stuffing style of politics, that San Francisco's Vigilance Committee had been formed. Their opponents were known as "long hairs," mostly for reasons of symmetry and not because of the length of their hair. See Philip Ethington, *The Public City: The Political Construction of Urban Life in San Francisco, 1850–1900* (New York: Cambridge University Press, 1994).

9. Davis, *Political Conventions*, 216.

10. Ibid., 217–18.

11. Ibid., 223.

12. For Lincoln's comments on his hopes for peace, see Carl Sandburg, *Abraham Lincoln: The War Years*, Vol. 4 (New York: Charles Scribner's Sons, 1949), 220. For the California State Legislature's reaction to Lincoln's plans for Reconstruction, see Davis, *Political Conventions*, 202–203. On San Franciscans' reaction to Lincoln's assassination, see Bancroft, *History of California*, Vol. 7, 311–12.

13. In his last speech before his death, Lincoln acknowledged the difficulties his plan had encountered in Louisiana, but he refused to accept failure and argued for staying the course. See Sandburg, *Abraham Lincoln: The War Years*, Vol. 4, 219–24.

14. On Johnson's threats to hang Confederates, see Sandburg, *Abraham Lincoln: The War Years*, Vol. 4, 189. On Benjamin Wade's comments, see p. 338 in the same volume.

15. For a more thorough discussion of these events, see Kenneth Stampp, *The Era of Reconstruction, 1865–1877* (New York: Knopf, 1965); Leon F. Litwack, *Been in the Storm So Long: The Aftermath of Slavery* (New York: Knopf, 1979); and Eric Foner, *Reconstruction*, esp. chaps. 3 and 4.

16. *Journal of the Senate of the United States of America*, 39th Congress, 1st Sess. 1865–1866 (Washington, D.C.: Government Printing Office, 1866), 10–23, quotes taken from 14–15.

17. On Reconstruction issues throughout the West, see Berwanger, *West and Reconstruction*; and Quintard Taylor, *In Search of the Racial Frontier: African Americans in the American West, 1528–1990* (New York: W. W. Norton, 1998), 103–29. The Radicals' plan was eventually incorporated into Section 2 of the Fourteenth Amendment.

18. *Daily Alta California*, Feb. 3, 1866.

19. On the ratio of men to women in California, see the *Daily Alta California*, Feb. 3, 1866; and Bancroft, *History of California*, Vol. 7, 699. For feelings of moderation among Californians, see *Daily Alta California*, Feb. 13, 1866.

20. For President Johnson's veto message concerning the Freedman's Bureau Bill, see *Journal of the Senate of the United States of America*, 39th Congress, 1st Sess., 1865–1866, 168–73, quote taken from 168. For Johnson's veto message concerning the civil rights bill, see ibid., 279–85.

21. For hopes that Johnson would befriend black Americans, see Foner, *Reconstruction*, 178. For the reaction of newspapers around the state, see *Daily Alta California*, Feb. 26, 1865. For the reaction of Union Party leaders, see Davis, *Political Conventions*, 233–35.

22. Davis, *Political Conventions*, 231–37.

23. On the various factions that splintered the Union Party in California, see Davis, *Political Conventions*, 237–39.

24. Berwanger, *West and Reconstruction*, 120.

25. For examples of early electioneering, see, for instance, the *Daily Alta California*, May 9, 17, and 27, 1867.

26. Davis, *Political Conventions*, 264–66.

27. Henry H. Haight to Charles Burns, Dec. 25, 1869, *Henry Huntley Haight Papers*, Huntington Library, Box 5, Folder HT 170.

28. Oscar T. Shuck, *Representative and Leading Men of the Pacific: Being Original Sketches of the Lives and Characters of the Principal Men, Living and Deceased, of the Pacific States and Territories—Pioneers, Politicians, Lawyers, Doctors, Merchants, Orators, and Divines—to Which Are Added Their Speeches, Addresses, Orations, Eulogies, Lectures, and Poems, Upon a Variety of Subjects, Including the Happiest Forensic Efforts of Baker, Randolph, McDougall, T. Starr King, and Other Popular Orators* (San Francisco: Bacon and Company, 1870), 663–666. Curiously, Shuck claims that prior to the 1867 campaign, Haight "had never been, but with one exception . . . engaged in any political struggle." Shuck elides Haight's Republican past entirely, casting him as a good Democrat. On Haight's decision to head to California, see Melendy and Gilbert, *Governors of California*, 143.

29. Melendy and Gilbert, *Governors of California*, 144; Shuck, *Representative Men*, 664; Bancroft, *History of California*, Vol. 7, 273.

30. Letter to George Bissell, quoted in Melendy and Gilbert, *Governors of California*, 144. On the Free Soil Movement, see Eric Foner, *Free Soil, Free Labor, Free Men: The Ideology of the Republican Party before the Civil War* (New York: Oxford University Press, 1970), esp. chap. 8.

31. On Haight's aborted candidacy, see Davis, *Political Conventions*, 287. Quotes taken from "Speech of Senator John Conness," *Proceedings of the San Francisco Union Ratification Meeting Held at Union Hall, San Francisco, Tuesday Evening, June 25, 1867* (San Francisco: Union State Central Committee, 1867), 5. Conness, whom Bret Harte once termed California's "only sober senator," was not above attacking Lincoln himself, and he once referred to the president as "a third rate clown in a third rate circus." See Bret Harte, *Bret Harte's California:*

Letters to the Springfield Republican and Christian Register, 1866–67, ed. Gary Scharnhorst (Albuquerque: University of New Mexico Press, 1990), letters May 1867 and August 9, 1867.

32. *Biographical Material Related to Henry H. Haight*, BANC MSS C-D 890, Bancroft Library, Statement of Mrs. Anna E. Haight, Dec. 30, 1890, *Biographical Materials Relating to Henry H. Haight*, BANC MSS C-D 890, Bancroft Library.

33. See, for instance, the *(San Francisco) Daily Morning Call*, July 7, 1867.

34. Henry H. Haight, *Speech of H. H. Haight, Esq. Democratic Candidate for Governor, Delivered at the Great Democratic Mass Meeting at Union Hall, Tuesday Evening, July 9, 1867* (San Francisco: n.p., 1867).

35. It might be worth remembering at this point that Haight was born in Rochester, N.Y., in 1825, precisely at the time that the region gained its reputation as the "Burned-Over District" because of the many religious revivals that swept through it as the Second Great Awakening unfolded. As Paul Johnson has argued, the new vision of Christianity expressed in the Second Great Awakening helped a newly emerging middle class to reconcile Christian precepts with a new capitalist order. See Paul Johnson, *A Shopkeeper's Millennium: Society and Revivals in Rochester, New York, 1815–1837* (New York: Hill and Wang, 1978); and Whitney R. Cross, *The Burned-Over District: The Social and Intellectual History of Enthusiastic Religion in Western New York, 1800–1850* (New York: Harper and Row, 1950).

36. Haight, *Speech of H. H. Haight, Esq.*

37. Bancroft, *History of California*, Vol. 7, 323. Gorham had been elected city clerk in Marysville in 1856. On Bret Harte's commentary, see Bret Harte, *Bret Harte's California*, Letter, May 1867. On the split in Union ranks, see Royce Delmatier, Clarence F. McIntosh, and Earl G. Waters, *The Rumble of California Politics, 1848–1970* (New York: Wiley, 1970), 58.

38. George C. Gorham, *Speech Delivered by George C. Gorham of San Francisco, Union Nominee for Governor, at Platt's Hall, San Francisco, Wednesday Evening, July 10th, 1867* (San Francisco: n.p., 1867).

39. *(San Francisco) Daily Morning Call*, July 23, 1867.

40. Ibid.

41. On the development of these ideas in the medical profession, see John S. Haller, Jr., *Outcasts from Evolution: Scientific Attitudes of Racial Inferiority, 1859–1900* (Urbana: University of Illinois Press, 1971).

42. Samuel B. Axtell, *Aloccucion de Samuel B. Axtell, Candidato Nominado por el Partido Democratico Para el Congresso Federal, por el Ier Distrito de California, Que Dirije a Los Nativos Californios y a la Hispano-Americanos* (San Francisco: n.p., 1867). Henry H. Haight, *Aloccucion Que Dirije A Los Hijos Del Pais H. H. Haight, Nominado por el Partido Democratico Para Gobernador Del Estado* (San Francisco: n.p., 1867).

43. David Montejano has described a similar process in the Rio Grande valley of Texas. See his *Anglos and Mexicans in the Making of Texas, 1836–1986* (Austin: University of Texas Press, 1987). On racial discrimination against Californios and Latinos in general, see Bancroft, *History of California*, Vols. 5 and 6; Leonard M. Pitt, *The Decline of the Californios: A Social History of the Spanish-Speaking Californians, 1846–1890* (Berkeley: University of California Press, 1966); and Douglas Monroy, *Thrown among Strangers: The Making of Mexican Culture in Frontier California* (Berkeley: University of California Press, 1990). On the supposed criminality of Mexicans, see Susan Lee Johnson, *Roaring Camp: The Social World of the California Gold Rush* (New York: W. W. Norton, 2000). On the economic and political prestige of Californios, see Lawrence E. Guillow, "The Origins of Race Relations in Los Angeles, 1820–1880: A Multi-Ethnic Study" (Ph.D. diss., Arizona State University, 1996).

44. *(San Francisco) Elevator*, March 23, 1866, and Feb. 23, 1866.

45. Ibid., August 30, 1867.

46. Ibid. On black literacy rates in the West, see Douglas Henry Daniels, *Pioneer Urbanites: A Social and Cultural History of Black San Francisco* (Philadelphia: Temple University Press, 1980), 18–19.

47. Bancroft, *History of California*, Vol. 7, 330.

48. On the assimilation of Irish immigrants in the eastern United States, see David Roediger, *Wages of Whiteness: Race and the Making of the American Working Class* (New York: Verso, 1991); Noel Ignatiev, *How the Irish Became White* (New York: Routledge, 1995); and Matthew Frye Jacobson, *Whiteness of a Different Color: European Immigrants and the Alchemy of Race* (Cambridge, Mass.: Harvard University Press, 1998).

49. Bret Harte, *Bret Harte's California*, 113–14.

50. On Haight's margin of victory, see Davis, *Political Conventions*, 267. The standard explanation for Haight's victory, both at the time and in later histories, claims that the Union Party lost the election because some twenty thousand disaffected Union Party voters stayed home on Election Day in protest of Gorham's candidacy and the manner in which he had secured the nomination. This would seem to undermine the argument that whites responded to Haight's racial message in large numbers and imply the notion that Haight's victory was a fluke unrelated to his message. That conclusion is bolstered by the fact that the total votes cast in the 1871 gubernatorial election jumped by roughly twenty thousand. This argument, however, incorrectly assumes a close correlation between Union Party support and adherence to Republican Party principles. For many Californians, support for the Union Party was a function of loyalty during the war rather than an embrace of Republican Party ideology. I argue that Haight's message about the dangers of Radical Reconstruction exposed the limits of that support. Further evidence of this can be found in California's vote counts in the presidential election the following year, when the absence of a Gorham candidacy and the presence of

war hero Ulysses S. Grant on the ballot as a Republican should have brought those twenty thousand voters back to the polls. Instead, Grant's margin of victory—*statewide*—was just 541, compared to Haight's margin of victory of more than 9,000 the previous fall. In 1868, Radical Reconstruction remained a significant electoral issue, and this suggests that concern over Reconstruction was indeed the primary reason for Haight's victory. By 1871, the issue had been settled at the federal level, and voters in California had turned to other issues. On the reaction of California's black community to Haight's election, see *Elevator* Sept. 13, 1867; *Pacific Appeal* Sept. 14, 1867.

51. Henry Haight to Andrew Johnson, January 18, 1868, Henry Huntley Haight Papers, BANC MSS C-B 646, Bancroft Library.

52. Henry H. Haight. *Message of H. H. Haight, Governor of California, Transmitting the Proposed Fifteenth Amendment to the Federal Constitution* (Sacramento: D. W. Gelwicks, State Printer, 1870), 9–10.

53. Ibid., 9–10, 13.

54. For an example of the use of such ideas in California, see Charles Loring Brace, *Races of the Old World: A Manual of Ethnology* (New York: C. Scribner, 1864); and Brace's *The New West: or California in 1867–1868* (New York: G. P. Putnam and Son, 1869).

55. *Sacramento Daily Union*, Jan. 14, 1870.

56. Ibid.

57. Ibid.

58. Ibid.

59. Ibid.

60. John S. Hager, *Speech of Honorable John S. Hager of San Francisco, In the Senate of California, January 28, 1870, on Senator Hager's Joint Resolution to reject the Fifteenth Amendment to the Constitution of the United States* (n.p., 1870), 10.

61. Ibid., 11.

62. Ibid.

Chapter 3. "The Most Satanic Hate"

1. *Ward v. Flood* Case File, WPA 3826, Supreme Court of California Records.

2. Ibid.

3. The development of California's system of public schools is a topic well covered. See John Swett, *History of the Public School System of California* (San Francisco: A. L. Bancroft and Company, 1876), and *Public Education in California: Its Origin and Development, with Personal Reminiscences of Half a Century* (New York: American Book Company, 1911); Richard Gauze Boone, *A History of Educational Organization in California* (n.p., n.d.); William G. Carr, *John Swett:*

The Biography of an Educational Pioneer (Santa Ana, Calif.: Fine Arts Press, 1933); William Warren Ferrier, *Ninety Years of Education in California, 1846–1936: A Presentation of Educational Movements and the Outcome of Education Today* (Berkeley, Calif.: Sather Gate Book Shop, 1937); Roy W. Cloud, *Education in California: Leaders, Organizations, and Accomplishments of the First Hundred Years* (Stanford, Calif.: Stanford University Press, 1952); Leighton H. Johnson, *Development of the Central State Agency for Public Education in California, 1849–1949* (Albuquerque: University of New Mexico Press, 1952); and Nicholas C. Polos, *John Swett: California's Frontier Schoolmaster* (Washington, D.C.: University Press of America, 1978). For examinations of race in California schools, see Nicholas P. Beck, "The Other Children: Minority Education in California Public Schools from Statehood to 1890" (Ph.D. diss., University of California, Los Angeles, 1975); Charles Wollenberg, *All Deliberate Speed: Segregation and Exclusion in California Schools, 1855–1975* (Berkeley: University of California Press, 1976); and Irving C. Hendrick, *Public Policy toward the Education of Non-White Minority Group Children in California, 1849–1970* (Riverside: University of California, Riverside, School of Education, 1975). On public attitudes toward public schools during the Jacksonian era and beyond, see David Tyack, Thomas James, and Aaron Benavot, *Law and the Shaping of Public Education, 1785–1954* (Madison: University of Wisconsin Press, 1987), 45–46, 53. See also Carl F. Kaestle, *Pillars of the Republic: Common Schools and American Society, 1780–1860* (New York: Hill and Wang, 1983); and Jean Baker, *Affairs of Party: The Political Culture of Northern Democrats in the Mid-Nineteenth Century* (Ithaca, N.Y.: Cornell University Press, 1983).

4. California's contribution came in the form of *U.S. v. Ryan*, a suit initiated after an African American was refused a seat in the dress circle of San Francisco's Maguire's Theater. See the *Civil Rights Cases*, 109 US 3 (1883).

5. On Swett's recommendations, see "Second Biennial Report of the Superintendent of Public Instruction of the State of California, 1866–67," *Appendix to the Journals of the Senate and Assembly of the State of California, 1868* (Sacramento: State Printing Office, 1868), 287. On conditions in California's schoolyards, see "Report of the Superintendent of Public Instruction," *Appendix to the Journals of the Senate, 12th Session, 1860* (Sacramento: State Printing Office, 1861), 31.

6. "Report of the Superintendent of Public Instruction," *Appendix to the Journals of the Senate and Assembly, 14th Session, 1862* (Sacramento: State Printing Office, 1863), 52. Californios, it will be remembered, were deemed legally white by the California Constitution of 1849, and so they were admitted to the schools, at least legally. The evidence suggests that they were admitted and even encouraged to attend by school officials. There was not much pressure over the matter, however, because of the existence of Catholic parish schools, which

siphoned off many Mexican children. By most accounts, de facto segregation for Mexican children did not begin in earnest until after the wave of immigration that followed the Mexican Revolution in 1910. See Beck, "Other Children"; Hendrick, *Public Policy*; and Lizbeth Haas, *Conquests and Historical Identities in California, 1769–1936* (Berkeley: University of California Press, 1995), esp. 190–96. On school officials' beliefs about Mexican students' potential for criminal behavior, see "Report of the Superintendent of Public Instruction," *Appendix to the Journals of the Senate and Assembly, 13th Session, 1861* (Sacramento: State Printing Office, 1862), 56. For a more detailed discussion of the link white Californians drew between the state's Californio population and crime, see Susan Johnson, *Roaring Camp: The Social World of the California Gold Rush* (New York: W. W. Norton, 2000).

7. *Los Angeles Star*, July 22, 1871. *Municipal Reports for the Fiscal Year 1865–6* (San Francisco Board of Supervisors, 1866), 301. On passage of the compulsory education law, see Cloud, *Education in California*, 60.

8. William Lee Miller, *Arguing about Slavery: The Great Battle in the United States Congress* (New York: Knopf, 1996), 106.

9. Quoted in "Second Biennial Report of the Superintendent of Public Instruction of the State of California, 1866 & 1867," *Appendix to the Journals of the Senate and Assembly* (Sacramento: State Printing Office, 1868). It should be noted that never once during this era did the legislature offer such decrees in favor of mathematics, grammar, or reading.

10. Tyack et al., *Law and the Shaping of Public Education*, 25–26.

11. On Swett's comments connecting the Civil War and education, see "First Biennial Report of the Superintendent of Public Instruction of the State of California, 1865–6," *Appendix to the Journals of the Senate and Assembly* (Sacramento: State Printing Office, 1866), 56. Caspar T. Hopkins, *A Manual of American Ideas* (San Francisco: n.p., 1873).

12. On the national debate over the role of education in Reconstruction, see Ward M. McAfee, *Religion, Race, and Reconstruction: The Public Schools in the Politics of the 1870s* (Albany: University of New York Press, 1998), esp. 21–22.

13. McAfee, *Religion, Race, and Reconstruction*, 106 and 23. The creation of a cabinet post devoted to education would have to wait one hundred years.

14. The efforts of these societies, and other institutions, to bring public education to the South are discussed in Ronald E. Butchart, *Northern Schools, Southern Blacks, and Reconstruction: Freedmen's Education, 1862–1875* (Westport, Conn.: Greenwood, 1980). On the "binding" nature of Southern schools, see Butchart, 54, 60.

15. On the actual wording of the legislation, see *California Statutes 1855*, ch. 185, § 12. On Judge Marvin's intentions, see Hendrick, *Public Policy*, 15. Superintendent Marvin apparently made this assumption while rampaging about the state as a militia leader, killing Indians, and enriching himself in the process.

Among his first acts as head of the state's school system was a demand for all-out war against the Indians around Mariposa. See David Frederic Ferris, *Judge Marvin and the Founding of the California Public School System* (Berkeley: University of California Press, 1962), 31–33.

16. Mai Ngai, *The Lucky Ones: One Family and the Extraordinary Invention of Chinese America* (New York: Houghton Mifflin Harcourt, 2010), 46–47. See also *Municipal Reports for the Fiscal Year 1866–7* (San Francisco Board of Supervisors, 1867), 375; and *Pacific Appeal*, Feb. 24, 1872.

17. See *Statutes of California, 1849–50*, chap. 133. On Indian education in California, see Wollenberg, *All Deliberate Speed*, 82–107.

18. "Annual Report of the Superintendent of Public Instruction," *Appendix to the Journals of the Senate, 10th Session* (Sacramento: State Printing Office, 1859), 14.

19. *San Francisco Daily Evening Bulletin*, Feb. 24, 1858. Lester made an appearance in chapter 1 when a white man beat him in his own shoe store, and the testimony laws made it impossible for him to seek redress for the beating.

20. "Annual Report of the Superintendent of Public Instruction," *Appendix to the Journals of the Senate, 10th Session, 1859* (Sacramento: State Printing Office, 1859), 14–15. *California Statutes 1860*, ch. 329, § 8.

21. The curriculum was mandated by law and applied, in later years, to black as well as white schools. It is unknown whether teachers were wicked enough to present these lessons to black children. Presumably black California schools received the same books as white schools did, but it is impossible to know whether they were used or whether teachers tempered the lessons. In most cases, teachers in black schools were white, a state of affairs which greatly agitated the black community and prompted calls for black teachers who "felt an interest in the education of their race." See the *Elevator*, July 24, 1868.

22. Arnold Guyot, *The Earth and Its Inhabitants: A Common School Geography* (New York: Charles Scribner and Company, 1869).

23. Ibid., 95.

24. Ibid.

25. Guyot, *The Earth and Its Inhabitants*, 29, 94–95, 124. For the quote about Arabs, see S. S. Cornell, *Cornell's Primary Geography, Forming Part First of a Systematic Series of School Geographies* (New York: D. Appleton and Company, 1857), 71.

26. Arnold Guyot, *The Earth and Its Inhabitants: Intermediate Geography* (New York: Charles Scribner and Company, 1875), 102–103.

27. Arnold Guyot, *The Earth and Man: Lectures on Comparative Physical Geography, in Its Relation to the History of Mankind* (Boston: Gould and Lincoln, 1865).

28. "Have Negroes Been Taught and Classed on Terms of Equality in a Public School Under the Charge of Mr. John Swett?" *Benjamin Ignatius Hayes*

Scrapbooks, Bancroft Library. Italics in the original. Janes had figured prominently in the flap over Peter Lester's daughter four years earlier. For Swett's response, see *Sacramento Daily Union*, Sept. 20, 1862.

29. For historians' judgments concerning Swett's tenure as superintendent of public instruction, see the sources in note 3. *California Statutes, 1865–6*, ch. 342, § 57–58. The reader is reminded that the liberality of the war years stemmed not from any genuine interest in black equality, but rather from a desire to rid California of any laws or institutions that smacked of Southern sympathy.

30. On the reaction of black Californians to the school board's decision, see the *Elevator*, July 31, 1868. For details on the construction of the school, see *Municipal Reports for the Fiscal Year 1863–64* (San Francisco Board of Supervisors, 1864), 271, 281.

31. On early schools for black Californians, see Delilah L. Beasley, *The Negro Trailblazers of California* (Los Angeles: Times Mirror Publishing and Binding Company, 1919), 172–73, 176–77; and Susan Bragg, "Knowledge Is Power: Sacramento Blacks and the Public Schools, 1854–1860," *California History* 75, 3 (1996): 216. The first school had been opened by a black woman, Elizabeth Thorn Scott, a year earlier, but had closed after a few months when she married. It was not considered acceptable for married women to teach school.

32. *Daily Alta California*, May 7, 1854. The article describes the intent to open a school and marks the location; the school really did open on May 22. See Stephen Lee Dolson, "The Administration of San Francisco Public Schools, 1847–1947" (Ph.D. diss., University of California, Berkeley, 1964), 117. William Leidsdorff's influence failed to outlast his own lifetime, which came to an end before California was admitted to the Union. In the years before the Civil War, virtually all education efforts for black Californians were private.

33. On the location of Sacramento's schools, see Winfield J. Davis, *History and Progress of the Public School Department of the City of Sacramento, 1849–1893* (Sacramento: D. Johnston, 1895), 46–47. On school furnishings in Los Angeles, see "Educational Matters in the Southern Counties," *California Teacher* 2, 11 (May 1865): 270.

34. *Municipal Reports for the Fiscal Year 1863–64* (San Francisco Board of Supervisors, 1864), 271.

35. *Pacific Appeal*, reprinted from *Zion's Standard*, Feb. 1, 1868.

36. On the reopening of the Broadway school, see the *Elevator*, July 24, 1868. The city superintendent's report appears in *Municipal Reports for the Fiscal Year 1866–7* (San Francisco Board of Supervisors, 1867), 351.

37. See the *Elevator*, July 31, 1868, and the *San Francisco Morning Call*, July 23, 1868.

38. *Elevator*, July 31, 1868.

39. Ibid., July 24, 1868, and *Pacific Appeal*, Feb. 1, 1868.

40. *Elevator*, Aug. 14, 1868.

41. Ibid., Nov. 6, 13, 1868.

42. On Superintendent Denman's promise to move the Broadway school, see the *Elevator*, May 28, 1869. On continued problems at the school, see *Pacific Appeal*, May 27, 1871. Classes in white schools were divided by grade, while children in black schools were often lumped together regardless of age or level of advancement.

43. On black Californians' reaction to ratification of the Fifteenth Amendment, see the *Sacramento Daily Union*, April 6, 19, 1870. On black Californians' demands for better facilities, see the *Sacramento Daily Union*, May 3, 1870, and *Pacific Appeal*, Sept. 3, 1870.

44. See the *Sacramento Daily Union*, April 7, 1870, and Jan. 17, 1871.

45. *Pacific Appeal*, May 27, 1871.

46. Ibid., Nov. 25, 1871.

47. Ibid., Feb. 10, 1872.

48. Ibid., Feb. 10 and 24, 1872.

49. On the Nevada case, see the *Pacific Appeal*, March 9, 1872. The case is found at *State ex. rel. Stoutmeyer v. Duffy*, 7 Nev. 342 (1872). On Sumner's efforts at the national level, see McAfee, *Religion, Race, and Reconstruction*, esp. chap. 4.

50. *Elevator*, April 27, 1872. *Ward v. Flood*, 48 Cal. 36 (1874). This case is often, and erroneously, cited as having occurred in 1872, and even the State Archives dates the case incorrectly. The case was submitted in 1872, but the decision was not handed down until January 1874.

51. Davis, *History and Progress*, 87. "School Board Minutes," *City of Sacramento School Board Records*, Sacramento City Archives, Dec. 29, Jan. 5, 8, 1873.

52. *Ward v. Flood*, 48 Cal. 39, 41, 52. On the Massachusetts case, see *Roberts v. The City of Boston*, 5 Cushing R. 198 (1849), quoted in *Ward v. Flood*, 48 Cal. 54. The *Roberts* case was the first in which the phrase "separate but equal" appeared and in part formed the basis for *Plessy* in 1896.

53. See a similar case that came to a similar end in Ohio: *State ex rel. Garnes v. McGann et al.*, 21 Ohio 198 (1871), 199.

54. On the reaction among black Californians to *Ward v. Flood*, see Beasley, *Negro Trailblazers*, 182. For the court's insistence on black access to public schools of some kind, see *Ward v. Flood*, 48 Cal. 56–57.

55. On the effects of the railroad and the depression of the mid-1870s, see Walton Bean and James J. Rawls, *California: An Interpretive History* (New York: McGraw-Hill, 1983), 165–72; and Lucille Eaves, *A History of California Labor Legislation, with an Introductory Sketch of the San Francisco Labor Movement* (Berkeley: University of California Press, 1910), 20.

56. On the desegregation of San Francisco schools, see "Report of the Superintendent of Common Schools," *Municipal Reports, 1879–80* (San Francisco

Board of Supervisors, 1880), 654–55. On desegregation around the state, see Wollenberg, *All Deliberate Speed*, 25–26.

57. On waning interest in the difficulties surrounding Reconstruction and on Redemption, see Eric Foner, *Reconstruction: America's Unfinished Revolution, 1863–1877* (New York: Harper and Row, 1988), chaps. 10–12.

58. Ngai, *Lucky Ones*, 47. On the number of black children enrolled in San Francisco schools, see San Francisco Board of Supervisors, *Municipal Reports, 1869–70*, 289. For Benicia, see *Benicia School Board Records*, BANC MSS C-A 147, Box 2, Folder 40, Bancroft Library, University of California, Berkeley. On the estimated enrollment at the Chinese school in San Francisco, see Wollenberg, *All Deliberate Speed*, 35.

59. On the history of San Francisco's Chinese school and the changes in the law that shaped it, see Ferrier, *Ninety Years of Education in California*, 102–103; Hendrick, *Public Policy*, 68–73; Wollenberg, *All Deliberate Speed*, 29–43; and Victor Low, *The Unimpressible Race: A Century of Educational Struggle by the Chinese in San Francisco* (San Francisco: East/West Publishing, 1982), 13–27. On Denman's decision to close the Chinese school, see San Francisco Board of Supervisors, *Municipal Reports, 1869–70*, 289.

60. *To the Honorable Senate and the Assembly of the State of California . . . petition for the establishment of separate schools for Chinese children, and for universal education* (n.p., n.d.). On fears for the safety of Chinese children in white schools, see Low, *Unimpressible Race*, 26.

61. *To the Honorable Senate and the Assembly of the State of California . . . petition for the establishment of separate schools for Chinese children, and for universal education* (n.p., n.d.).

62. On the economic crisis in California and the rise of the Workingmen's Party of California, see Hubert Howe Bancroft, *History of California*, Vol. 7 (San Francisco: History Company, 1890), 335–406; Henry George, "The Kearney Agitation in California," *Popular Science Monthly* 17 (August 1880); Eaves, *History of California Labor Legislation*; and Neil Larry Shumsky, *The Evolution of Political Protest and the Workingmen's Party of California* (Columbus: Ohio State University Press, 1991).

63. *Tape v. Hurley*, 66 Cal. 473 (1885). For contemporary discussion of Joseph Tape's adoption of a distinctly American lifestyle, see the *(San Francisco) Daily Evening Bulletin*, Jan. 15, 1885. Both Joseph and Mary Tape had been born in China and had immigrated to the United States as children, Joseph at the age of twelve and Mary at the age of eleven. Joseph found work as a drayman, and Mary was rescued from prostitution by women of the Ladies' Society. Mary dropped her Chinese name and adopted the name of her mentor in the Ladies' Society home, Mary McGladery. Ngai, *Lucky Ones*, 3–23.

64. *Tape v. Hurley*, 66 Cal. 473. For the text of the school law as amended in 1880, see *Tape v. Hurley*, 66 Cal. 473–37, emphasis added. The law had been

amended following the drafting of a new state constitution, and given the addition of specific legal disabilities aimed at the Chinese included in the document, the State Legislature had felt safe in writing such a generously worded law. On Tape's appeal to Bee, see the *(San Francisco) Daily Evening Bulletin*, Oct. 22, 1884.

65. *(San Francisco) Daily Evening Bulletin*, Oct. 22, 1884.

66. Two school board members voted against the resolution, although not, it must be said, out of any fellow feeling for the Chinese. Rather, they argued that native-born Chinese would be able to vote once they reached adulthood under the Fifteenth Amendment, and they feared the consequences that would flow from so many uneducated potential voters. See the *(San Francisco) Daily Evening Bulletin*, Oct. 22, 1884. For the instructions from the San Francisco School Board to the district's principals and teachers, see *Circular No. 52*, Circular Scrapbook, San Francisco Unified School District Records, San Francisco Public Library.

67. Ngai, *Lucky Ones*, 51. *(Sacramento) Daily Record-Union*, Jan. 10, 1885.

68. *(San Francisco) Daily Evening Bulletin*, Jan. 15, 1885. For the full text of Welcker's letter, see the *(Sacramento) Daily Record-Union*, Jan. 16, 1885.

69. *Tape v. Hurley*, 66 Cal. 473. For discussion among school officials following the Supreme Court's decision, see the *(San Francisco) Daily Evening Bulletin*, April 2, 1885. For information on Assembly bill 268, see the *(San Francisco) Daily Evening Bulletin*, March 19, 1885; and Wollenberg, *All Deliberate Speed*, 42.

70. *(San Francisco) Daily Evening Bulletin*, April 14, 1885.

Chapter 4. "Wa Shing and His Tireless Fellows"

1. The two ordinances were Order Nos. 1569 and 1587, passed May 24, 1880, and July 28, 1880, respectively. *In re Yick Wo*, 68 Cal. 294 (1885); *In re Wo Lee*, 26 Fed. 471 (1886); and *Yick Wo v. Hopkins, Sheriff/Wo Lee v. Hopkins, Sheriff*, 118 U.S. 356 (1886). See also *In re Wo Lee* Case File, Civil Case Files, U.S. District Court, Northern District of California RG21.

2. On early taxes imposed on Chinese migrants, see Charles J. McClain, *In Search of Equality: The Chinese Struggle against Discrimination in Nineteenth-Century America* (Berkeley: University of California Press, 1994), 9–42.

3. Carl Brent Swisher, *Motivation and Political Technique in the California Constitutional Convention, 1878–79* (Claremont, Calif.: Pomona College, 1930), 6. On the effects of the railroad, see Walton Bean and James J. Rawls, *California: An Interpretive History* (New York: McGraw-Hill, 1983), 165; and Lucille Eaves, *A History of California Labor Legislation, with an Introductory Sketch of the San Francisco Labor Movement* (Berkeley: University of California Press, 1910), 20.

4. Bean and Rawls, *California*, 172; Swisher, *Motivation and Political Technique*, 7; Royce Delmatier, Clarence F. McIntosh, and Earl G. Walters, eds., *The Rumble of California Politics* (New York: John Wiley and Sons, 1970), 70–71. For

banking and stock gambling in general, see Hubert Howe Bancroft, *History of California* (San Francisco: History Company, 1890), Vol. 7, esp. chap. 7.

5. On the Burlingame Treaty and its effects, see Najia Aarim-Heriot, *Chinese Immigrants, African Americans, and Racial Anxiety in the United States, 1848–82* (Urbana: University of Illinois Press, 2003), 109–12; and McClain, *In Search of Equality*, 30–31. U.S. Census Office, *Historical Census Statistics on Population Totals by Race, 1790 to 1990, and by Hispanic Origin, 1970 to 1990, for the United States, Regions, Divisions, and States, Working Paper Series No. 56* (Washington, D.C.: Government Printing Office, 2002).

6. On the Workingmen's Party of California, see Bancroft, *History of California*, Vol. 7, 335–406; Henry George, "The Kearney Agitation in California," *Popular Science Monthly* 17 (August 1880); Eaves, *History of California Labor Legislation*; and Neil Larry Shumsky, *The Evolution of Political Protest and the Workingmen's Party of California* (Columbus: Ohio State University Press, 1991). On anti-Chinese measures at the California Constitutional Convention, see *Debates and Proceedings of the Constitutional Convention of the State of California, Convened at the City of Sacramento, Saturday, September 28, 1878*, Vol. 3 (Sacramento: State Printing Office, 1880); Swisher, *Motivation and Political Technique*; and McClain, *In Search of Equality*, 79–97.

7. On the Cubic Air and Queue Ordinances, see *Ho Ah Kow v. Nunan*, 5 Sawy. 552 (1879). For a general overview of anti-Chinese legislation and Chinese legal challenges to such laws, see Benjamin S. Brooks, *Brief of the Legislation and Adjudication Touching the Chinese Question Referred to the Joint Commission of Both Houses of Congress* (San Francisco: n.p., 1877); Eaves, *History of California Labor Legislation;* Elmer Clarence Sandmeyer, *The Anti-Chinese Movement in California* (Chicago: University of Chicago Press, 1939), William J. Courtney, *San Francisco Anti-Chinese Ordinances, 1850–1900* (San Francisco: R and E Research Associates, 1974); and McClain, *In Search of Equality*, 9–132.

8. For the connection between the laundry war and suburbanization, I am heavily indebted to the work of Paul Man Ong, whose unpublished paper, "The Development and Decline of an Ethnic Enterprise: Chinese Laundries in Early California" (Ethnic Studies Library, University of California, Berkeley, n.d.), and master's thesis, "The Chinese and the Laundry Laws: The Use and Control of Urban Space" (University of Washington, 1975), first made the observation. On state party demands for a Chinese exclusion bill, see Winfield J. Davis, *History of Political Conventions in California, 1849–1892* (Sacramento: California State Library, 1893), 423, 425.

9. On the origins of the Chinese laundry trade, see Paul C. P. Siu, *The Chinese Laundryman: A Study in Social Isolation* (New York: New York University Press, 1987), 1; Joan S. Wang, "Race, Gender, and Laundry Work: The Roles of Chinese Laundrymen and American Women in the United States, 1850–1950," *Journal of Ethnic History* 24, 1 (Fall 2004): 58–99; and Ronald Takaki, *Strangers*

from a Different Shore: A History of Asian Americans (New York: Penguin, 1990), 92–93.

10. On the role of Chinese in the California economy, see Ping Chiu, *Chinese Labor in California, 1850–1880: An Economic Study* (Madison: University of Wisconsin Press, 1963), esp. 27, 32, 48. On the movement of Chinese laborers into California agriculture, see Sucheng Chan, *This Bittersweet Soil: The Chinese in California Agriculture, 1860–1910* (Berkeley: University of California Press, 1989). See also Siu, *Chinese Laundryman*, 46; and Takaki, *Strangers from a Different Shore*, 88–92.

11. On racial hostility in the mines, see Bancroft, *History of California*, Vol. 7, *1860–1890* (San Francisco: History Company, 1890), 335–40; Chiu, *Chinese Labor in California*, 17–32, 54; and Ong, "Chinese and the Laundry Laws," 20, 29. On the controversy over Chinese employment on public works in San Francisco, see Courtney, *San Francisco Anti-Chinese Ordinances*, 48–49; and the *(San Francisco) Daily Evening Bulletin*, Feb. 12, 1867.

12. On the difficulties of housekeeping in nineteenth-century America, see Sarah Deutsch, *Women and the City: Gender, Space, and Power in Boston, 1870–1940* (New York: Oxford University Press, 2000), esp. 18. On the Chinese desire to avoid the *bok kwei*, see Ong, "Chinese and the Laundry Laws," 45. On competition, see Ong, "Development and Decline of an Ethnic Enterprise."

13. Takaki, *Strangers from a Different Shore*, 92–93; Ong, "Development and Decline of an Ethnic Enterprise," 12; *Yick Wo v. Hopkins*, 118 U.S. 356. In 1880, officials in the city of San Francisco estimated that there were 240 Chinese laundries with a total capitalization of $200,000. This yields an average capitalization of $833.33.

14. Takaki, *Strangers from a Different Shore*, 92–92; McClain, *In Search of Equality*, 47; Chiu, *Chinese Labor in California*, 65; "John Chinaman in San Francisco," *Scribner's*, October 1876, 864; Ong, "Development and Decline of an Ethnic Enterprise," 3; and Ong, "Chinese and the Laundry Laws," 38, 52.

15. Much of what follows is drawn from Siu's *The Chinese Laundryman*. Siu was the son of a Chinese immigrant and laundryman in Chicago. As a student of Robert Park in the sociology department at the University of Chicago during the 1930s, Siu researched the Chinese laundry trade and later wrote *The Chinese Laundryman* as his doctoral dissertation. His experience in that world gave him unique access. He visited and studied 591 Chinese laundries and found patterns of work and construction repeated in each. Siu argued that the patterns he described had been static for three generations or more. Descriptions and drawings in contemporary San Francisco newspapers bear out his assertion that little had changed between the 1870s and the 1920s.

16. *Yick Wo v. Hopkins*, 118 U.S. 356; Ong, "Chinese and the Laundry Laws," 50; Siu, *Chinese Laundryman*, 57; and Hubert Howe Bancroft, "Mongolianism in America," in *Essays and Miscellany* (San Francisco: History Company, 1890), 322.

17. Siu, *Chinese Laundryman*, 60–61; *Daily Alta California*, June 24, 1873.

18. Siu, *Chinese Laundryman*, 62–63. See also the *San Francisco Chronicle*, June 6, 1880, for a report of a tragic fire in a Chinese laundry. The bodies of eight laundrymen were found in the ironing room where they had been sleeping when the fire broke out during the night. Three others were found in living quarters farther back in the shop.

19. Siu, *Chinese Laundryman*, 60; Takaki, *Strangers from a Different Shore*, 93; and McClain, *In Search of Equality*, 46–47.

20. Siu, *Chinese Laundryman*, 2–3, 85; Ong, "Chinese and the Laundry Laws," 23.

21. Ong, "Chinese and the Laundry Laws," 23; McClain, *In Search of Equality*, 13–16, 85.

22. Ong, "Chinese and the Laundry Laws," 23–24.

23. Ong, "Development and Decline of an Ethnic Enterprise," 15.

24. *Daily Alta California*, May 23, 1870.

25. Ibid. See also the *Sacramento Reporter*, May 23, 1870, printed in *Chinese Laundries Ordinance, and Other Articles from Chinese American Newspapers* (University of California, Berkeley, Asian American Studies Library, 1983). Dupont Street has since been renamed Grant Street, and it is Chinatown's central tourist corridor.

26. *Yick Wo v. Hopkins* 118 U.S. 356; *In re Wo Lee* Case File.

27. Ong, "Development and Decline of an Ethnic Enterprise," 18.

28. On suburbanization, see Janet L. Abu-Lughod, *New York, Chicago, Los Angeles: America's Global Cities* (Minneapolis: University of Minnesota Press, 1999), 129. Ong, "Development and Decline of an Ethnic Enterprise," 18.

29. On the early development of nineteenth-century suburbs, see Sam Bass Warner, *Streetcar Suburbs: The Process of Growth in Boston, 1870–1900* (Cambridge, Mass.: Harvard University Press, 1962). Ong, "Chinese and the Laundry Laws," 73; Shumsky, *Evolution of Political Protest*, 108.

30. On the issue of domesticity in suburbs, see William Cronon, *Nature's Metropolis: Chicago and the Great West* (New York: W. W. Norton, 1991), 347–48; Olmsted is quoted on p. 347. For an example of nineteenth-century domestic advice literature, see "John Chinaman in San Francisco," 862–72.

31. Ong, "Chinese and the Laundry Laws," 67; Siu, *Chinese Laundryman*, 137.

32. *San Francisco Chronicle*, May 5, 1882. On petitions to the board of supervisors, see McClain, *In Search of Equality*, 104.

33. On black Californians' consistent support for Chinese exclusion, see Leigh Dana Johnson, "Equal Rights and the 'Heathen Chinee': Black Activism in San Francisco, 1865–1875," *Western Historical Quarterly* 11, 1 (1980): 57–68. On the decline of the California Indian population, see Albert Hurtado, *Indian Survival on the California Frontier* (New Haven, Conn.: Yale University Press, 1988).

Between the onset of American occupation in 1846 and the census of 1890, California's Indian population fell from an estimated 150,000 to fewer than 17,000.

34. For a detailed discussion of the role played by the rhetoric of disease in the racialization of the Chinese, see Nayan Shah, *Contagious Divides: Epidemics and Race in San Francisco's Chinatown* (Berkeley: University of California Press, 2001).

35. H. N. Clement, *The Conflict of Races in California*, in Horace Davis, ed. *Chinese Immigration Pamphlets*, Bancroft Library, University of California, Berkeley. Bancroft, "Mongolianism in America," 315.

36. Romualdo Pacheco, *Remarks of Hon. Romualdo Pacheco, of California, in the House of Representatives, Saturday, March 18, 1882.* [The House Having Under Consideration the Bill (S. No. 71) to Enforce Treaty Stipulations Relating to the Chinese.] (Washington, D.C.: Government Printing Office, 1882), 6; Bancroft, "Mongolianism in America," 309–10.

37. Charles Loring Brace, *The Races of the Old World: A Manual of Ethnology* (New York: Scribner, 1864), 155–58.

38. Bancroft, "Mongolianism in America," 310, 313.

39. William B. Farnell, *The Chinese at Home and Abroad. Together with the Report of the Special Committee of the Board of Supervisors of San Francisco, on the Condition of the Chinese Quarter of that City* (San Francisco: San Francisco Board of Supervisors, 1885), 3–44.

40. Ibid., 3, 44, 114.

41. *Chinese Immigration: Its Social, Moral, and Political Effect. Report to the California State Senate of its Special Committee on Chinese Immigration* (Sacramento: State Printing Office, 1878), 109; *Report of the Special Committee of the Board of Supervisors of San Francisco, on the Condition of the Chinese Quarter of that City*, printed in Farnell, *Chinese at Home and Abroad*, 5; "John Chinaman in San Francisco." *Scribner's* (October 1876): 866, 868.

42. *San Francisco Chronicle*, Feb. 17, 1880.

43. Farnell, *Chinese at Home and Abroad*, 114; Lauren E. Crane, ed., *Newton Booth of California: His Speeches and Addresses* (New York: Putnam's, 1894), 326; *Report of the Special Committee of the Board of Supervisors of San Francisco, on the Condition of the Chinese Quarter of that City*, printed in Farnell, *Chinese at Home and Abroad*, 63.

44. *Chinese Immigration: Its Social, Moral, and Political Effect. Report to the California State Senate of its Special Committee on Chinese Immigration*, 9–10; "John Chinaman in San Francisco," 864.

45. "John Chinaman in San Francisco," 865; *San Francisco Chronicle*, May 5, 1882.

46. *San Francisco Chronicle*, February 22, 24, 1880.

47. Ibid., May 24, 1882; Siu, *Chinese Laundryman*, 66; see also "John Chinaman in San Francisco," 864.

48. *San Francisco Chronicle*, May 4, 19, 1882.

49. Ibid., Feb. 16, 1880; *Report of the Special Committee of the Board of Supervisors of San Francisco, on the Condition of the Chinese Quarter of that City*, printed in Farnell, *Chinese at Home and Abroad*, 14–16.

50. *Report of the Special Committee of the Board of Supervisors*, 12–14; *San Francisco Chronicle*, Feb. 7, 1880.

51. For legal contests in other California cities, see *In re Tie Loy*, 26 F. 611 (1886) and *In re Hang Kie*, 69 Cal. 149 (1886), which discuss laundry ordinances in Stockton and Modesto, respectively.

52. *San Francisco Chronicle*, Feb. 6, 1880; McClain, *In Search of Equality*, 100–101.

53. *Yick Wo v. Hopkins*, 118 U.S. 356; Alfred Clarke, *Report of Alfred Clarke, Special Counsel for the City and County of San Francisco in the Laundry Order Litigation. February 24, 1885* (San Francisco: W. A. Woodward and Company, 1885), 1; McClain, *In Search of Equality*, 100–101; Ong, "Chinese and the Laundry Laws," 5. For a thorough discussion of the legal and constitutional issues surrounding the laundry ordinances, see Charles McClain, *In Search of Equality*, 47–131. My purpose here is not so much to retry the cases as to illuminate the racial issues upon which they touched.

54. *In re Quong Woo*, 7 Sawy. 526 (1882); *In re Quong Woo* Case File, Civil Case Files, U.S. District Court, Northern District of California, RG 21. *San Francisco Chronicle*, July 21, 1882.

55. *In re Quong Woo*, 7 Sawy. 526.

56. See *In re Ah Fong*, 1 F. Cas. 213 (1874); and *Chy Lung v. Freeman*, 92 U.S. 275 (1876).

57. *San Francisco Chronicle*, August 9, 11, 1882.

58. *Soon Hing v. Crowley*, 113 U.S. 703 (1885), 711.

59. *Yick Wo v. Hopkins*, 118 U.S. 373–74; McClain, *In Search of Equality*, 124.

60. Andrew Gyory, *Closing the Gate: Race, Politics, and the Chinese Exclusion Act* (Chapel Hill: University of North Carolina Press, 1998).

Chapter 5. "The Chinese Must Go!"

1. On the destruction of California Indians, see Albert Hurtado, *Indian Survival on the California Frontier* (New Haven, Conn.: Yale University Press, 1988).

2. For a detailed examination of violence against Chinese immigrants in the nineteenth-century American West, see Jean Pfaelzer's excellent *Driven Out: The Forgotten War against Chinese Americans* (New York: Random House, 2007).

3. Winfield J. Davis, *History of Political Conventions in California, 1849–1892* (Sacramento: California State Library, 1893), 442, 432–33.

4. Alexander Saxton, *The Indispensable Enemy: Labor and the Anti-Chinese Movement in California* (Berkeley: University of California Press, 1971), 177–178; Ronald Takaki, *Strangers from a Different Shore: A History of Asian Americans* (New York: Penguin, 1990), 40; Lucy Salyer, "Captives of Law: Judicial Enforcement of the Chinese Exclusion Laws, 1891–1905," *Journal of American History* 76, 2 (1989): 97; Christian G. Fritz, "A Nineteenth-Century 'Habeas Corpus Mill': The Chinese before the Federal Courts in California," *American Journal of Legal History* 32, 4 (1988): 353, 360. See also *In re Tung Yeong*, 19 F. 184 (1884).

5. Davis, *Political Conventions*, 432; *Truth*, May 17 and 11, 1882, quoted in Saxton, *Indispensable Enemy*, 179.

6. Saxton, *Indispensable Enemy*, 176–77, 188.

7. Takaki, *Strangers from a Different Shore*, 40.

8. Fritz, "Nineteenth-Century 'Habeas Corpus Mill,'" 348.

9. Ibid.; *In re Tie Loy*, 26 F. 611 (1886). On the success rate of Chinese habeas corpus cases, see *Daily Alta California*, Jan. 25, 1888; Fritz, "Nineteenth-Century 'Habeas Corpus Mill,'" 368; and Salyer, "Captives of Law," 92.

10. On Ogden Hoffman's feelings about the Chinese, see Fritz, "Nineteenth-Century 'Habeas Corpus Mill,'" 349–50; and Christian G. Fritz, *Federal Justice in California: The Court of Ogden Hoffman, 1851–1891* (Lincoln: University of Nebraska Press, 1991). On Lorenzo Sawyer's racial ideas, see Lorenzo Sawyer, *Lorenzo Sawyer Dictations, Biographical Sketches and Related Materials (ca. 1886–1890)*. Banc MSS C-D 321, Bancroft Library, University of California, Berkeley.

11. Fritz, "Nineteenth-Century 'Habeas Corpus Mill,'" 352, 354, 357, 367; *In re Jung Ah Lung*, 25 F. 141 (1885).

12. *San Francisco Chronicle*, Oct. 15, 1885.

13. *In re Tung Yeong*, 19 F. 185, 187.

14. *San Francisco Chronicle*, Oct. 15 and 22, 1885; Fritz, "Nineteenth-Century 'Habeas Corpus Mill,'" 361.

15. *In re Tung Yeong*, 19 F. 187–89; Fritz, "Nineteenth-Century 'Habeas Corpus Mill,'" 353, 360–61.

16. Saxton, *Indispensable Enemy*, 215; *New York Times*, July 31, 1883, and Dec. 8, 1884, in *Chinese Laundry Ordinances and Other Articles from Chinese American Newspapers* (Berkeley, University of California, Berkeley, Asian American Studies Library, 1983).

17. *San Francisco Chronicle*, Oct. 19 and 20, 1885.

18. *San Francisco Chronicle*, Oct. 20, 1885.

19. *San Francisco Chronicle*, Oct. 18 and 22, 1885. After a 1957 law offered limited amnesty to "paper sons," some eight thousand Chinese men admitted to having entered the country through fraudulent documentation. See Salyer, "Captives of the Law," 108 n. 38.

20. *San Francisco Chronicle*, Nov. 22, 1885, Oct. 19, 1885, and Oct. 21, 1885. John S. Hager, it will be remembered, had vigorously opposed the Fifteenth Amendment as a Democratic U.S. senator from California in 1870.

21. *San Francisco Chronicle*, Oct. 19 and 20, 1885.

22. *San Francisco Chronicle*, Nov. 6 and Oct. 23, 1885. San Francisco's Chinatown was widely regarded as an "impregnable" fortress from which Chinese immigrants might safely defend themselves against attack. See Saxton, *Indispensable Enemy*, 148–51.

23. Daniel Cornford, "To Save the Republic: The California Workingmen's Party in Humboldt County," *California History* 66, 2 (June 1987): 130–42; Pfaelzer, *Driven Out*, 121–66.

24. Pfaelzer, *Driven Out*, 130–31.

25. Ibid., 122–27.

26. Clayton D. Laurie, "Civil Disorder and the Military in Rock Springs, Wyoming: The Army's Role in the 1885 Chinese Massacre," *Montana: The Magazine of Western History* 40, 3 (September 1990): 44–59; Charles J. McClain, *In Search of Equality: The Chinese Struggle against Discrimination in Nineteenth-Century America* (Berkeley: University of California Press, 1994), 173; *Harper's* quoted in Pfaelzer, *Driven Out*, 213.

27. *San Francisco Chronicle*, Nov. 5, 1885.

28. Ibid., Nov. 6, 1885.

29. Ibid., Nov. 8, 1885; *(Sacramento) Daily Record-Union*, Nov. 9, 1885.

30. *San Francisco Chronicle*, Nov. 8 and 14, 1885. On the reporting of events in Eureka, see Pfaelzer, *Driven Out*, 138.

31. Saxton, *Indispensable Enemy*, 125.

32. *San Francisco Chronicle*, Nov. 7 and 8, 1885; Sacramento *Daily Record-Union*, Nov. 9, 1885.

33. *(Sacramento) Daily-Record-Union*, Nov. 9, 1885; *San Francisco Chronicle*, Nov. 14, and 15, 1885.

34. *San Francisco Chronicle*, Nov. 22, 1885.

35. *(Sacramento) Daily Record-Union*, Nov. 14–23, 1878.

36. *(Truckee) Republican*, Nov. 25, 1885.

37. *San Francisco Chronicle*, Dec. 13 and 20, 1885. Pfaelzer, *Driven Out*, 167–85.

38. *San Francisco Chronicle*, Dec. 13 and 20, 1885; *(Sacramento) Daily Record Union*, Jan. 18 and Feb. 15, 1885.

39. Ibid. On the Ku Klux Klan in the South, see Eric Foner, *Reconstruction: America's Unfinished Revolution, 1863–1877* (New York: Harper and Row, 1988), 425–44.

40. *San Francisco Chronicle*, Dec. 11, 1885; *(Sacramento) Daily Record-Union*, Feb. 10, 16, and 17, 1886; Saxton, *Indispensable Enemy*, 207 n. 14.

41. Davis, *Political Conventions*, 479–504; Saxton, *Indispensable Enemy*, 208–209.

42. *(Sacramento) Daily Record-Union*, July 2, 1886; McClain, *In Search of Equality*, 175.

43. *(Sacramento) Daily-Record Union*, Feb. 19 and July 2, 1886; McClain, *In Search of Equality*, 176.

44. *(Sacramento) Daily Record-Union*, March 13, 1886; McClain, *In Search of Equality*, 176.

45. *(Sacramento) Daily Record-Union*, March 13, 1886.

46. Ibid., Feb. 25, 1886.

47. McClain, *In Search of Equality*, 177–79; *Baldwin v. Franks*, 120 U.S. 678 (1887).

48. McClain, *In Search of Equality*, 178–79; *United States v. Harris*, 106 U.S. 629 (1882).

49. McClain, *In Search of Equality*, 179–81.

50. Ibid., 179–81, 184; *(Sacramento) Daily Record-Union*, April 1, 1886.

51. *Baldwin v. Franks*, 120 U.S. 685–89.

52. McClain, *In Search of Equality*, 188–90; *Baldwin v. Franks*, 120 U.S. 707.

53. Takaki, *Strangers from a Different Shore*, 111; McClain, *In Search of Equality*, 191–93.

Conclusion

1. *Gandolfo v. Hartman*, 49 F. 181 (1892).

2. Ibid., 181–83. See also *Ho Ah Kow v. Nunan*, 5 Sawy. 552 (1879); *United States v. Harris*, 106 U.S. 629 (1882); and *Baldwin v. Franks*, 120 U.S. 678 (1887).

3. On the persistence of segregation in California's public schools, see Irving C. Hendrick, *Public Policy toward the Education of Non-White Minority Group Children in California, 1849–1970* (Riverside: University of California, Riverside, School of Education, 1975); and Charles Wollenberg, *All Deliberate Speed: Segregation and Exclusion in California Schools, 1855–1975* (Berkeley: University of California Press, 1976). On the persistence of exclusionary legislation aimed at Asian Americans, see Ronald Takaki, *Strangers from a Different Shore: A History of Asian Americans* (New York: Penguin, 1990). On California's Proposition 14 and racial discrimination in general, see Walton Bean and James J. Rawls, *California: An Interpretive History* (New York: McGraw-Hill, 1983).

4. On Mexican immigration to California during the twentieth century, see George J. Sanchez, *Becoming Mexican American: Ethnicity, Culture, and Identity in Chicano Los Angeles, 1900–1945* (New York: Oxford University Press, 1993). On the "Okie" migration, see James N. Gregory, *American Exodus: The Dust Bowl*

Migration and Okie Culture in California (New York: Oxford University Press, 1989). On California and the West during the war years, see Gerald D. Nash, *The American West Transformed: The Impact of the Second World War* (Bloomington: Indiana University Press, 1985). On civil rights in California, see Josh Sides, *L.A. City Limits: African American Los Angeles from the Great Depression to the Present* (Berkeley: University of California Press, 2003). On California's Proposition 187, see Kent A. Ono and John M. Sloop, *Shifting Borders: Rhetoric, Immigration, and California's Proposition 187* (Philadelphia: Temple University Press, 2002).

5. On the black migration of the early twentieth century, see James R. Grossman, *Land of Hope: Chicago, Black Southerners, and the Great Migration* (Chicago: University of Chicago Press, 1989). On municipal segregation ordinances and racial covenants in the early twentieth century, see Roger L. Rice, "Residential Segregation by Law, 1910–1917," *Journal of Southern History* 34, 2 (May 1968): 179–99; and David Delaney, *Race, Place, and the Law, 1836–1948* (Austin: University of Texas Press, 1998).

Bibliography

Manuscript Collections

Benicia School Board Records, Bancroft Library, University of California–Berkeley

Biographical Material Related to Henry H. Haight, Bancroft Library, University of California–Berkeley

Blacks in California Petition, 1862, California Historical Society, North Baker Research Library, San Francisco

Breen, Harry, Scrapbooks, California Historical Society, North Baker Research Library, San Francisco

City of Sacramento School Board Records, Sacramento City Archives

Civil Case Files, U.S. District Court Northern District of California, National Archives and Records Administration, Washington, D.C.

Davis, Winfield J., Scrapbooks, Huntington Library, San Marino, Calif.

Haight, Henry Huntley, Papers, Huntington Library, San Marino, Calif.

Hayes, Benjamin Ignatius, Scrapbooks, Bancroft Library, University of California–Berkeley

Maclay, Charles, Papers, Huntington Library, San Marino, Calif.

Roney, Frank, Papers, Bancroft Library, University of California–Berkeley

San Francisco Unified School District Records, San Francisco Public Library

Sawyer, Lorenzo, Dictations, Biographical Sketches and Related Materials (ca. 1886–1890), Bancroft Library, University of California–Berkeley

Supreme Court of California Records, California State Archives, Sacramento

Newspapers and Magazines

Antioch (Calif.) Ledger

California Teacher (San Francisco)

Daily Alta California (San Francisco)

Daily Evening Bulletin (San Francisco)

Daily Evening Signal (San Francisco)

Daily Morning Call (San Francisco)

Daily Record-Union (Sacramento)

Elevator (San Francisco)

Harper's Weekly

Los Angeles Star

Mirror of the Times (San Francisco)
Pacific Appeal (San Francisco)
Penny Magazine of the Society for the Diffusion of Useful Knowledge
Sacramento Daily Record Union
Sacramento Daily Union
Sacramento Reporter
San Francisco Chronicle
Scribner's Monthly

Court Records

Baldwin v. Franks, 120 U.S. 707 (1887)

Chy Lung v. Freeman, 92 U.S. 275 (1875)

Gandolfo v. Hartman, 49 F. 181 (1892)

Ho Ah Kow v. Nunan, 5 Sawy. 552 (1879).

In re Ah Fong, 1 F. Cas. 213 (1874)

In re Hang Kie, 69 Cal. 149 (1886)

In re Jung Ah Lung, 25 F. 141 (1885)

In re Qwong Woo, 7 Sawy. 526 (1882)

In re Quong Woo Case File, Civil Case Files, U.S. District Court, Northern District of California, RG 21, National Archives and Records Administration, San Bruno, Calif.

In re Tiburcio Parrott 1 F. 481 (1880)

In re Tie Loy 26 F. 611 (1886)

In re Tung Yeong, 19 F. 184 (1884)

In re Wo Lee Case File, Civil Case Files, U.S. District Court, Northern District of California RG21, National Archives and Records Administration, San Bruno, Calif.

In re Yick Wo, 68 Cal. 294 (1885)

Lin Sing v. Washburn, 20 Cal 534 (1862)

People v. George Washington, 30 Cal. 658 (1869)

People v. Hall, 4 Cal 402 (1854)

People v. Hall Case File, Supreme Court of California Records, California State Archives, Sacramento

People v. James Brady, 40 Cal. 198 (1870)

Soon Hing v. Crowley, 113 U.S. 703 (1885)

Tape v. Hurley, 66 Cal. 473 (1885)

United States v. Harris, 106 U.S. 629 (1882)

Ward v. Flood, 48 Cal. 52 (1874)

Ward v. Flood Case File, Supreme Court of California Records, California State Archives, Sacramento

Yick Wo v. Hopkins, 118 U.S. 356 (1886)

Published Sources

Aarim-Heriot, Najia. *Chinese Immigrants, African Americans, and Racial Anxiety in the United States, 1848–82*. Urbana: University of Illinois Press, 2003.

Abu-Lughod, Janet L. *New York, Chicago, Los Angeles: America's Global Cities.* Minneapolis: University of Minnesota Press, 1999.

Acuna, Rodolfo. *Occupied America: A History of Chicanos*. New York: Harper and Row, 1981.

Almaguer, Tomas. *Racial Fault Lines: The Historical Origins of White Supremacy in Race Relations in California.* Berkeley: University of California Press, 1994.

Axtell, Samuel B. *Aloccucion de Samuel B. Axtell, Candidado Nominado por el Partido Democratico Para el Congresso Federal, por el 1er Distrito de California, Que Dirije a Los Nativos Californios y a la Hispano-Americanos.* San Francisco: n.p., 1867.

Baker, Jean H. *Affairs of Party: The Political Culture of the Northern Democrats in the Mid-Nineteenth Century.* Ithaca, N.Y.: Cornell University Press, 1983.

Bakken, Gordon Morris. *The Development of Law in Frontier California: Civil Law and Society, 1850–1890.* Westport, Conn.: Greenwood, 1985.

———. *Practicing Law in Frontier California.* Lincoln: University of Nebraska Press, 1991.

Bancroft, Hubert Howe. *California Inter Pocula.* San Francisco: History Company, 1888.

———. *California Pastoral, 1769–1848.* San Francisco: History Company, 1888.

———. *History of California.* Vol. 5. San Francisco: History Company, 1888.

———. *History of California.* Vol. 6. San Francisco: History Company, 1888.

———. *History of California.* Vol. 7. San Francisco: History Company, 1890.

Barth, Gunther. *Bitter Strength: A History of Chinese in the United States, 1850–1870.* Cambridge, Mass.: Harvard University Press, 1964.

Bean, Walton, and James J. Rawls. *California: An Interpretive History.* San Francisco: McGraw-Hill, 1983.

Beasley, Delilah. *The Negro Trailblazers of California.* Los Angeles: Times Mirror Printing and Binding House, 1919.

Beck, Nicholas Patrick. "The Other Children: Minority Education in California Public Schools from Statehood to 1890." Ph.D. diss., University of California, Los Angeles, 1975.

Beckert, Sven. *The Monied Metropolis: New York City and the Consolidation of the American Bourgeoisie, 1850–1896.* Cambridge: Cambridge University Press, 2001.

Bell, Derrick. *Race, Racism, and American Law.* Boston: Little Brown, 1992.

Bemis, Samuel Flagg. *John Quincy Adams and the Union.* New York: Knopf, 1956.

Benedict, Michael Les. "Victorian Moralism and Civil Liberty in the Nineteenth-Century United States." In *The Constitution, Law, and American Life: Critical Aspects of the Nineteenth-Century Experience.* Athens: University of Georgia Press, 1992.

Bensel, Richard Franklin. *Yankee Leviathan: The Origins of Central State Authority in America, 1859–1877.* Cambridge: Cambridge University Press, 1990.

Berthoff, Roland. "Conventional Mentality: Free Blacks, Women, and Business Corporations as Unequal Persons, 1820–1870." *Journal of American History* 76, 3: 753–84.

Berwanger, Eugene. *The West and Reconstruction.* Urbana: University of Illinois Press, 1981.

Boone, Richard Gauze. *A History of Educational Organization in California.* N.p., n.d.

Bowes, John P. *Exiles and Pioneers: Eastern Indians in the Trans-Mississippi West.* Cambridge: Cambridge University Press, 2007.

Brace, Charles Loring. *The Life of Charles Loring Brace, Chiefly Told in His Own Letters.* Edited by Emma Brace. New York: Scribner's Sons, 1894.

———. *The New West: Or, California in 1867–1868.* New York: G. P. Putnam, 1869.

———. *Races of the Old World: A Manual of Ethnology.* New York: C. Scribner, 1864.

Bragg, Susan. "Knowledge Is Power: Sacramento Blacks and the Public Schools, 1854–1860." *California History* 75 (1996): 215–21.

Brooks, Benjamin S. *Brief of the Legislation and Adjudication Touching the Chinese Question Referred to the Joint Commission of Both Houses of Congress.* San Francisco: n.p., 1877.

Brown, Thomas J., ed. *Reconstructions: New Perspectives on the Postbellum United States.* New York: Oxford University Press, 2006.

Browne, J. Ross. *The Indians of California.* San Francisco: Colt Press, 1944.

———. *Report of the Debates in the Convention of California on the Formation of the State Constitution.* Washington, D.C.: J. T. Towers, 1850.

Burchell, R. A. *The San Francisco Irish, 1848–1880.* Manchester, England: Manchester University Press, 1979.

Butchart, Ronald E. *Northern Schools, Southern Blacks, and Reconstruction: Freedmen's Education, 1862–1875.* Westport, Conn.: Greenwood, 1980.

California Labor Exchange. *Facts about California: A Circular Issued to Workingmen.* San Francisco: n.p., 1869.

Carr, William G. *John Swett: The Biography of an Educational Pioneer.* Santa Ana, Calif.: Fine Arts Press, 1993.

Carson, James H. "Early Recollections of the Mines." In *Bright Gem of the Western Seas: California, 1846–1852,* ed. Peter Browning. Lafayette, Calif.: Great West Books, 1991.

Chan, Sucheng. *This Bittersweet Soil: The Chinese in California Agriculture, 1860–1910.* Berkeley: University of California Press, 1989.

Chance, John K. *Race and Class in Colonial Oaxaca.* Stanford, Calif.: Stanford University Press, 1978.

Chen, Yong. *Chinese San Francisco, 1850–1943: A Trans-Pacific Community.* Stanford, Calif.: Stanford University Press, 2000.

Chinese Immigration: Its Social, Moral, and Political Effect. Report to the California State Senate of the Special Committee on Chinese Immigration. Sacramento, Calif.: State Printing Office, 1878.

Chinese Laundries Ordinance, and Other Articles from Chinese American Newspapers. Berkeley: University of California, Berkeley, Asian American Studies Library, 1983.

Chiu, Ping. *Chinese Labor in California, 1850–1880: An Economic History.* Madison: State Historical Society of Wisconsin for the Department of History, University of Wisconsin, 1963.

Chun Chuen Lai. *Remarks of the Chinese Merchants of San Francisco upon Governor Bigler's Message, and Some Common Objections With Some Explanations of the Character of the Chinese Companies and the Laboring Class of California.* Trans. Rev. William D. Speer. San Francisco: Office of the Oriental, 1855.

Clarke, Alfred. *Report of Alfred Clarke, Special Counsel for the City and County of San Francisco in the Laundry Order Litigation. February 24, 1885.* San Francisco: W. A. Woodward and Company, 1885.

Cloud, Roy W. *Education in California: Leaders, Organizations, and Accomplishments of the First Hundred Years.* Stanford, Calif.: Stanford University Press, 1952.

Coben, Stanley. "Northeastern Business and Radical Reconstruction: A Reexamination." *Mississippi Valley Historical Review* 156 (June 1959): 67–90.

Colored Citizens of California. *Proceedings of the First State Convention of the Colored Citizens of the State of California.* Sacramento: Democratic State Journal Printer, 1855; rpt. San Francisco: R and E Research Associates, 1969.

———. *Proceedings of the Second Annual Convention of the Colored Citizens of the State of California.* San Francisco: J. H. Udell and W. Randall, 1856.

Cook, Sherburne F. *The Population of the California Indians, 1769–1974.* Berkeley: University of California Press, 1976.

Coolidge, Mary Roberts. *Chinese Immigration.* New York: H. Holt and Co., 1909.

Cornell, S. S. *Cornell's Primary Geography, Forming Part First of a Systematic Series of School Geographies.* New York: D. Appleton and Company, 1857.

Cornford, Daniel. "To Save the Republic: The Workingmen's Party in Humboldt County." *California History* 66, 2 (June 1987): 130–42.

Courtney, William J. *San Francisco Anti-Chinese Ordinances, 1850–1900.* San Francisco: R and E Research Associates, 1974.

Crane, Lauren E., ed. *Newton Booth of California: His Speeches and Addresses.* New York: Putnam's, 1894.

Cronon, William. *Changes in the Land: Indians, Colonists, and the Ecology of New England.* New York: Hill and Wang, 1983.

———. *Nature's Metropolis: Chicago and the Great West.* New York: W. W. Norton, 1991.

Crosby, Alfred E. *The Columbian Exchange: Biological and Cultural Consequences of 1492.* Westport, Conn.: Greenwood, 1972.

———. *Ecological Imperialism: The Biological Expansion of Europe, 900–1900.* New York: Cambridge University Press, 1986.

Cross, Ira B. *A History of the Labor Movement in California.* Berkeley: University of California Press, 1935.

Cross, Whitney. *The Burned-Over District: The Social and Intellectual History of Enthusiastic Religion in Western New York, 1800–1850.* New York: Harper and Row, 1950.

Daniels, Douglas Henry. *Pioneer Urbanites: A Social and Cultural History of Black San Francisco.* Philadelphia: Temple University Press, 1980.

Davis, Winfield J. *History and Progress of the Public School Department of the City of Sacramento, 1849–1893.* Sacramento, Calif.: D. Johnson, 1895.

———. *History of Political Conventions in California, 1849–1892.* Sacramento: California State Library, 1893.

Dayton, Dello Grimmett. "The California Militia, 1850–1866." Ph.D. diss., University of California, Berkeley, 1951.

Debates and Proceedings of the Constitutional Convention of the State of California, Convened at the City of Sacramento, Saturday, September 28, 1878. Vol. 3. Sacramento: State Printing Office, 1880.

Degler, Carl. *Neither White nor Black: Slavery and Race Relations in Brazil and the United States.* New York: Macmillan, 1971.

Delaney, David. *Race, Place, and the Law, 1836–1948.* Austin: University of Texas Press, 1998.

del Castillo, Richard Griswold. *The Los Angeles Barrio, 1850–1890: A Social History.* Berkeley: University of California Press, 1979.

Delmatier, Royce, Clarence F. McIntosh, and Earl G. Waters. *The Rumble of California Politics, 1848–1970.* New York: Wiley, 1970.

Deutsch, Sarah. *Women and the City: Gender, Space, and Power in Boston, 1870–1940.* New York: Oxford University Press, 2000.

Dippie, Brian. *The Vanishing American: White Attitudes and U.S. Indian Policy.* Middletown, Conn.: Wesleyan University Press, 1982.

Dobie, Charles Caldwell. *San Francisco's Chinatown.* New York: D. Appleton, 1936.

Dolson, Stephen Lee. "The Administration of San Francisco Public Schools, 1847–1947." Ph.D. diss., University of California, Berkeley, 1964.

DuBois, W. E. B. *Black Reconstruction: An Essay toward a History of the Part Which Black Folk Played in the Attempt to Reconstruct Democracy in America, 1860–1880.* New York: Russell and Russell, 1935.

Dykstra, Robert. *Bright Radical Star: Black Freedom and White Supremacy on the Hawkeye Frontier.* Cambridge, Mass.: Harvard University Press, 1993.

Eaves, Lucille. *A History of California Labor Legislation, with an Introductory Sketch of the San Francisco Labor Movement.* Berkeley: The University Press, 1910.

Edwards, Laura F. *Gendered Strife and Confusion: The Political Culture of Reconstruction.* Urbana: University of Illinois Press, 1997.

Edwards, Rebecca. *Angels in the Machinery: Gender in American Party Politics from the Civil War to the Progressive Era.* New York: Oxford University Press, 1997.

Ellison, Joseph. *California and the Nation, 1850–1869: A Study of the Relations of a Frontier Community with the Federal Government.* Berkeley: University of California Press, 1927.

Ellison, William H. *A Self-Governing Dominion: California, 1849–1860.* Berkeley: University of California Press, 1950.

Ethington, Philip. *The Public City: the Political Construction of Urban Life in San Francisco, 1850–1900.* New York: Cambridge University Press, 1994.

Evans, George Heberton. *Business Incorporations in the United States, 1800–1943.* New York: Bureau of Economic Research, 1948.

Farnell, William B. *The Chinese at Home and Abroad. Together with the Report of the Special Committee of the Board of Supervisors of San Francisco, on the Condition of the Chinese Quarter of that City.* San Francisco: San Francisco Board of Supervisors, 1885.

Fernandez, Ferdinand F. "Except a California Indian: a Study in Legal Discrimination." *Southern California Quarterly* 50 (Spring 1968): 161–75.

Ferrier, William Warren. *Ninety Years of Education in California, 1846–1936: A Presentation of Educational Movements and the Outcome of Education Today.* Berkeley: Sather Gate Book Shop, 1937.

Ferris, David Frederic. *Judge Marvin and the Founding of the California Public School System.* Berkeley: University of California Press, 1962.

Fisher, James J. "The Struggle for Negro Testimony in California, 1851–1863." *Southern California Quarterly* 51 (December 1969): 313–24.

Foner, Eric. *Free Soil, Free Labor, Free Men: The Ideology of the Republican Party before the Civil War.* New York: Oxford University Press, 1970.

———. *Nothing but Freedom: Emancipation and Its Legacy.* Baton Rouge: Louisiana State University Press, 1983.

————. *Reconstruction: America's Unfinished Revolution, 1863–1879.* Chapel Hill: University of North Carolina Press, 1988.

Frederickson, George. *White Supremacy: A Comparative Study in American and South African History.* New York: Oxford University Press, 1981.

Friedman, Lawrence. *A History of American Law.* New York: Simon and Schuster, 1985.

Fritz, Christian G. *Federal Justice in California: The Court of Ogden Hoffman, 1851–1891.* Lincoln: University of Nebraska Press, 1991.

————. "A Nineteenth-Century 'Habeas Corpus Mill': The Chinese before the Federal Courts in California." *American Journal of Legal History* 32 (1988): 347–72.

Genovese, Eugene. *Roll Jordan Roll: The World the Slaves Made.* New York: Vintage, 1975.

George, Henry. "The Kearney Agitation in California," *Popular Science Monthly* 17 (August 1880).

————. *Progress and Poverty: An Inquiry Into the Cause of Industrial Depressions and of Increase of Want with Increase of Wealth, the Remedy.* Garden City, N.Y.: Doubleday, Page and Company, 1879.

————. "Why Work is Scarce, Wages Low, and Labor Restless," a Lecture by Henry George, Delivered in Metropolitan Temple, San Francisco, Cal., March 26, 1878. San Francisco: California Tax Reform League, 1878.

Gibbs, Mifflin W. *Shadow and Light: An Autobiography, with Reminiscences of the Last and Present Century.* Lincoln: University of Nebraska Press, 1902.

Gibson, Arrell Morgan. *The American Indian: Prehistory to the Present.* New York: D.C. Heath and Company, 1980.

Gomez-Quinones, Juan. *The Roots of Chicano Politics, 1600–1940.* Albuquerque: University of New Mexico Press, 1994.

Goodrich, Chauncey Shafter. "The Legal Status of the California Indian: Introductory." *California Law Review* 14 (1926): 83–100.

Gorham, George C. *Speech Delivered by George C. Gorham of San Francisco, Union Nominee for Governor, at Platt's Hall, San Francisco, Wednesday Evening, July 10, 1867.* San Francisco: n.p., 1867.

Gregory, James N. *American Exodus: The Dust Bowl Migration and Okie Culture in California.* New York: Oxford University Press, 1989.

Grivas, Theodore. *Military Governments in California, 1846–1850: With a Chapter on Their Prior Use in Louisiana, Florida, and New Mexico.* Glendale, Calif.: A. H. Clark Co., 1962.

Grossman, James R. *Land of Hope: Chicago, Black Southerners, and the Great Migration.* Chicago: University of Chicago Press, 1989.

Guillow, Lawrence E. "The Origins of Race Relations in Los Angeles, 1820–1880: A Multi-Ethnic Study." Ph.D. diss., Arizona State University, 1996.

Guyot, Arnold. *The Earth and Its Inhabitants: A Common School Geography.* New York: Charles Scribner and Company, 1869.

————. *The Earth and Its Inhabitants: Intermediate Geography.* New York: Charles Scribner and Company, 1875.

————. *The Earth and Man: Lectures on Comparative Physical Geography, in Its Relation to the History of Mankind.* Boston: Gould and Lincoln, 1865.

Gyory, Andrew. *Closing the Gate: Race, Politics, and the Chinese Exclusion Act.* Chapel Hill: University of North Carolina Press, 1998.

Haas, Lizbeth. *Conquests and Historical Identities in California, 1769–1936.* Berkeley: University of California Press, 1995.

Hager, John S. *Speech of Honorable John S. Hager of San Francisco, in the Senate of California, January 28, 1870, on Senator Hager's Joint Resolution to Reject the Fifteenth Amendment to the Constitution of the United States.* n.p., 1870.

Haight, Henry H. *Inaugural Address of H. H. Haight, Governor of the State of California, at the Seventeenth Session of the Legislature.* Sacramento: D. W. Gelwicks, State Printer, 1867.

————. *Message of H. H. Haight, Governor of California, Transmitting the Proposed Fifteenth Amendment to the Federal Constitution.* Sacramento: D. W. Gelwicks, State Printer, 1870.

————. *Speech of H. H. Haight, Esq. Democratic Candidate for Governor, Delivered at the Great Democratic Mass Meeting at Union Hall, Tuesday Evening, July 9, 1867.* San Francisco: n.p., 1867.

Haller, John S., Jr. *Outcasts from Evolution: Scientific Attitudes of Racial Inferiority, 1859–1900.* Urbana: University of Illinois Press, 1971.

Haney-López, Ian. *White by Law: The Legal Construction of Race.* New York: New York University Press, 1996.

Harris, Marvin. *Patterns of Race in the Americas.* New York: Walker, 1964.

Harte, Bret. *Bret Harte's California: Letters to the Springfield Republican and Christian Register, 1866–67.* Edited and with an introduction by Gary Scharnhorst (Albuquerque: University of New Mexico Press, 1990).

Hendrick, Irving C. *Public Policy toward the Education of Non-White Majority Group Children in California, 1849–1970.* Riverside: University of California, Riverside, School of Education, 1975.

Hittell, Theodore H. *History of California,* Vol. 3. San Francisco: Pacific Press Publishing House, 1898.

Holliday, J. S. *The World Rushed In: The California Gold Rush Experience.* New York: Simon and Schuster, 1981.

Hopkins, Caspar T. *Common Sense Applied to the Immigrant Question: Showing Why the "California Immigrant Union" was Founded and What it Expects to Do.* San Francisco: Turnbull and Smith, Printers, 1869.

————. *A Manual of American Ideas.* San Francisco: 1873.

Horowitz, Morton J. *The Transformation of American Law, 1780–1860.* Cambridge, Mass.: Harvard University Press, 1977.

————. *The Transformation of American Law, 1870–1960: The Crisis of Legal Orthodoxy.* New York: Oxford University Press, 1992.

Horsman, Reginald. *Race and Manifest Destiny: The Origins of American Racial Anglo-Saxonism.* Cambridge, Mass.: Harvard University Press, 1981.

Huggins, Dorothy H. "Continuation of the Annals of San Francisco." *California Historical Society Quarterly* 16, 3 (September 1937): 283–85.

Hull Hoffer, Williamjames. *To Enlarge the Machinery of Government: Congressional Debates and the Growth of the American State, 1858–1891.* Baltimore: Johns Hopkins University Press, 2007.

Humfreville, J. Lee. "Early Recollections of the Mines." In *Bright Gem of the Western Seas: California, 1846–1852,* ed. Peter Browning. Lafayette, Calif.: Great West Books, 1991.

Hurtado, Albert. "Clouded Legacy: California Indians and the Gold Rush." In *Riches for All: The California Gold Rush and the World,* ed. Kenneth N. Owens, 90–117. Lincoln: University of Nebraska Press, 2002.

————. Indian *Survival on the California Frontier.* New Haven, Conn.: Yale University Press, 1988.

Ignatiev, Noel. *How the Irish Became White.* New York: Routledge, 1995.

Israel, J. I. *Race, Class, and Politics in Colonial Mexico, 1610–1670.* London: Oxford University Press, 1975.

Jacobson, Matthew Frye. *Whiteness of a Different Color: European Immigrants and the Alchemy of Race.* Cambridge, Mass.: Harvard University Press, 1998.

"John Chinaman in San Francisco," *Scribner's,* October 1876, 862–72.

Johnson, David. *Founding of the Far West: California, Oregon, and Nevada, 1840–1890.* Berkeley: University of California Press, 1992.

Johnson, Leigh Dana. "Equal Rights and the 'Heathen Chinee': Black Activism in San Francisco, 1865–1875." *Western Historical Quarterly* 11 (1980): 57–68.

Johnson, Leighton H. *Development of the Central State Agency for Public Education in California, 1849–1949.* Albuquerque: University of New Mexico Press, 1952.

Johnson, Paul. *A Shopkeeper's Millennium: Society and Revivals in Rochester, New York, 1815–1837.* New York: Hill and Wang, 1978.

Johnson, Susan Lee. *Roaring Camp: The Social World of the California Gold Rush.* New York: W. W. Norton, 2000.

Jordan, Winthrop. *White over Black: American Attitudes toward the Negro, 1550–1802.* Chapel Hill: Published for the Institute of Early American History and Culture at Williamsburg, Va., by the University of North Carolina Press, 1968.

Kaestle, Carl F. *Pillars of the Republic: Common Schools and American Society, 1780–1860.* New York: Hill and Wang, 1983.

Kantrowitz, Stephen David. *Ben Tillman and the Reconstruction of White Supremacy.* Chapel Hill: University of North Carolina Press, 2000.

Kearney, Dennis. *Speeches of Dennis Kearney, Labor Champion.* New York: Jesse Haney, 1878.

Kens, Paul. *Justice Stephen J. Field: Shaping Liberty from the Gold Rush to the Gilded Age.* Lawrence: University Press of Kansas, 1997.

Kroeber, Alfred L. *Types of Indian Culture in California.* Berkeley: University Press, 1904.

Lamoreaux, Naomi. *Insider Lending: Banks, Personal Connections, and Economic Development in Industrial New England.* New York: Cambridge University Press, 1994.

Langum, David J. *Law and Community on the Mexican California Frontier: Anglo-American Expatriates and the Clash of Legal Traditions, 1821–1846.* Norman: University of Oklahoma Press, 1987.

Lansing, Gerritt. "Chinese Immigration: A Sociological Study." *Popular Science Monthly*, April 1882.

Lapp, Rudolph M. *Blacks in Gold Rush California.* New Haven, Conn.: Yale University Press, 1977.

———. "Negro Rights Activities in Gold Rush California." *California Historical Society Quarterly* 45 (March 1966): 3–20.

Laurie, Clayton D. "Civil Disorder and the Military in Rock Springs, Wyoming: The Army's Role in the 1885 Chinese Massacre." *Montana: The Magazine of Western History* 40, 3 (September 1990): 44–59.

Litwack, Leon F. *Been in the Storm So Long: The Aftermath of Slavery.* New York: Knopf, 1979.

Lonnberg, Allan. "The Digger Indian Stereotype in California." *Journal of California and Great Basin Anthropology*, 3, 2 (1981): 217–18.

Lovejoy, Arthur O. *The Great Chain of Being: A Study of the History of an Idea.* Cambridge, Mass.: Harvard University Press, 1942.

Low, Victor. *The Unimpressible Race: A Century of Educational Struggle by the Chinese in San Francisco.* San Francisco: East/West Publishing, 1982.

Lyman, Stanford. *The Asian in the West.* Reno: University of Nevada System, Western Studies Center, Desert Research Institute, 1970.

Lynn-Sherow, Bonnie. *Red Earth: Race and Agriculture in Oklahoma Territory.* Lawrence: University Press of Kansas, 2004.

McAfee, Ward M. *Religion, Race, and Reconstruction: The Public Schools in the Politics of the 1870s.* Albany: University of New York Press, 1998.

McClain, Charles J. *In Search of Equality: The Chinese Struggle against Discrimination in Nineteenth-Century America.* Berkeley: University of California Press, 1994.

McKanna, Clare V. "Enclaves of Violence in Nineteenth-Century California." *Pacific Historical Review* 73, 3 (2004): 391–423.

———. *Race and Homicide in Nineteenth-Century California*. Reno: University of Nevada Press, 2002.

Meier, Matt S., and Feliciano Ribera. *Mexican Americans/American Mexicans: From Conquistadors to Chicanos*. New York: Hill and Wang, 1993.

Melendy, H. Brett, and Benjamin F. Gilbert. *The Governors of California: Peter H. Burnett to Edmund G. Brown*. Georgetown, Calif.: Talisman Press, 1965.

Miller, Stuart. *The Unwelcome Immigrant: The American Image of the Chinese, 1785–1882*. Berkeley: University of California Press, 1970.

Miller, William Lee. *Arguing about Slavery: The Great Battle in the United States Congress*. New York: Knopf, 1996.

Monroy, Douglas. *Thrown among Strangers: The Making of the Mexican Culture in Frontier California*. Berkeley: University of California Press, 1990.

Montejano, David. *Anglos and Mexicans in the Making of Texas, 1836–1986*. Austin: University of Texas Press, 1987.

Montgomery, David. *Beyond Equality: Labor and the Radical Republicans, 1862–1872*. New York: Vintage, 1972.

———. *The Fall of the House of Labor: The Workplace, the State, and American Labor Activism, 1865–1925*. Cambridge: Cambridge University Press, 1987.

Moody, William Penn. "The Civil War and Reconstruction in California Politics." Ph.D. diss., University of California, Los Angeles, 1950.

Moorhead, Dudley T. "Sectionalism and the California Constitution of 1879." *Pacific Historical Review* 12 (June 1943): 287–93.

Morgan, Edmund. *American Slavery, American Freedom: The Ordeal of Colonial Virginia*. New York: Norton, 1975.

Morner, Magnus. *Race and Class in Latin America*. New York: Columbia University Press, 1970.

———. *Race Mixture in the History of Latin America*. Boston: Little Brown, 1967.

Nash, Gerald D. *The American West Transformed: The Impact of the Second World War*. Bloomington: Indiana University Press, 1985.

Ngai, Mai. *The Lucky Ones: One Family and the Extraordinary Invention of Chinese America*. New York: Houghton Mifflin Harcourt, 2010.

Omi, Michael, and Howard Winant. *Racial Formation in the United States from the 1960s to the 1980s*. New York: Routledge and Kegan Paul, 1986.

Ong, Paul Man. "The Chinese and the Laundry Laws: the Use and Control of Urban Space." M.A. Thesis, University of Washington, 1975.

———. "The Development and Decline of an Ethnic Enterprise: Chinese Laundries in Early California." Ethnic Studies Library, University of California, Berkeley.

Ono, Kent A., and John M. Sloop. *Shifting Borders: Rhetoric, Immigration, and California's Proposition 187*. Philadelphia: Temple University Press, 2002.

Pacheco, Romualdo. *Remarks of Hon. Romualdo Pacheco, of California, in the House of Representatives, Saturday, March 18, 1882*. Washington, D.C.: Government Printing Office, 1882.

Palladino, Grace. *Another Civil War: Labor, Capital, and the State in the Anthracite Regions of Pennsylvania, 1840–1868*. Urbana: University of Illinois Press, 1990.

Paul, Rodman W. *California Gold: the Beginning of Mining in the Far West*. Lincoln: University of Nebraska Press, 1947.

———. *Mining Frontiers of the Far West, 1848–1880*. New York: Holt, Rinehart, and Winston, 1963.

Perman, Michael. *The Road to Redemption: Southern Politics, 1869–1879*. Chapel Hill: University of North Carolina Press, 1984.

Pfaelzer, Jean. *Driven Out: The Forgotten War against Chinese Americans*. New York: Random House, 2007.

Phillips, George H. *The Enduring Struggle: Indians in California History*. San Francisco: Boyd and Fraser, 1981.

Pitt, Leonard M. *The Decline of the Californios: A Social History of the Spanish-Speaking Californians, 1846–1890*. Berkeley: University of California Press, 1966.

Polos, Nicholas C. *John Swett: California's Frontier Schoolmaster*. Washington, D.C.: University Press of America, 1978.

Powell, Richard R. *Compromises of Conflicting Claims: A Century of California Law, 1760–1860*. Dobbs Ferry, N.Y.: Oceans Publications, 1977.

Rawls, James J. *Indians of California: The Changing Image*. Norman: University of Oklahoma Press, 1984.

Rice, Roger L. "Residential Segregation by Law, 1910–1917." *Journal of Southern History* 34, 2 (May 1968): 179–99.

Richardson, Heather Cox. *West from Appomattox: The Reconstruction of America after the Civil War*. New Haven, Conn.: Yale University Press, 2007.

Ridge, Martin. "Disorder, Crime, and Punishment in the California Gold Rush." In *Riches for All: The California Gold Rush and the World*, ed. Kenneth N. Owens. Lincoln: University of Nebraska Press, 2002.

Roberts, Brian. *American Alchemy: The California Gold Rush and Middle-Class Culture*. Chapel Hill: University of North Carolina Press, 2000.

Roediger, David R. *The Wages of Whiteness: Race and the Making of the American Working Class*. New York: Verso, 1991.

Roney, Frank B. *Frank Roney, Irish Rebel and California Labor Leader: An Autobiography*. Edited by Ira B. Cross. Berkeley: University of California Press, 1931.

Royce, Josiah. *California: a Study of American Character.* Boston: Houghton, Mifflin, 1886.

Salyer, Lucy. "Captives of Law: Judicial Enforcement of the Chinese Exclusion Laws, 1891–1905." *Journal of American History* 76 (1989): 91–117.

Sanchez, George J. *Becoming Mexican American: Ethnicity, Culture, and Identity in Chicano Los Angeles, 1900–1945.* New York: Oxford University Press, 1993.

Sandburg, Carl. *Abraham Lincoln: The War Years.* Vol. 4. New York: Charles Scribner's Sons, 1949.

Sandmeyer, Elmer Clarence. *The Anti-Chinese Movement in California.* Urbana: University of Illinois Press, 1939.

Saxton, Alexander. *The Indispensable Enemy: Labor and the Anti-Chinese Movement in California.* Berkeley: University of California Press, 1971.

———. *The Rise and Fall of the White Republic: Class Politics and Mass Culture in Nineteenth-Century America.* New York: Verso, 1990.

Schuck, Oscar T. *Representative and Leading Men of the Pacific.* San Francisco: Bacon and Company, 1870.

Scott, Anne Firor. *Natural Allies: Women's Associations in American History.* Urbana: University of Illinois Press, 1992.

Shah, Nyan. *Contagious Divides: Epidemics and Race in San Francisco's Chinatown.* Berkeley: University of California Press, 2001.

Sheehan, Bernard. *Seeds of Extinction: Jeffersonian Philanthropy and the American Indian.* Chapel Hill: Published for the Institute of Early American History and Culture at Williamsburg, Va., by the University of North Carolina Press, 1973.

Shinn, Charles H. *Mining Camps: A Study in Frontier Government.* New York: Charles Scribner's Son, 1885.

Shuck, Oscar T. *Representative and Leading Men of the Pacific: Being Original Sketches of the Lives and Characters of the Principal Men, Living and Deceased, of the Pacific States and Territories—Pioneers, Politicians, Lawyers, Doctors, Merchants, Orators, and Divines—to Which Are Added Their Speeches, Addresses, Orations, Eulogies, Lectures, and Poems, Upon a Variety of Subjects, Including the Happiest Forensic Efforts of Baker, Randolph, McDougall, T. Starr King, and Other Popular Orators.* San Francisco: Bacon and Company, 1870.

Shumsky, Neil Larry. *The Evolution of Political Protest and the Workingmen's Party of California.* Columbus: Ohio State University Press, 1991.

Sides, Josh. *L.A. City Limits: African American Los Angeles from the Great Depression to the Present.* Berkeley: University of California Press, 2003.

Silbey, Joel. *The American Political Nation, 1838–1893.* Stanford, Calif.: Stanford University Press, 1991.

Siu, Paul C. P. *The Chinese Laundryman: A Study in Social Isolation.* New York: New York University Press, 1987.

Sklar, Martin J. *The Corporate Reconstruction of American Capitalism, 1890–1916: The Market, the Law, and Politics.* Cambridge: Cambridge University Press, 1988.

Slotkin, Richard. *The Fatal Environment: The Myth of the Frontier in the Age of Industrialization, 1800–1890.* New York: Atheneum, 1985.

———. *Regeneration through Violence: The Mythology of the American Frontier, 1600–1860.* Middletown, Conn.: Wesleyan University Press, 1973.

Snyder, David. *Negro Civil Rights in California: 1850.* Sacramento: California State Library, 1969.

Soule, Frank, John H. Gihon, and James Nesbitt. *The Annals of San Francisco.* San Francisco: D. Appleton, 1855.

"Speech of Senator John Conness." *Proceedings of the San Francisco Ratification Meeting Held at Union Hall, San Francisco, Tuesday Evening, June 25, 1867.* San Francisco: Union State Central Committee, 1867.

Speer, Reverend William. *An Answer to Common Objections to Chinese Testimony: And an Earnest Appeal to the Legislature of California for Their Protection by Our Law.* San Francisco: Chinese Mission House, 1857.

———. *An Humble Plea, Addressed to the Legislature of California, in Behalf of Immigrants from the Empire of China to this State.* San Francisco: Office of the Oriental, 1856.

———. *The Oldest and Newest Empire: China and the United States.* Hartford: S. S. Scranton, 1870.

Stampp, Kenneth. *The Era of Reconstruction, 1865–1877.* New York: Knopf, 1965.

Stanley, Gerald. "The Slavery Issue and Election in California." *Mid-America* 62, 1 (Spring 1980): 35–45.

———. "Slavery and the Origins of the Republican Party in California." *Southern California Quarterly* 60 (Spring 1978): 1–16.

Stanton, William. *The Leopard's Spots: Scientific Attitudes toward Race in America, 1815–59.* Chicago: University of Chicago Press, 1960.

Swett, John. *History of the Public School System of California.* San Francisco: A. L. Bancroft and Company, 1876.

———. *Public Education in California: Its Origin and Development, with Personal Reminiscences of Half a Century.* New York: American Book Company, 1911.

Swisher, Carl Brent. *Motivation and Political Technique in the California Constitutional Convention, 1878–79.* Claremont, Calif.: Pomona College, 1930.

Takaki, Ronald. *Strangers from a Different Shore: A History of Asian Americans.* New York: Penguin, 1990.

Taylor, Quintard. *In Search of the Racial Frontier: African Americans in the American West, 1528–1990.* New York: W. W. Norton, 1998.

Truesdell, Dr. A. P. *The People's Champion. The Voice of the People Must Be Heard. Land Monopoly: Its Origin and End. Mob Law vs. Revolution. The*

Starving. The Chinese Question. San Francisco: A. L. Bancroft and Company 1878.

Tyack, David, Thomas James, and Aaron Benavot. *Law and the Shaping of Public Education, 1785–1954.* Madison: University of Wisconsin Press, 1987.

U.S. Census Office. *Historical Census Statistics on Population Totals by Race, 1790 to 1990, and by Hispanic Origin, 1970 to 1990, For The United States, Regions, Divisions, and States, Working Paper Series No. 56.* Washington, D.C.: Government Printing Office, 2002.

U.S. Senate. *Journal of the Senate of the United States of America, 39th Congress, First Session, 1865–1866.* Washington, D.C.: Government Printing Office, 1866.

Wang, Joan S. "Race, Gender, and Laundry Work: The Roles of Chinese Laundrymen and American Women in the United States, 1850–1950." *Journal of Ethnic History* 24, 1 (Fall 2004): 58–99.

Warner, Sam Bass. *Streetcar Suburbs: The Process of Growth in Boston, 1870–1900.* Cambridge, Mass.: Harvard University Press, 1962.

Waugh, Joan. *Unsentimental Reformer: The Life of Josephine Shaw Lowell.* Cambridge: Cambridge University Press, 1997.

Welke, Barbara Young. *Recasting American Liberty: Gender, Race, Law, and the Railroad Revolution, 1865–1920.* Cambridge: Cambridge University Press, 2001.

West, Elliot. "Reconstructing Race." *Western Historical Quarterly* 34, 1 (Spring 2003): 6–26.

Whittlesly, Edgar Camp. "Hugh C. Murray: California's Youngest Chief Justice." *California Historical Society Quarterly* 20 (December 1941): 366–369.

Wollenberg, Charles. *All Deliberate Speed: Segregation and Exclusion in California Schools, 1855–1975.* Berkeley: University of California Press, 1976.

Workingmen's Party of California. *The Labor Agitators; or the Battle for Bread. The Party of the Future: the Workingmen's Party of California, its Birth and Organization—its Leaders and its Purposes. Corruption in Our Local and State Governments. Venality of the Press.* San Francisco: Geo. Greene, 1878.

Index

References to illustrations are in italic type.

Abolitionists, 215n23 (chap. 1). *See also* Slavery
Abyssinians, 110
Act for the Government and Protection of Indians, An, 23–24, 27
African Americans. *See* Blacks
Agassiz, Louis, 25. *See also* Evolution
Agriculture, 141, 200–201
Alameda, California, 140
Alcoholism, 19, 20
Alien Land Act, 204
Aliens. *See* Immigrants
American Indians. *See* Indians
Anderson, Peter, 118–19, 120
Anglo-Africans. *See* Blacks
Anglo-Saxons, 43–44. *See also* Whites
Anti-Chinese Club, 187–88, 193, 195
Apaches, 153. *See also* Indians
Arabs, 110
Arthur, Chester Alan, 173
Assassination, of Lincoln, 62–63, 64
Assimilation, of Irish, 85
Atlantic Monthly (magazine), 103–104
Axtell, Samuel B, 82

Baldwin, Thomas, 198
Baldwin v. Franks, 196–97, 199–200, 203
Banbury, Jabez, 187
Banbury, Thomas, 187
Bancroft, Hubert Howe: on blacks, 84; on Chinese, 154; on Democratic Party, 84; on Indians, 27; and Sawyer, 175; on suffrage, 84

Bangor, California, 39
Bank of California, 137
Bee, Frederick: and Chinese, 190; and Meares, 159; and Moulder, 131; and Six Companies, 159; and Tapes, 131
Bell, Phillip A., 114–15, *116,* 117
Benicia, California, 127
Berwanger, Eugene, 9
Bigelow, S. C., 41
Bigler, John, 216n30 (chap. 1)
Black codes, defined, 65
Blacks: Anderson on, 120; aspirations of, 46–47, 48; Axtell on, 82; Bancroft on, 84; in Benicia, 127; Berwanger on, 9; and Butte County Union Convention, 61; and Chinese, 30, 34, 35, 41–42, 45–46, 86, 88, 120, 131, 152, 153, 197–98; as citizens, 96; and Civil Rights Act of 1866, 6, 49; and Civil Rights Acts of 1871, 6; and Civil Rights Act of 1875, 6; civil rights of, 66–67, 129; and Civil War, 169–70, 228n29 (chap. 3); and Colorado Territory, 34, 67; conventions of, 30–31; and Cowdery, 119, 120; *Daily Morning Call* on, 79, 81; and *Dred Scott* decision, 38; and equal protection clause, 12, 122; and exclusionary testimony laws, 27–28, 30, 31–32, 47, 53–54, 58–59, 83; exodus from California of, 38; and Fay, 217n39 (chap. 1); and Fifteenth Amendment, 119–20, 170; and Fourteenth

257

Lee, Wo, arrest of, 136, 139, 140, 149, 162
Leidsdorff, William, 113, 228n32
Lester, Peter, 28, 106–107, 227n19
Levanter (ship), 215n24
Licenses, for Chinese laundries, 162–63
Lincoln, Abraham: assassination of, 62–63, 64; Conness on, 221n31; and Emancipation Proclamation, 74; and Haight, 55, 73; and Louisiana, 220n13; and McClellan, 74; and Reconstruction, 62, 63–64; and slavery, 63; and 10 Percent Plan, 63; and Wade-Davis Bill, 64
Ling, Wong Poo, 163
Linnaeus, Carl, 43, 218n45
Literacy, of blacks, 46–47
Livermore, California, 192
Long Bar, California, 39
Long-hair faction, 61, 78, 220n8
Lorenzo, California, 187–88
Los Angeles, California, 52–53, 113, 192
Los Angeles Star (newspaper), 101
Louisiana, 220n13
Low, Frederick F., 55, 71, 77
Lyell, Charles, 2
Lynching, 39

Maguire, James, 132
Maguire's Theater, 225n4
Mariposa, California, 227n15 (chap. 3)
Martin, R. M., 89–90
Marvin, John G., 104, 226n15
Masons, 74
Massacres, 26–27
Matthews, Stanley, 166
McAllister, Hall, 196, 198
McAllister, Matthew Hall, 215n24
McClellan, George B., 74
McConnell, J. R., 14, 16–17

McDonald, A. H., 121
McDougall, James A., 73
McGlashan, Charles F., 189, 192
Meares, J. L., 158–59
Merchants, 177–78
Mexican Californians, 82
Mexican Revolution, 206
Mexicans: in California Constitution of 1849, 26; Henley on, 91; and racial hierarchy, 206; and schools, 226n6 (chap. 3)
Middle class, blacks in, 46, 48
Miners, Chinese. *See* Chinese miners
Minorities. *See* Blacks; Chinese; Indians
Mirror of the Times (newspaper), 32, 33
Missionary schools, 105. *See also* Schools
Mississippi, 93
Modesto, California, 140, 204
"Mongolians." *See* Chinese
Montana Territory, 7, 67
Moore, J. J., 113, 114
Moral science, 99–101. *See also* Schools
Moulder, Andrew Jackson, *106*; and Bee, 131; on blacks, 107; on black schools, 107; on Chinese, 106, 107, 131, 132; on Chinese schools, 128, 133; and Hurley, 131; on Indians, 107; on racial segregation, 105–106, 107–108; on schools, 131; on separate but equal principle, 133; on *Ward v. Flood*, 133; and Welcker, 131, 132–33
Murray, Hugh C.: as alcoholic, 19, 20; beatings by, 20; on blacks, 25; and California State Supreme Court, 19, 20; as chief justice, 19, 20; on Chinese, 17, 24, 25, 35; and Conness, 19–20; and Democratic Party, 19; and exclusionary testimony laws,